TIME TO PREPARE THE WAY
IN THE WILDERNESS

STUDIES ON THE TEXTS
OF THE DESERT OF JUDAH

EDITED BY

F. GARCIA MARTINEZ
A. S. VAN DER WOUDE

VOLUME XVI

TIME TO PREPARE THE WAY IN THE WILDERNESS

*Papers on the Qumran Scrolls by Fellows of
the Institute for Advanced Studies of
the Hebrew University, Jerusalem, 1989-1990*

EDITED BY

DEVORAH DIMANT

AND

LAWRENCE H. SCHIFFMAN

E.J. BRILL
LEIDEN · NEW YORK · KÖLN
1995

The paper in this book meets the guidelines for permanence and durability of the Committee on Production Guidelines for Book Longevity of the Council on Library Resources.

BM
487
.T55
1995

Library of Congress Cataloging-in-Publication Data

Time to prepare the way in the wilderness : papers on the Qumran scrolls / by the fellows of the Institute for Advanced Studies of the Hebrew University, Jerusalem, 1989-90 ; edited by Devorah Dimant and Lawrence H. Schiffman.
    p. cm. — (Studies on the texts of the desert of Judah, ISSN 0169-9962 ; v. 16)
    Includes bibliographical references.
    ISBN 9004102256
    1. Dead Sea scrolls—Criticism, interpretation, etc.   I. Dimant, Devorah.   II. Schiffman, Lawrence H.   III. Universiṭah ha-'Ivrit bi -Yerushalayim. Makhon le-limudim miṭḳadmim.   IV. Series.
BM487.T55   1994
296.1′55—dc20   94-38809
                                                                               CIP

Die Deutsche Bibliothek – CIP-Einheitsaufnahme

Time to prepare the way in the wilderness : papers on the Qumran scrolls by the Fellows of the Institute for Advanced Studies of the Hebrew University, Jerusalem, 1989-90 / ed. by Devorah Dimant and Lawrence H. Schiffman. - Leiden ; New York ; Köln : Brill, 1995
    (Studies on the texts of the desert of Judah ; Vol. 16)
    ISBN 90-04-10225-6
NE: Dimant, Devorah [Hrsg.]; ham - Mākôn lal-Limûdîm Mitqaddemîm < Yerûšālayim>; GT

ISSN   0169-9962
ISBN   90 04 10225 6

PRINTED IN THE NETHERLANDS

CONTENTS

PREFACE

Some forty years ago the remains of more than 800 Hebrew and Aramaic manuscripts came to light unexpectedly in eleven caves on the western shore of the Dead Sea, near ruins known as Khirbet Qumran. The antiquity of these manuscripts, dating to a few centuries BCE and immediately after, as well as their large number and peculiar character, electrified and captured the imagination of both scholars and the wider public. Expectations ran high for exceptional discoveries regarding the origins of Christianity and its Jewish background. These expectations were soon disappointed, and excitement and interest gradually died out. Most of the readers, both within and outside the scholarly world, were under the impression that most of the scrolls were published and that what there was to be said about them had already been said. Few were aware of the fact that the largest part of the major cave, cave 4, was still unpublished and remained practically unknown, except to the few who worked at leisure on its publication. In the last five years a real change began to be felt, as more and more texts from cave 4 were made known. New texts and younger scholars have raised a whole new range of questions. A new excitement was born, and students of the Qumran documents felt that a new era, and perhaps a rediscovery of the scrolls, was at hand. It was precisely at this moment, and in order to advance the publication of texts from cave 4, that the Institute for Advanced Studies at the Hebrew University, Jerusalem, decided to aid in this process by providing fellowships to a group of scholars working on the Qumran scrolls. The research group included: Joseph M. Baumgarten, Magen Broshi, Devorah Dimant, Jacob Milgrom, Émile Puech, Lawrence H. Schiffman, John Strugnell, Emanuel Tov, Eugene Ulrich, and Moshe Weinfeld. Esti Eshel served as research assistant.

It so happened that shortly after the year of their tenure at the Institute, all the scrolls were opened to the public. With this development, a new era in Qumran studies has indeed been inaugurated. Working within the already changing context, members of this group felt the need to share their new knowledge with colleagues and to indicate to the wider public the new trends emerging in our understanding of the Dead Sea Scrolls. This collection of articles is the fruit of such an initiative. The editors have agreed to accept responsibility for preparing it for publication on behalf of the entire group. Originally we had hoped to cover more topics and to address wider issues. But it may be too early for such an ambitious perspective. At best this collection represents the ongoing work of editing and interpreting one of the greatest discoveries of our century, and we offer it as a contribution to fulfilling the words of the Rule of the Community (1QS 9:19-20): "It is time to prepare the way in the Wilderness."

We wish to thank the Institute for Advanced Studies for providing the means and framework for the research of the group, part of which is published in this volume. Professors Moshe Weinfeld and Emanuel Tov of the Hebrew University directed the group. Dr. Elisheva Yaron, the Associate Director of the Institute, was most helpful in the organization of this project. We especially wish to thank Rama Friedlander of the Institute for expertly preparing the manuscript for camera-ready publication. Erik Larson of New York University was kind enough to proofread the final copy. We thank Dr. Florentino García Martínez and Dr. Adam S. van der Woude for accepting the volume for publication in the series under their editorship, *Studies on the Texts of the Desert of Judah*. The final stages in the editing of this volume took place during our tenure as fellows at the Annenberg Research Institute, Philadelphia.

Devorah Dimant
Lawrence H. Schiffman

4QTOHORAª (PAM 43.309)

THE LAWS ABOUT FLUXES IN 4QTOHORA[a] (4Q274)

Joseph M. Baumgarten

4QToh[a] is the provisional designation given by J.T. Milik to one of a group of fragments from Qumran Cave 4 which deal with the subject of ritual purity. This group has been numbered 4Q274. The text is written on relatively small strips of leather in columns which measure only c. 10 cm in width and c. 4.5 cm in height. The proportionately small size of the letters allows an average of c. 65 letters per line in three of the four partially preserved columns; the fourth column is written with letters only half this size. The writing is in an early Herodian formal script which in Cross's palaeographic sequence may be estimated to come from the end of the first century BCE.

The column transcribed below, dealing with the impurity resulting from fluxes (Lev 15) is relatively well preserved, despite two tears in the lower half. It has an upper margin of c. 0.5 cm and a lower one of 0.7 cm with intercolumnar stitching on the right.

TRANSCRIPTION

1 יחל להפיל את ת..ונו מ[ש]כב יג[ו]ן ישכ]ב ומו[שב אנחה ישב
בדד לכול הטמאים ישב ורחוק מן

2 הטהרה שתים עשרה [ב]אמה בדברו אליו ומערב צפון לכול מושב ישב
רחוק כמדה הזות

3 איש מכול הטמאים [אש]ר [יגע ב]ו ורחץ במים ויכבס בגדיו ואחר יואכל כי
הוא אשר אמר טמא טמא

4 יקרא כול ימי היו[ת   ]ע והובה דם לשבעת הימים אל תגע בזב
ובכול כלי [א]שר יגע בו הזב וש[כב]

5 עליו אׁוׁ אשר ישב עליו וא[ם] נגעה תכבס בגדיה ורחצה ואחר תוכל ובכול
מודה [א]ל תתערב בשבעת

6 ימיה בעבור אשר לו[א]   תגאל את מ... קד[שי] ישראל וגם אל תגע בכול
אשה [זבה] דם לימים רב[י]ם

7 והסופר אם [ז]כר ואם נקבה אל יג[ע   ]ו בדוה בנדתה כי אם טהרה
[מנד]תה כי הנה דם

8 הנדה כזוב ואשר נוגע בו ואם תצ]א ממנו ש[כבת הזרע מגעו יטמא ה] נ]וגע
באדם מכול

9 הטמאיׁם האלה בשבעת ימי טה]רתו א[ל יוכל כאשר יטמא לנפ]ש האדם
ורח[ץ וכבס ואה]ר[

NOTES ON THE READINGS

L.1

The word following להפיל את is most likely to be restored as ת]חנ[ונו,
as orally suggested by J. Milgrom on the basis of Dan 9:18.[1] The
vertical stroke visible after the *taw* may be taken to be the right
leg of a *ḥet*. The crease which follows has apparently obscured the
next two letters.

    The *shin* of משכב has been distorted by a vertical crease and only
the base of the *waw* in יגון remains.

L.2

A faint trace of the *bet* in באמה may be discerned.

L.3

Part of the *resh* in אשר remains. The restoration of the next two
words is suggested by the context.

L.4

The phraseology, deriving from Lev 13:45-46, and the extant *ᶜayin*
lend cogency to Milgrom's suggested restoration: כל ימי היו]ת בו הנג[ע.

L.6

Milik has proposed the reading מ]חני [קד]שי [ש]ראל ; cf. Deut 23:15.

L.7

On the basis of Lev 15:33 and the length of the lacuna, Milik's
restoration אל ינ]ע בוב את זוב[ו seems plausible.

L.8

For the first restoration cf. Lev 15:32. The second lacuna was
completed by Milik as וטמא ה]וא וכול נ[וגע. We prefer the reading
יטמא, which supplies a verb for the preceding מגעו, although the
following *heᵓ* remains problematical.

---

1   For Milgrom's treatment of this text, see below, 59-68 [eds.].

TRANSLATION

[Let him not]

1. begin to cast his supplication. In a bed of sorrow shall he lie and in a seat of sighing shall he sit. Apart from all the unclean shall he sit and at a distance of

2. twelve cubits from the purity when he speaks to him; towards the northwest of any dwelling place shall he sit distant by this measure.

3. Anyone of the unclean who touches him shall bathe in water and wash his clothes and afterwards he may eat, for this is what he said, "'Unclean, unclean'

4. shall he call out all the days [when the plague is upon him]." And a woman who has a flow of blood, during the seven days she shall not touch a man who has a flux, nor any vessel which he touches, nor anything that he lies

5. upon or sits upon. If she touches (these), she shall wash her clothes and bathe; afterwards she may eat. During her seven days she shall by no means mingle (with others).

6. so that she may not contaminate the [camp?] of sacred things of Israel; also, she is not to touch any woman with a blood flow lasting many days.

7. Moreover, one who is counting (seven days), whether male or female, shall not touch [one who has a flux] or a menstruating woman in her uncleanness, unless she cleansed herself of her uncleanness; for the menstrual blood

8. is like the flux and the one touching it. And when he has an emission of semen his touch is defiling. [Whoever] touches any person among

9. these unclean ones during the seven days of his purification [is not] to eat just as if he had become unclean [by a corpse]; he must bathe and wash (his clothes), afterwards...

COMMENTS

L.1

The mention of מֹשְׁכָּב and מוֹשָׁב strongly suggests that the subject of lines 1-4 is the *zab*, who transmits defilement to the bed upon which he lies and the objects upon which he sits (Lev 15:4). We assume a negative before יחל, thus implying restrictions upon his recitation of prayers during the period of uncleanness. This is in accordance with the indications of 4Q512 that the *zab* may recite blessings only after his purification.[2] For the pairing of יגון and אנחה see Isa 35:10 and 51:10. The phraseology for the isolation of the *zab* is derived from that employed for those afflicted with skin disease in Lev 13:46.

Ll.1-2

ורחוק מן הטהרה apparently refers to the distance he must keep from pure food or objects in the possession of those with whom he converses; cf. 4QMMT C 64-65 (forthcoming in a volume by J. Strugnell and E. Qimron):

ואף על הצרועים אנחנו א[ומרים שלוא י]בואו עם טהרת הקודש כי בדד יהיו

Likewise, concerning the lepers we [say that they must not] come (in contact) with sacred purities, for they are to be segregated.

For the location to the northwest compare 11QT 46:14 where the latrines are located "to the northwest of the city." However, 11QT 46:17 locates persons with fluxes as well as others who are unclean "to the east of the city." The latter would be readily explainable on the basis of the prevailing westerly winds, but the reason for placing the latrines to the northwest is not so patent.[3] Does it have something to do with the Essene veneration of the rising sun (J.W. 2.128) and their care to prevent its rays from being sullied by the sight of excrement (2.148)? Our text is concerned with segregating the *zab* from other unclean persons, presumably all located to the east of the city, by confining him "to the northwest of any dwelling place." This apparently would serve to accentuate his social isolation. Compare the rabbinic rule about the *meṣora*ᶜ:

בדד ישב שלא יהיו טמאים אחרים יושבים עמו

"Alone shall he dwell" (Lev 13:46), (this means) that other unclean persons may not dwell with him (b. Pes. 67a).

However, rabbinic halakhah did not exclude the *zab* from the city.

Ll. 3-4

For the restriction on eating before purification compare 4Q512 col. XI, frag. 9 and 4Q514.[4]

---

2   See J.M. Baumgarten, "The Purification Rituals in DJD 7," *The Dead Sea Scrolls: Forty Years of Research* (ed. D. Dimant and U. Rappaport; Jerusalem: Magnes and Yad Itzhak Ben-Zvi, Leiden, New York, Köln: E.J. Brill, 1992) 199-209.

3   Cf. Y. Yadin, *The Temple Scroll* (Jerusalem: Israel Exploration Society, 1983) 1.296-8.

4   M. Baillet, *Qumran Grotte 4, III (4Q484-4Q520)* (DJD VII; Oxford: Clarendon Press, 1982) 271 and 296; Baumgarten, "Purification Rituals."

The quotation from Lev 13:45-46 pertains to the *meṣoraᶜ*, but is extended here by analogy to the *zab*. Compare *Sifra*, Tazriaᶜ 12.9 where the repetition טמא טמא serves as the source of the rule that not only the *meṣoraᶜ*, but also other defiled persons must give warning of their uncleanness:

ומנין לרבות שאר הטמאים תלמוד לומר וטמא טמא יקרא

And whence (do we know) to include other impure persons? (Scripture) teaches: "'Unclean, unclean' shall he cry out."

In our text, the apparent intent is to show from the repetition of טמא that even one who is already טמא requires purification to remove the טומאה contracted from the *zab*.

L.4

הזבה refers here, as in Lev 15:19, to a menstruant woman whose period of uncleanness lasts seven days. Unlike the *zab*, she does not require the counting of clean days after the cessation of her flow. She is to avoid contact with a *zab* and requires purification if it should occur.

L.5

We take ובכול מודה in the sense which it apparently has in CD 12:10 אל ימכר להם בכל מאודו, "let him by no means sell to them," although מאד can also signify "property" as in מאד המחנה, CD 9:11. The meaning of the verb התערב in connection with ritual purity is illustrated in 11QT 45:4 where the departing and entering priestly courses are enjoined from intermingling themselves and their utensils:

ולוא יהיו מתערבים אלה באלה ובכליהמה

So that they not mingle with each other and with their utensils.

E. Qimron[5] has proposed to interpret our passage, as well as CD 11:4 (אל יתערב איש מרצונו בשבת), to refer specifically to sexual intercourse. However, it seems difficult to harmonize this with the specification that he must not intermingle "voluntarily;" nor does it seem plausible that the menstruant in our text is called upon to avoid sexual relations in order not to spread contamination, when these are offenses subject to a capital penalty in Lev 20:18. The contamination of "the sacred things of Israel" (cf. טהרת ישראל in 4Q512 col. XI frag. 8, which pertains to the *zab*) refers, in our

5   "'אל יתערב איש מרצונו בשבת' (ברית דמשק יא,4)", *Proceedings of the Ninth World Congress of Jewish Studies*, Division D, I (Jerusalem: World Union of Jewish Studies, 1986) Hebrew section, 9-15.

opinion, to the proliferation of impurity through the intermingling of foods and utensils.

L.6

The text goes on to prohibit also contact between a menstruant woman and a woman who suffers from a flux of blood extending for "many days" (Lev 15:25). The latter is subject to a more severe form of impurity requiring seven clean days after the end of her flow.

L.7

Those who are counting clean days, whether man or woman, are further enjoined to avoid contact with a menstruant woman before her purification. The rationale is that clean days mean the absence of flux from the person who is counting, but contact with another person suffering from the flux, whether of menstrual blood, the discharge of a *zab*, or an emission of semen, is likewise contaminating.

L.8

The parity between menstrual blood and the discharges (including semen) of the *zab* is strikingly similar to the mishnaic ranking of the different degrees of impurity in m. Kel. 1.3 and Zab. 5.7. Samaritan tradition, by contrast, considered contact with menstrual blood to result in seven days of uncleanness, but only one day for contact with the discharge of the *zab*.[6]

L.9

When one who is counting clean days touches any of the aforementioned unclean persons he must bathe and wash his clothes before eating any food, just as if he had been defiled by corpse uncleanness. However, our text apparently does not require him to begin counting the seven clean days anew.

Discussion

Laws pertaining to the impurity resulting from fluxes (Lev 15) are found in a number of Qumran sources. CD 5:7 lists the failure to separate from women during the menses among the major transgressions of the sect's contemporaries. In 4QD[a], the largest of the cave 4 manuscripts of the *Damascus Document*, a fragmentary passage elaborates on the laws of the *zab* after a section dealing

---

6   I.R.M. Bóid, *Principles of Samaritan Halachah* (Leiden: E.J. Brill, 1989) 145, 287, and 302.

with the laws of skin disease. 4QD[a] lists both those afflicted with skin disease and those suffering from fluxes in a catalogue of transgressors. We have elsewhere noted the markedly penitential tone of the liturgy for the purification rituals in 4Q512, which include blessings to be recited by the *zab* after his immersion at the end of the seven pure days (4Q512 cols. X and XI). It is furthermore noteworthy that *Temple Scroll* 46:16-18 provides for three distinct and separated areas (מובדלים זה מזה) for 'lepers', *zabim*, and men after a seminal emission. This concern for segregating those in different categories of impurity is one of the salient characteristics of our text.

The *zab* is to be kept, not only outside the city, but at a distance from the dwelling place of others who are unclean. The *zabah* must not touch the *zab*, and those counting clean days must avoid contact with those still experiencing a flow. This segregation is reminiscent of Josephus's observation concerning the grades of purity among the Essenes, "A senior if but touched by a junior, must take a bath, as after contact with an alien" (J.W. 2.150). Josephus, however, also refers to the banishment of those afflicted with fluxes from the city as a requirement of the law of Moses (J.W. 5.227 and Ant. 3.261).

Rabbinic halakhah did not generally impose such rigid barriers. We do have a tannaitic ruling forbidding a *zab* to eat together with his wife who is a *zabah* (m. *Shabb.* 1:3), but this may perhaps be a precaution against illicit intercourse, although the parallel Tosefta (Shab. 1:14) cites it as an example of stringency with regard to purity in former times. The *zab* was permitted to remain in the city, though excluded from the Temple precincts (m. Kel. 1:8). Yet the principle of segregating different categories of ritually unclean persons from each other is not unknown in rabbinic sources, as we noted above with regard to the isolation of the *meṣoraᶜ* (Lev 13:46).

Another stringency in our text is the restriction on eating before purification (lines 3, 5, and 9). As we noted above this is known from other Qumran texts. G. Alon[7] had earlier maintained that this was also reflected in the references in *Yerushalmi Berakhot* to bathing before ordinary meals, despite the efforts of L. Ginzberg to read them otherwise.[8]

We also observed above that extension of Lev 13:45 ("'Unclean, unclean' shall he cry") from the *meṣoraᶜ* to other unclean persons was paralleled in *Sifra*. A late midrashic source, *Leqaḥ Ṭob* (Lev 13:45) specifically refers to those suffering from fluxes:

---

7   מחקרים בתולדות ישראל (Tel Aviv: Hakkibutz Hameuchad, 1967) 1.150.
8   Baumgarten, "Purification Rituals."

אפילו הזב והזבה שאינה יכולה לטהר היתה מכרזת להודיע לרבים
Even the *zab* and the *zabah* who were not able to purify themselves
would call out to warn the public.

Finally, we take note of the vestigial isolation still imposed
upon the *zab* as reflected in the responsum of Hai Gaon (d. 1038). In
answer to the question whether a *zab* may participate in synagogue
services, he responded that this was permissible, but

> Let there be assigned for him something to sit upon alone. Let him
> not adorn himself, but appear disheveled. If he sees someone ap-
> proaching who does not recognise him, he is to warn him not to
> touch him until God has mercy upon him and restores him to his
> health and his purity.[9]

---

9   L. Ginzberg, *Geonica* (New York: Hermon Press, 1967) 2.38.

VISIONARY ARCHITECTURE AND TOWN PLANNING IN THE DEAD SEA SCROLLS

Magen Broshi

The composition known as the "Description of New Jerusalem" (henceforth DNJ) is one of the more popular of the non-biblical and non-Qumranic Dead Sea Scrolls. Remains of six exemplars were found in five caves, and though their state of preservation leaves much to be desired, we still can get a fair idea regarding the contents of this work.[1] This is another link in a chain that started with Ezekiel and ended with Revelation. In this literary genre an angel takes the author and shows him the eschatological Temple and the Temple City in great detail, including exact measurements of the various components of the Temple and City. The compositions regarding this genre do not necessarily agree with one another in details, but all are characterised by a fantastic scale. The later the work, the greater the measurements of the Temple and City. The *Temple Scroll* (henceforth TS) devotes some one third of its length to the description of the Temple. Indeed, this is not an eschatological temple, nor is it revealed through the guidance of an angel (the authority here is the Lord); but, as we shall see below, there is a great kinship between the two compositions.

Although DNJ deals with subjects that loom large in archaeology, it has hardly attracted the attention of scholars, despite the fact that it is already over thirty years since its main parts were

---

1   The six exemplars are:
    1Q32 (J.T. Milik, DJD I, (134-35).
    2Q24 (M. Baillet, DJD III, 84-89 and *RB* 62 [1955] 222-25).
    5Q15 (J.T. Milik, DJD III, 183-93).
    4Q549 (partially described in J. Starcky, "Jerusalem et les manuscrits de la Mer Morte," *Le Monde de la Bible* 1 (1977) 38-40, to be published by É. Puech).
    4Q550 (three tiny fragments, probably from DNJ, also to be published by É. Puech).
    11Q Jer Nouv ar (B. Jongeling, "Publication provisoire d'un fragment provenant de la grotte 11 de Qumran," *JSJ* 1 (1970) 58-64, 185-186. Final publication has been entrusted to F. García Martínez).
    In addition to the above mentioned copies, 4Q232 seems to be a Hebrew version of the Aramaic DNJ (J.T. Milik, *The Books of Enoch* [Oxford: Oxford University Press, 1976] 59).
    English translations: J.A. Fitzmyer-D.J. Harrington, *A Manual of Palestinian Aramaic Texts* (Rome: Biblical Institute Press, 1978) 46-65; Licht (below, n. 21). German: K. Beyer, *Die aramäischen Texte vom Toten Meer* (Göttingen: Vandenhoeck & Ruprecht, 1984) 214-21.

published.[2] A partial explanation of this disregard is the visionary nature of the DNJ and its fantastic scale, but this disregard is certainly a wrong attitude. One finds in this text a rare expression of the *Zeitgeist* and conceptions of architecture and town planning current in the Hellenistic period. The TS fared much better, as in the last twenty years it was the most discussed scroll, but it deals only with the Temple and has nothing to say about the appearance of the City. We will attempt here to prove the relationship of these two texts and to show how together they provide important information on the architecture and town planning of the Second Temple period.

I. The Relation Between the Two Works

The differences between the TS and the DNJ are numerous and significant. One is in Hebrew, the other is in Aramaic; in one God speaks in the first person singular, in the other a heavenly surveyor is the source of information; the TS deals with a temple for the 'here and now,' while DNJ is concerned with a temple for the End of Days; the TS, most probably, is a sectarian work, while DNJ lacks any sectarian ingredients (even its use of Aramaic points to its non-sectarian origin).[3]

Nevertheless, there is a close relationship between the two. Not only do both deal with the Temple, and both display strong Hellenistic character, but they share many identical elements. This cannot be a coincidence and it is quite certain that one depended on the other or that both borrowed from a common source. As we shall see below, remains of such a source (or sources?) were found at Qumran. Yadin, in his *editio princeps* of TS, has not devoted a special discussion to the relation between the two, but *en passant* has pointed out parallels and similarities. In a fragment of DNJ (1Q32), for instance, wheels and pillars are mentioned, and Yadin compared to it the description of the slaughterhouse in the

---

2 A book on town planning in Hellenistic Palestine published recently does not mention this text. See R. Arav, *Hellenistic Palestine, Settlement Pattern and City Planning 331-37 BC*, BAR Int. Series 485 (Oxford, 1989).

3 S. Segert, "Die Sprachenfrage in der Qumrangemeinschaft," *Qumran-Probleme: Vorträge des Leipziger Symposions über Qumran-Probleme* (Berlin: Deutsche Akademie der Wissenschaften zu Berlin, 1963) 315-39; Idem, "Sprachliche Bemerkungen zu einigen aramäischen Texten von Qumran," *Archiv Orientalni* 33 (1965) 190-206, (esp. 205-20) (I owe these two references to Prof. J.A. Fitzmyer). The Aramaic Testament of Amram is perhaps the only exception to this rule.

TS.[4] Another passage in DNJ (2Q24), which describes the altar, resembles a similar passage in TS.[5] The term חלונות (חלונים) אטמות (frequently used in Ezekiel, first used in Kings), translated in DNJ as כוין אטימן, is used in both texts.[6] Great similarity has been noted in regard to the description of the House with the Winding Stair.[7] The houses in DNJ have the same measurements as the House of the Laver in TS, 21 cubits square.[8] In both works, the measurements of the House with the Winding Stair are 20 cubits square.[9] The measurements of the gates of the House of the Laver in the TS are identical to those of the houses of DNJ.[10]

Wise, who compared the two texts meticulously, pointed to further similarities of which we will mention three.[11] In both scrolls the most frequent figures are divisible by 7, while in Ezekiel the basic figure is 25.[12] The gates of the Temple's Middle and Outer Courts are named after the twelve sons of Jacob in an order unknown from any biblical or intertestamental book, but this is the order in DNJ.[13] The outer measurements of the Temple compound according to TS are 1700x1700 cubits, a figure very close to the size of a mega-block made of four insulae (1680x1680 cubits, i.e. 7x12x20 cubits) in DNJ.[14] This could hardly be an accident. Last, but not least, the height of the city wall in DNJ is 49 cubits, which is the height of the wall of the Outer Court in TS.

Undoubtedly both scrolls ought to be discussed together, not only because they deal with the same subjects but also, as we shall try to show below, because they must have been composed in the same period.

---

4   Y. Yadin, *The Temple Scroll* I (Jerusalem: Israel Exploration Society, 1983) 235 (hereafter *Temple Scroll*).
5   Ibid., 241
6   Ibid., 225-26.
7   Ibid., 214-17.
8   Ibid., 220.
9   Ibid., 212-17.
10   Ibid., 220.
11   M. O. Wise, *A Critical Study of the Temple Scroll* (Chicago: Oriental Institute, 1990) 61-81.
12   Ibid., 100-5.
13   Ibid., 116; On the order of the gates in the TS cf. *Temple Scroll* 1.244, 252; On their order in the DNJ, cf. Starcky (above, n. 1) 39. An unpublished Hebrew text from 4Q (364-365), 'an expansionist Pentateuchal text,' has a similar order of gates (J. Strugnell, personal communication). On this text cf. F. García Martínez, "La 'Nueva Jerusalén' y el Templo Futuro de los Mss. de Qumrán," *Salvación en la Palabra, Homenaje al Prof. A. Díez Macho* (Madrid: Editiones Cristiandad, 1986) 563-4 n. 2. An English version appeared in F. García Martínez, *Qumran and Apocalyptic, Studies on the Aramaic Texts from Qumran* (Leiden: E.J. Brill, 1992) 180-213. The text is reproduced in part in *Temple Scroll* III, supplementary plate 38*:5.
14   Cf. Wise (above, n. 11) 123.

II. The Gigantic Dimensions

Short perusal shows that most of the dimensions used in DNJ are very big, indeed extravagant, and bear very little relation to the topography and geography of Jerusalem or to the technology of the time. It is a pity that we do not know the exact value of the cubit mentioned in these two scrolls, and it seems that all the labor spent by scholars who tried to find the precise metric equivalent of the cubit was spent in vain.[15] Therefore, and in view of the fact that the majority of the figures are fantastic, there is no harm if we use a rounded figure: 1 cubit=50 cm. This is also quite close to the average of the two estimates of the long and the short cubits (42+56=98/2=49cm).

The size of the City according to DNJ is 140x100 *ris*, which equals, according to our system, (rounded) 21 kmx30 km=6300 sq. km.[16] This is an area greater than that of the West Bank. If we suppose that the density of such a city was 250 people per hectare, quite a reasonable density, then the population of the city according to DNJ would have reached 150 million.[17] This is, though, a modest city in comparison with the heavenly city described in the Revelation of John, the area of which exceeds 6,000,000 sq. km (12,000 *ris* square, Rev 21:16).

The Temple complex according to TS, as I have shown elsewhere,[18] equaled in area the entire Herodian city. It spread all the way from Damasus Gate to the Mount of Olives. Leveling such an area would have necessitated the removal of millions of cubic meters of rock, as well as the filling in of lower areas such as the Kidron Valley. Despite the fantastic proportions, the authors of both TS and DNJ treated their figures with utmost care and with extreme earnestness. DNJ quotes every figure twice: in cubits and reeds, although the conversion is very simple (1:7), all to avoid any possible error or confusion.

---

15   E.g. J. Maier, "The Architectural History of the Temple in Jerusalem in the Light of The Temple Scroll," *Temple Scroll Studies* (ed. G.J. Brooke; *JSPS* 7; Sheffield: JSOT Press, 1989) 23-62; García Martínez (above, n. 13) 570-72.

16   Our computation is based on the assumption that the *ris* (*stadion*) equals 60 reeds, i.e. 420 cubits (see Starcky [above n. 1] and García Martínez [above n. 13]). In our system 1 *ris*=210m.

17   We believe that 250 persons per hectare is not far off the mark. Cf. M. Broshi, R. Gophna, "Middle Age Bronze Palestine: Its Settlements and Population," *BASOR* 261 (1986) 73-90. For ancient Jerusalem we suggested 400 persons per hectare. Cf. M. Broshi, "La population de l'ancienne Jérusalem," *RB* 82 (1975) 5-14.

18   M. Broshi, "The Gigantic Dimensions of the Visionary Temple in the *Temple Scroll*," *BAR* 13, 6 (1987) 36-37.

In both compositions there is a successful attempt to use sacred figures (mostly 7, but also 12, and in one case 52).[19] Needless to say, the authors were very careful to calculate all measurements without any error.

III. DNJ AS A SOURCE REFLECTING THE ARCHITECTURAL CONCEPTIONS OF ITS TIME

In ancient Jewish literature DNJ is the only composition that treats town planning in a professional and detailed manner. Even in classical literature such works are rare.[20] Accordingly, detailed examination of this text from an architectural point of view is in order.

The following résumé of DNJ is based primarily on 5Q15, the fullest preserved text: The angel who guides the author shows him first the city from the outside, a city of 140x100 *ris*.[21] In the wall there are twelve gates and four hundred and eighty posterns—three gates in each side and a postern for each *ris*.[22] Each gate is flanked by two towers (35 cubits square) the roofs of which are reached by outer stairways. The width of the gates is 21 cubits, that of the posterns is 14 cubits, quite an exaggerated size for a postern. Inside the city the angel shows him the insulae, each one 357 cubits square. Each insula is surrounded by an open space (but according to Milik it is a peristyle).[23] Between the insulae pass streets of 42 cubits wide. These are the narrow streets of a city which has a

---

19   The most frequent measurements are multiples of seven, but there are also multiples of twelve (more so in the TS). See the meticulous treatment in Wise (above, n. 11) 66-70. The figure fifty-two that appears once in the TS and once in the War Scroll is, of course, the number of weeks according to the Qumranic calendar. Cf. *Temple Scroll* 1.265. The book of Ezekiel which exercised a strong influence on both scrolls uses, in contradistinction, the programmatic number twenty-five. Cf. Wise, ibid., 70.

20   Discussions of town planning are quite rare in ancient literature. One of the notable exceptions is Vitruvius I,VI-VII.

21   García Martínez (above, n. 13) 566, 569. J. Licht, "An Ideal Town Plan from Qumran," *IEJ* 29 (1979) 45-59, the best architectural analysis of DNJ, was not aware of Starcky (above, n. 1) and reconstructed the measurements of the city according to Ezekiel, erroneously of course. Ezekiel's city (48:16-17) is only 5000 cubits.

22   So García Martínez (pace Milik), ibid. 570.

23   Milik (DJD III, 185) interpreted the word שבק as "peristyle" (French: passage couvert), but Greenfield ("The Small Caves of Qumran" [a critique of the above], *JAOS* 89 (1969) 134 is of the opinion that it should be translated "space left open." Some scholars follow Milik (Vermes, Fitzmyer-Harrington, Beyer, García Martínez) and others Greenfield (Licht, Wise). Archaeologically, both interpretations are possible, but Milik's is less likely since normal insulae were not adorned with porticoes. But we should remember that our planned city is not a normal one.

strict hierarchy of roads. The most important is a thoroughfare 126 cubits wide which runs in the direction east-west, north of the Temple. The main street which crosses the city from north to south is 92 cubits wide. Two E-W main streets are 70 cubits wide, while the two N-S streets are 67 cubits wide. This network of highways divides the city into 16 'super blocks,' each 35x25 *ris* in size.[24]

Each insula, of 357 cubits square, is made up of a strip of houses that surrounds an inner court. The size of a house is 21x14 cubits, i.e. ca. 73.5 sq. m. If Licht's reconstruction is correct, and we know of no other way to interpret the text, it means that only a small part of the area was occupied by buildings: 17,640 sq. cubits (14x21x60) out of 127,449 sq. cubits.[25] Thus, only one seventh of the area of the insulae was built upon, and if we consider also the open spaces, streets, etc., the proportion of occupied area in the city was particularly low. Contrary to what some authors have claimed about the Oriental character of this work, inner courts were common not only in the East but also in Greece.[26]

Each insula had four gates, one for each side. Here too, we propose to accept Licht's ingenious reconstruction.[27] The construction of the gates is absurdly large for *intra muros* construction (ca. 26x15 m) and its shape anachronistic. The only proper element, time-wise, is the tower with spiral staircase attached to it. Here one may wonder why such a tower should be built for a regular housing block. The tower is described accurately and clearly and its reconstruction is fairly certain. The houses have a second floor, but unfortunately its description has been poorly preserved. An interesting element in the upper floor is a hall (19x12 cubits) furnished with twenty-two beds. This hall has eleven 'blind windows,' i.e. niches. There is no telling what this hall was intended for. Milik's opinion that this is a dining hall seems to be unfounded, and the niches must have been used to store garments, as we learn from the TS, the Mishnah, as well as the archaeological evidence.[28] It is well worth noting that except for the Temple, and perhaps for the above mentioned 'dormitory,' the scroll does not

---

24   This division is not mentioned in the scroll, but can be inferred from the layout of the main streets (avenues). According to our system, each 'mega-block' was 38.5 sq. km large (7.35x5.25 km).

25   Licht (above, n. 21) 52-53.

26   A.W. Lawrence, *Greek Architecture* (Harmondsworth: Penguin Books, 1957) 238-49; W. Hoepfner, E.L. Schwander, *Haus und Stadt im klassischen Griechenland* (München: Deutscher Kunstverlag, 1986) passim.

27   Licht (above, n. 21) 54-58.

28   Milik's reading (=מאכלא, dining) is not supported by the photograph and should be regarded as a guess (DJD III, 190, pl. xli). On the niches, cf. *Temple Scroll* 1. 220-21.

discuss any public building. Is this to be ascribed to an accident of preservation?

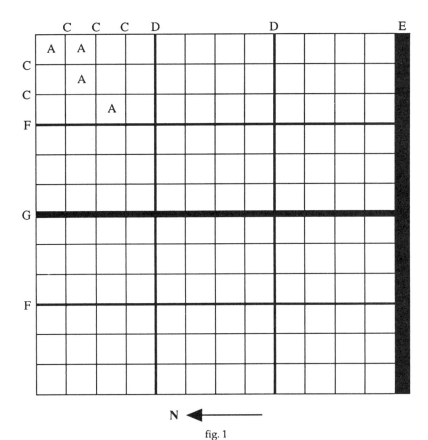

fig. 1

The city plan (partial) and street hierarchy. A—insula; C—narrow streets (24 cubits wide); D—main streets, east-west (70 cubits wide); E—main thoroughfare, east-west (126 cubits); F—main street, north-south (67 cubits); G—main street, north-south (92 cubits). After J. Licht (cf. note 21).

How much we depend on the chances of preservation can be deduced also from this scroll. Had we only the fragments from cave 5, we might have thought that this was the first case of an apocalyptic book that deals with the City and ignores the Temple. However, this is not the case, for the fragments from caves 2 and 11 are concerned with the Temple, with its cult rather than its architecture. But this, too, might be fortuitous.

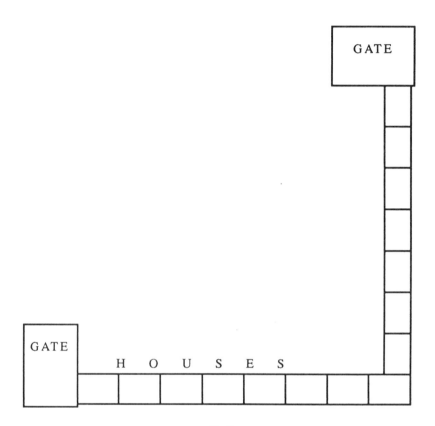

Fig. 2
Arrangement of houses along quarter-perimeter of an insula.
After J. Licht (cf. note 21).

We shall conclude this summary with some information supplied by Starcky regarding a fragment from cave 4.[29] Among other things, it tells about a 49 cubit high wall which has 1432 towers—two flanking each of the 480 posterns and one midway between the posterns. The careful author has not included the large gate towers nor the eight corner towers (two for each corner) that must have been of different size. The computation must have been 480x3=1440-8=1432. Doubtless, the complete publication of the fragments from caves 4 and 11 will add new data and will clarify our understanding of the architectural details of the City described in DNJ.

---

29   Starcky (above, n. 1); García Martínez (above, n. 13) 577.

IV. The TS as a Source of Information on Contemporary Architecture

The TS is far better preserved than the DNJ. This, among other reasons, accounts for the fact that the TS was the main topic of Dead Sea Scroll research in the last two decades. However, very few archaeologists (except Yadin, of course) bothered to study it.[30]

The scroll devotes over a third of its space to the description of the Temple as it should be. The first unit (cols. 3-13) discusses the Temple, while the second and larger one (cols. 30-46) deals with the courts. The author of the TS displays exceptional proficiency with his subject, something to be appreciated all the more since he describes a visionary complex rather than an existing one.

V. The Date of the Two Works According to Various Scholars

Yadin was of the opinion that the *Temple Scroll* was composed at the time of the Hasmonean king John Hyrcanus or a little later, i.e. the second half of the second century BCE,[31] and so far this date has been adopted by scholars. Other scholars suggested different dates and in the following we will enumerate some of them, from the latest to the earliest.

Barbara Thiering ascribes the scroll to the times of Herod the Great (37-4 BCE).[32] Hengel, Charlesworth and Mendels believe that it was composed under Alexander Jannaeus (103-76 BCE).[33] Similar dates, though for different reasons, are suggested also by other scholars: Laperrousaz (the first quarter, or third of the first century BCE);[34] Schiffman is even more precise (110-90 BCE).[35]

---

30   Some exceptions are I. Magen, "Bet Ha-Mesibbah in the *Temple Scroll* and in the Mishnah," *EI* 17 (1984) 226-35 (Hebrew); J. Patrich, "The Mesibbah of the Temple according to the Tractate Middot," *IEJ* 36 (1986) 215-33.
31   *Temple Scroll* 1.386-90.
32   B. Thiering, "The Date of the Composition of the Temple Scroll," *Temple Scroll Studies* (ed. G.J. Brooke; Sheffield : JSOT Press, 1989) 99-120.
33   M. Hengel, J.H. Charlesworth, D. Mendels, "The Polemical Character of 'On Kingship' in the Temple Scroll: An Attempt at Dating 11Q Temple," *JJS* 37 (1986) 28-38.
34   E.M. Laperrousaz, "Does the *Temple Scroll* Date from the First or Second Century BCE?" apud Brooke (above, n. 32) 91-97.
35   L.H. Schiffman, "The Temple Scroll and the Systems of Jewish Law of the Second Temple Period," apud Brooke, ibid., 239-55.

Wacholder is of the opinion that the scroll was written by the Teacher of Righteousness in 200 BCE and that it was revealed to his followers in 196 BCE (sic!).[36]

Maier suggests the beginning of the Hellenistic period or even the Persian period.[37] Stegemann offers the earliest dating, sometime between the second half of the fifth century BCE and the third century BCE, most probably the fourth.[38]

In the following we shall try to prove that the scroll could not have been composed before the Hellenistic period, and that it was most likely composed in one of the advanced stages of this era.

DNJ has not occupied the attention of scholarship as much as has TS. Therefore, the opinions on its date are fewer. The manuscripts we possess are quite late and cannot be used as palaeographical evidence to establish the date of composition.[39] Beyer ascribes it precisely to 142 BCE and Wise is of the opinion that it was composed in 170 BCE.[40] Kutscher places the language of the DNJ on the same level as that of the Genesis Apocryphon—i.e. a transitory stage between Imperial Aramaic and Middle Aramaic— and he dates this language to the first century BCE or the first century CE. However, he does not rule out a date in the second century CE.[41]

VI. ARCHITECTURAL DETAILS POINTING TO THE DATE OF THE COMPOSITION OF THE TWO WORKS

These two works contain at least three architectural elements (each text has two), dating them to the Hellenistic period: the tower with spiral staircase (found in both works); the peristyle (repeatedly referred to in the TS, and probably appearing also in DNJ); the Hippodamic town plan (only in DNJ). The presence of each one of these elements can certainly be used as a chronological indicator; and their appearance together lends them extra weight.

---

36   B.Z. Wacholder, *The Dawn of Qumran* (Cincinnati: Hebrew Union College Press, 1983) 211, 215; Cf. also the sober critique of Devorah Dimant, *Zion* 51 (1986) 246-50.

37   Cf. above, n. 15.

38   H. Stegemann, "The Literary Composition of the *Temple Scroll* and its Status at Qumran," apud Brooke (above, n. 32) 123-48.

39   García Martínez (above, n. 13) 580-81.

40   Beyer (above, n. 1) 34-35; Wise (above, n. 11) 130.

41   E.Y. Kutscher, "The Language of the Genesis Apocryphon," *Scripta Hierosolymitana* 4 (1957) 6, 15.

The House with the Winding Stair

The tower with the spiral staircase should stand, according to the TS, near the northwestern corner of the Temple (30:3-31:9) and it agrees in function (though not in shape) to the one described in the Mishnah (Mid. 4:5). Similar structures are used, according to TS, to ascend the upper colonnades of the outer court (42:6-7). In DNJ such a tower is described in great detail (5Q15, II, 2-5), but here such towers flank the gates. As we remarked above, the outer measurements of the towers in both works are identical.[42] The reconstruction accepted by most scholars is based on clear data that does not call for great contributions of the imagination.

This tower is a characteristic Hellenistic edifice that appears frequently from the third century BCE.[43] In Palestine as well it appears during this period. Thus far it has been found at three sites: Dor, Beth Yeraḥ and Tel Zeror.[44] In the first two sites, towers function as city-wall towers; in the third, as a watch tower.[45] Before the third century there is only one case of a construction that can be interpreted as a spiral-staircase tower—room M of Palace 1723 at Megiddo, from Solomon's times. The identification of this room as such is far from certain, as the remains are too scanty.[46] It should also be borne in mind that some seven hundred years have elapsed between the Megiddo tower and the Hellenistic towers.

In short, this architectural element makes the third century BCE the earliest possible date for the composition of the two scrolls.

---

42   *Temple Scroll* 1.211-17; 2.131-33. Recently an attempt was made to use the tower described in both works to reconstruct the Mishnaic Temple. It seems to us that Patrich (above, n. 30) is correct in claiming that the Mishnaic Temple had its staircase inside the Temple wall, while the tower described in our works was an independent one.

43   Arav (above, n. 2) 157 (=257).

44   Beit Yeraḥ: P. Bar-Adon, "Beit Yerah," *IEJ* 5 (1955) 273. Dor: E. Stern, "Excavations at Tel Dor 1981: Preliminary Report, 1981," *IEJ* 32 (1982) 110; Y. Yadin, *The Temple Scroll, The Hidden Law of the Dead Sea Sect* (London: Weidenfeld and Nicolson, 1985) 126. Tel Zeror: K. Ohata, *Tel Zeror* 3 (Tokyo: The Society for Near Eastern Studies in Japan, 1970) 36-37, pl. vii. Since this paper was completed, A. Kloner unearthed a fourth one at Maresha.

45   A. Negev, "The Staircase-Tower in Nabatean Architecture," *EI* 11 (1973) 197-207 (Hebrew). We cannot agree with Negev in ascribing the invention of this tower to the Nabateans and placing its earliest use in the second century.

46   Speaking about a Solomonic building, Yadin (above, n. 44) must have had in mind Room M in Palace 1723 at Megiddo. Cf. R.S. Lamon, G.M. Shipton, *Megiddo* I (Chicago: University of Chicago, 1939) 23, figs. 12, 29, 30.

The Peristyle

One of the salient features in the description of the Temple courts is the stoas, the colonnades that surround the courts and thus form the peristyles of all three courts.[47] In two of the courts, the middle and the outer, the peristyles have an intricate system of chambers and rooms. There are no clear cases of complete peristyles before the Hellenistic period.[48] Moreover, though freestanding colonnades are known from the seventh century BCE on, stoas with rooms are known outside Athens only from the end of the fourth century.[49] The Amrit temple from the sixth-fifth centuries BCE mentioned by Maier is not a very clear case, and at best this is a solitary, undeveloped peristyle.[50] We have already mentioned above Milik's idea that the insulae were surrounded by colonnades [cf. n. 23], but his interpretation is doubtful.

The peristyle seemed in the Hellenistic period to be such an indispensible element that the Septuagint translators imposed it, anachronistically, on Solomon's Temple. The translation of Ezek. 40:17-18 reads for רצפה, which stands undoubtedly for floor, once στοαί and the other time Περίστυλα.[51] Josephus also, in his description of Solomon's Temple (Ant. 8.96), ascribes to it spacious stoas.[52]

DNJ does not mention any peristyles, but there is good reason to believe that it is only because of the fragmentary nature of the texts that reached us. One fragment mentions 12 cubit high columns and the distance (the exact figure is unfortunately lost) between the columns (5Q15, II, 4-5). Another fragment also has columns (1Q32, 1 and 5), but the mention of wheels nearby means, perhaps, that it deals with the slaughterhouse.[53]

---

47   On the term פרור, the scroll's equivalent of portico, cf. *Temple Scroll* 1. 237-39, and passim.
48   D.S. Robertson, *A Handbook of Greek and Roman Architecture* (Cambridge: Cambridge University Press, 1943) 297.
49   J.J. Coulton, *The Architectural Development of the Greek Stoa* (Oxford: Clarendon Press, 1976) 55, 85ff., figs. 24, 25.
50   M. Dunand, "Le Temple d'Amrit dans la Pérée d'Aradus," *Akten des VII. Internationalen Kongresses für Iranische Kunst und Archaeologie* (Berlin: Dietrich Reimer Verlag, 1979) 247-48. This is a preliminary report lacking fundamental data.
51   Cf. commentaries on Ezekiel; *Temple Scroll* 1. 263-64 tries to find an unusual meaning for רצפה (paving) to explain the LXX's anachronistic ascription of peristyles to Solomon's Temple. Apparently, Yadin's solution is unacceptable.
52   *Temple Scroll* 1.192-93.
53   Ibid., 235.

The Hippodamic Plan

Straight streets that intersect each other at right angles have existed from time immemorial, but it was Hippodamos of Miletus who codified the idea of a gridiron-planned city.[54] He began his career in 479 BCE when he reconstructed his city, and as a matter of fact built a new one over its ruins, since it had been destroyed fifteen years earlier by the Persians. This system was introduced into Asia (excluding Western Anatolia where it was conceived) and Egypt, after the conquests of Alexander the Great. From then on very intensive building activity took place in the East. In the Hellenistic period more than 350 cities were founded there.[55]

As we have noted above, DNJ is a characteristic Hippodamic composition. Not only is the city built like a chessboard, but its houses have standard shapes and sizes and its streets have hierarchical order (126, 92, 70, 67, 42 cubits wide). It has been noted that certain Hippodamic plans have absorbed certain elements from the Pythagorean numerical theories.[56] We have dwelt already on the fact that measurements in our works are not arbitrary. They may follow Jewish traditions. As to the street-width measurements of DNJ, the logic of three of them is clear: that of the narrow standard one ($2 \times 3 \times 7 = 42$ cubits), the widest ($42 \times 3 = 126$), and the mean ($7 \times 10 = 70$). The determination of the other two escapes us.

VII. ANACHRONISMS

In treatises such as the two works under discussion, which display a strong link to old sources, one would expect anachronistic elements; but in fact, only one is discernible. The gates to the insulae in DNJ are the sole example of an out-of-place element. The closest structure to these gates can be found only in the Iron Age. However, the gates are out-of-place in any case, as the insulae are not meant to be fortified units and they do not need gigantic gates flanked by mighty towers.

---

54   Cf. R.E. Wycherley, *How the Greeks Built Cities* (2nd. ed; New York: W.W. Norton, 1976); J.B. Ward Perkins, *Cities of Ancient Greece and Italy: Planning in Classical Antiquity* (New York: F. Braziller, 1974) 14-21; Hoepfner and Schwander (above, n. 26); F.E. Peters,"City Planning in Greco-Roman Syria," *Damaszener Mitteilungen* 1 (1983) 269-77.
55   V. Tcherikover, *Die hellenistischen Städtegründungen* I (Leipzig: Dieterich'sche Verlagbuchhandlung, 1927).
56   Hoepfner and Schwander (above, n. 26), 253-56.

In the TS the gates of the Temple courts as reconstructed by Yadin have eight chambers, like those described in Ezekiel 40.[57] The scroll, however, does not furnish us with data that justifies such a reconstruction. Yadin's reconstruction is logical, but the gates Yadin draws find no explicit support in the *Temple Scroll.*[58]

VIII. The Date of the Two Works

It seems to us that the data adduced above excludes the attribution of the TS to the Persian period, as suggested by Stegemann and Maier.[59] Even without the archaeological considerations, the Qumranic nature of the scroll precludes a dating earlier than the mid-second century BCE.

DNJ was composed in our view close to 200 BCE, two or three generations before the TS. It is a pre-Qumranic composition, but linguistically it cannot be dated too early.[60] Unlike the TS, which deals only with the Temple and its courts—a preoccupation that befits Qumranic predilections and says nothing about the Temple City—DNJ is concerned mostly with the City.[61] It seems that only the extreme anti-Hasmonean feelings typical of the Qumran sect could have given rise to so strong an aversion to the existing Temple, and could have brought about such a detailed preoccupation with the image of the proper Temple.[62]

---

57   Cf. the reconstruction of Ezekiel's gates by M. Haran, *Encyclopaedia Biblica* 5 (Jerusalem: Bialik Institute, 1968) cols. 347-49 (Hebrew).
58   *Temple Scroll* 1.246.
59   Cf. above, n. 15, 38.
60   Cf. Kutscher (above, n. 41).
61   It is worthwhile noting that nowhere in the two works is the name Jerusalem mentioned. This is, of course, in the tradition of Deuteronomy. In other scrolls the name Jerusalem is spelled out explicitly. Cf. E. Qimron, "The Holiness of the Holy Land in the Light of a New Document from Qumran," *Pillars of Smoke and Fire, The Holy Land in History and Thought* (ed. M. Sharon; Johannesburg: Southern Book Publishers, 1986) 9-13.
62   I wish to thank my colleagues G. Foerster, E. Netzer, É. Puech, and L.H. Schiffman for their advice in the preparation of this paper.

THE QUMRAN MANUSCRIPTS: CONTENTS AND SIGNIFICANCE

Devorah Dimant

Ever since J.T. Milik and F.M. Cross published their surveys on the Qumran documents at the beginning of the sixties, it has become customary to speak of the Library of Qumran.[1] Scholars are in the habit of talking about the contents of the Library, its significance and its historical context. But whereas Milik and Cross had first-hand knowledge of the entire collection and, therefore, were justified to some extent in using this catch-phrase, the case was different with scholars who were not members of the scroll editors' team. They were familiar with only a handful of scrolls from caves 1, 11 and 4. Important and well-preserved as these scrolls are, they represent only a small segment of the entire Qumran collection. The lion's share of it comes from cave 4, most of which has remained unpublished for many years. Denied access to this major share, and not always realizing the scope and importance of the missing part, scholars formulated interpretations and theories on the narrow basis of the available data. Thus, most of the discussion on the nature and provenance of the Qumran manuscripts was, and to a large extent still is, conducted on the basis of only part of the evidence.[2] At present, however, the situation is changing rapidly. An increasing number of new texts from cave 4 is now being brought to light, and the publication of a complete list of the still unedited materials allows us to draw a fairly precise picture of the Qumran collection as a complete entity.[3] In my judgement, the drawing of

---

1   See J.T. Milik, *Ten Years of Discovery in the Wilderness of Judaea* (London: SCM Press, 1959) where the chapter on the manuscripts is entitled: "The Qumran Library." F.M. Cross called his book *The Ancient Library of Qumran and Modern Biblical Studies* (rev. ed.; Garden City: Doubleday, 1961; repr., Grand Rapids: Baker, 1980).

2   Virulent critics of the prevalent theories about the scrolls, such as the outspoken Norman Golb (cf. n. 24), base themselves on the same narrow and partial evidence.

3   Cf. the lists published by E. Tov, "The Unpublished Qumran Texts from Caves 4 and 11," *JJS* 43 (1992) 101-36; "The Unpublished Qumran Texts from Caves 4 and 11," *BA* 55 (1992) 94-104. For bibliographical resources the reader is referred to these lists. However, wherever updating or clarification was needed I have supplied the necessary information in the footnotes. I thank Emanuel Tov for placing at my disposal a more up-to-date version of his list. Also helpful were the lists compiled by S.A. Reed, *Dead Sea Scrolls Inventory Project: Lists of*

such a picture is indispensable for understanding the phenomenon of Qumran as a whole, as it is for the advancement of the editorial work on individual texts. To the best of my knowledge no attempt at drawing such a picture has yet been undertaken.[4] Because of its importance and its potential benefit for my own editorial work, I venture to offer a preliminary sketch of such a picture. Inevitably, the following is a modest beginning of such an undertaking, and in its present form is still rudimentary. The complete and precise inventory of the entire Qumran collection is an ongoing project which can be brought to completion only when all the Qumran documents are fully published. Nonetheless, even at this stage of research the reader will benefit, I hope, from the following list. My own perusal of recent publications for the purpose of this presentation has given me the impression that many of the yet unpublished fragments are rather small and, therefore, the actual amount of text yet unknown is smaller than one would be led to suppose by the manuscripts' serial numbering.

Documents, Photographs and Museum Plates (Claremont: Ancient Biblical Manuscript Center, 1991-1992) fascs. 8-10. I am also indebted to my colleagues, fellows during 1992-93 at the Annenberg Research Institute in Philadelphia, who made helpful comments, and particularly to those who shared with me information on unpublished material they are editing: Shemaryahu Talmon on the 4Q calendrical texts, Joseph Baumgarten on halakhic texts, Emanuel Tov on the Pentateuch Reworked, Bilhah Nitzan on 4QBerakhot, and Lawrence Schiffman on pseudepigraphic texts (=4Q459-4Q460). Special thanks are due to George Brooke and Lawrence Schiffman who improved upon my English and made helpful suggestions.

4   An overall list was published by L. Rosso Ubigli, "Italian-English Index of Qumran Texts," *Henoch* 11 (1989) 233-69, in which the author has attempted to classify the manuscripts according to their content and literary genre. The attempt was commendable but premature, for it was based on the still incomplete list published by F. García Martínez, "Lista de MSS procedentes de Qumran," *Henoch* 11 (1989) 149-232. One of its other shortcomings is that it does not make the distinction between works which contain terminology distinctive of the Qumran community and works which do not. Useful but incomplete is the listing provided by J.A. Fitzmyer, *The Dead Sea Scrolls: Major Publications and Tools for Study* (*SBL Resources for Study* 20; rev. ed.; Atlanta: Scholars Press, 1990). Separate listing of cave 11's contents is given by F. García Martínez, "Texts from Qumran Cave 11," *The Dead Sea Scrolls: Forty Years of Research* (eds. D. Dimant and U. Rappaport; *Studies on the Texts of the Desert of Judah* 10; Jerusalem–Leiden: Magnes–E.J. Brill, 1992) 18-26. Just before submitting the present article for publication, a copy has reached me of the volume by F. García Martínez, *Textos de Qumrán* (Madrid: Editorial Trotta, 1992). It contains translations of most of the non-biblical texts from Qumran published to date, classified according to genres and contents. The reader will note, however, that the principles of classification employed by me in the present listing are significantly different from those used by García Martínez. Thus, for instance, he does not make a systematic distinction between community and non-community works. As for the Aramaic works, he includes them together with the Hebrew ones.

PRINCIPLES OF THE PRESENT DESCRIPTION

Among the written documents from the Second Temple period found in Eretz-Israel the Qumran collection is unique in its size and literary character. It constitutes an unprecedented literary corpus from the Second Temple period which has surfaced in the twentieth century. The primary description of such a corpus must, therefore, be a literary one. Elements for such a description are scattered in various commentaries and discussions written during the sixties and the seventies. But they were never assembled and organized into a systematic and overall framework. The need for a well-founded, comprehensive literary description of the Qumran collection is particularly felt at present, because of the constant confusion between literary considerations and historical evaluations. To be sure, the texts in question are ancient ones and as such must be understood in terms of a well-defined historical framework. Without such a framework no critical discussion is possible.

In the case of the Qumran manuscripts a few facts are firmly established: the manuscripts extend over a period of more than three centuries, from the second century B.C.E to the eve of the fall of Jerusalem in 70 C.E.[5] Written predominantly in Hebrew and Aramaic (and a few in Greek) as they are, and having been unearthed in Eretz-Israel, there is no reason to place their origin elsewhere. In their literary forms, styles and language they fall well within the general picture of the period known to us from other contemporary sources. But beyond these general features, not much else about the scrolls can be established beyond doubt. Aiming at a definition based on non-controversial literary data, the present review attempts at providing a more precise, commonly accepted frame of reference which could serve in turn as the basis for future discussion. Bearing this in mind, and given the limitations of the available literary terminology, the definitions offered below are formulated in as strict literary terms as possible.[6] Historical evaluations are discussed separately.

---

5   As was recently reestablished by new, more advanced carbon-14 tests. Cf. G. Bonnani, M. Broshi, I. Carmi, S. Ivy, J. Strugnell, W. Wölfli, "Radiocarbon Dating of the Dead Sea Scrolls," ʿAtiqot 20 (1991) 27-32. These tests have independently confirmed the soundness and precision of the dating achieved by paleographical typological chronology. For the paleographical charts of the scrolls see F.M. Cross, "The Development of the Jewish Scripts," The Bible and the Ancient Near East: Essays in Honor of William Foxwell Albright (Garden City: Doubleday, 1965) 170-264.

6   In the absence of more adequate ones, the terms 'pseudepigrapha' and 'apocrypha' are used not in their historical-canonical sense but in a literary-

Finally, it should be noted that the present review reconstructs the library as consisting of units of complete manuscripts. This is done in order to give the student an idea of the components which constituted the original collection. In this way each manuscript is considered as one unit, regardless of its size. Thus, individual small fragments are given numerical value equal to those of large scrolls. The description, therefore, does not aim at providing the precise amount of text preserved, but at reconstructing the library as an intact collection. The original collection undoubtedly possessed many more manuscripts, but they are lost forever.[7] The basic computation is that of manuscript units, and the percentage calculations are conducted on that basis. The listing according to works should, however, help the reader to figure out the number of individual works as compared to the number of manuscripts, and to gain a sense of the distribution and number of copies of each work.

For the purpose of this article I have checked all the cave 4 materials available in print. Information on a number of as yet unpublished 4Q manuscripts was obtained from their respective editors. Where necessary and possible, photographs of unpublished texts were consulted.[8] The group of "unidentified manuscripts" contains fragments illegible or too small to be analyzed. Although they do preserve little or no actual text, they were included in order to give some idea of the size of the original collection. The Qumran manuscripts may be divided into three distinct groups:

a. Biblical manuscripts
b. Works containing terminology linked with the Qumran Community (shortened to CT=Community Terminology)
c. Works not containing such terminology (shortened to NCT=No Community Terminology).

Such a classification has proved to be particularly fruitful in assessing the character and provenance of the collection.

---

descriptive sense, namely, 'pseudepigraphic' designates works using a pseudepigraphic framework and 'apocryphal' designates works closely related to or reworking the Hebrew Bible.

7　　Cave 8, for instance, yielded only five manuscripts, but also sixty-eight reinforcing tabs used to fasten scrolls. The cave, then, must have originally contained many more manuscripts. Cf. J. Carswell, "Fastenings on the Qumrân Manuscripts," *Qumrân Grotte 4, II. Tefillin, Mezuzot et Targums (4Q128-4Q157)*, DJD VI (Oxford: Clarendon Press, 1977) 24.

8　　For photographic verification cf. R.H. Eisenman, J.M. Robinson, *A Facsimile Edition of the Dead Sea Scrolls* (Washington: Biblical Archaeology Society, 1991) vols. I-II.

Biblical Manuscripts

Biblical texts form a group of distinct character. In the present list this category covers only books of the Hebrew Bible. The status at Qumran of works later considered as apocryphal, such as Ben Sira and Jubilees, is uncertain. They are therefore included here together with NCT works. This, however, does not imply taking a stand with regard to views currently expressed on the biblical canon and its development. Perhaps at a more advanced stage of research the need will arise to introduce a category intermediate between proper biblical texts and "apocryphal" ones. But to do this at this stage of the inquiry would be premature. In any case, this paper is not concerned with Qumran biblical manuscripts, for which there exist other good surveys.[9] They are, however, included in the overall list of manuscripts, mainly for the purpose of comparison and completeness. Manuscripts other than the biblical ones vary in character and literary form. But all of them fall roughly into two groups.

Documents Employing Terminology Connected to the Qumran Community (=CT)

Since the beginning of Qumran studies a group of scrolls was discerned which employed a distinctive terminology, linked with a peculiar set of ideas. Such clusters of terms and ideas concern roughly four major areas: (1) the practices and organization of a particular community,[10] (2) the history of this community and its contemporary circumstances,[11] (3) the theological and metaphysical outlook of that community,[12] and (4) the peculiar biblical

---

9   E. Tov, *The Textual Criticism of the Hebrew Bible* (Assen: Van Gorcum, 1992) 104-5. In the computation below I have used this list and an additional one placed in my hands by Emanuel Tov. For a previous list and discussion of this material cf. E. Ulrich, "The Biblical Scrolls from Qumran Cave 4: An Overview and a Progress Report on their Publication," *RQ* 14 (1989-90) 207-28.

10   Typical examples of such terms are יחד ="community" (e.g. 1QS 1:16; 6:10; 1QSa 1:26; CD 20:32); סרך ="rule," "a collection of rules" (e.g. 1QS 1:10, 6:8; 1QM 3:3, 5:4; 1QSa 1:1; CD 7:6); and מבקר ="overseer" (e.g. 1QS 6:12, 20; CD 9:8, 13:6).

11   See, for example, the term חלקות ="smooth things," as a derogatory sobriquet for the exegetical method of the community's opponents (e.g. CD 1:18; 1QH 2:32; 4QpNah 3-4 i 2); מורה הצדק ="Teacher of Righteousness," for the community's leader (e.g. 1QpHab 1:13, 11:5; CD 1:11, 20:32; 4QpPs 2:15); איש / מטיף הכזב = "Man/Spouter of Lies," for his opponent (e.g. 1QpHab 2:2, 5:11; CD 8:13, 20:15).

12   Cf., for instance, terms related to dualism, such as the Spirits of Light and Darkness (e.g. 1QS 2:18, 3:25; 1QM 13:11) and to predestination, such as תעודה = "appointed time" (e.g. 1QS 1:9; 3:10,16; 1QM 3:4; 11:8; 1QH 1:19; and רזי אל ="mysteries of God," e.g. 1QpHab 7:8; 1QS 3:23; 1QM 3:9). The theological category is, however, problematic. Theological vocabulary which now appears as

exegesis espoused by that community.[13] The distinctiveness of such clusters in the context of this peculiar corpus lies precisely in the close connection between terms and ideas.[14] In contradistinction, some of the religious ideas and concepts found in this group of texts figure also in works known outside Qumran, such as the book of Jubilees and 1 Enoch. This is, for instance, the case with regard to ideas on the role of the righteous, the presence of evil angels, and eschatological expectations. However, in these works such ideas are not associated with the peculiar terminology related to the community, a terminology distinctive of the CT works. Hence, in themselves concepts and ideas are insufficient criteria for assigning a given text to the group of the CT works. Only the combination of the distinctive terminology with the respective ideas provides such criteria.[15] Restricting the definition in this way enables us to

---

distinctive of the CT works may in the future turn up in non-Qumranic texts. To some extent the problem exists already with regards to defining the relationship between certain pseudepigraphic works, such as Jubilees and 1 Enoch, and Qumranic literature. Nevertheless, at the present stage of inquiry this category is still useful.

13   The term most characteristic of the *pesharim* is the word פשר (=pesher- "interpretation") itself. But there are other technical terms which go together with specific methods of exegesis characteristic of the *pesharim*. For the exegesis in the *pesharim* see M. P. Horgan, *Pesharim* (*CBQ Monograph Series* 8; Washington: Catholic Biblical Association, 1979) 229-59; B. Nitzan, *Pesher Habakkuk* (Jerusalem: Bialik Institute, 1986) 29-79 and my summary in "Pesharim, Qumran," *The Anchor Bible Dictionary*, ed. D.N. Freedman with G.A. Herion, D.F. Grant and J.D. Pleins (New York: Doubleday, 1992) 5.244-51.

14   As a matter of fact, only the presence of such distinctive terminology defines a given text as belonging to the community. It is therefore meaningless to talk about members of the community authoring documents "compatible" with the community's ideology but using none of its distinctive terminology as argued in connection with the provenance of the *Words of the Luminaries* by E.G. Chazon, "Is *Divrei ha-Me'orot* a Sectarian Prayer?" *The Dead Sea Scrolls: Forty Years*, 14. In such a case we simply do not have any basis for connecting such a document with the community. For the same reason it is meaningless to speak about genres and literary forms which by their very nature are not expected to employ terminology of the community (for instance, liturgical units). If works found at Qumran do not employ distinctive CT terminology due to the use of particular genres, we have no way of knowing whether or not they were authored within the community. In itself the presence of a text at Qumran is insufficient to posit community authorship of that text.

15   E. Tov has recently proposed using the scribal character of the scrolls as a criterion in determining whether they originated in the Qumran community or outside it. Cf. his "Hebrew Biblical Manuscripts from the Judaean Desert: Their Contribution to Textual Criticism," *JJS* 39 (1988) 5-37. Taking note of the full orthography and peculiar linguistic forms predominant in the writings of the community, as distinct from the defective orthography and forms similar to those used by the biblical Massoretic text found in other scrolls, he posited that the existence of two systems of orthography and language are involved, and that they reflect two scribal schools current at the time. According to his view the first system is used almost exclusively in copies containing works of the community, whereas copies of various apocryphal works use the defective

distinguish the literature of the community proper from other texts similar, but not identical, to it.[16] It is not always easy or possible to decide whether or not a given term is actually distinctive of the Qumran community. Nevertheless, a considerable body of sufficiently distinctive texts is now available, and it provides the criteria necessary for making the distinction between community and non-community works.[17]

Works which do not Contain Clusters of Terms and Ideas Related to the Community (=NCT).

As a rule, each text which is found not to contain any of the distinctive terms related to the community was assigned to this category. However, a certain margin of error should be allowed, since it is not always easy to judge, especially with regards to partly published or unpublished texts, whether a given fragment,

---

system. He therefore concluded that the fuller system is characteristic of the scribal school practiced at Qumran, and that its use in a given Qumranic document indicates its origin in the community. It may, however, be assumed that if two such schools existed, they would be prevalent in Israel at large without being necessarily connected to the community, or to any other particular circle. The degree of distinctiveness of each mode of orthography and their precise significance are yet to be established by further research. As a matter of fact, one often finds a mixture of the two types of orthography in one and the same text, as pointed out to me by Elisha Qimron. In an unpublished paper he notes that contrary to the assumptions of Tov, a copy of the typical CT work the *Manual of Discipline* (4Q264) is written throughout in defective and not full orthography (I thank Elisha Qimron for putting the manuscript of his article at my disposal). A reverse case is provided by the Temple Scroll. Written throughout in full orthography it however does not contain terminology of the community (cf. n. 26). Another criterion suggested for identifying works of the community is the avoidance of using the Tetragrammaton. See H. Stegemann, "Religionsgeschichtliche Erwägungen zu den Gottesbezeichnungen in den Qumrantexten," *Qumrân, sa piété, sa théologie et son milieu* (ed. M. Delcor; BETL 46; Paris-Gembloux: Duculot, 1978) 200-17. However, whereas the avoidance of the Tetragrammaton in CT works seems clear, the use of it in NCT ones has not been sufficiently studied.

16 Along similar lines, but of a more limited scope, is the categorization proposed by C. Newsom, "'Sectually Explicit' Literature from Qumran," *The Hebrew Bible and its Interpreters* (eds. W.H. Propp, B. Halpern and D.N. Freedman; Winona Lake: Eisenbrauns, 1990) 167-87. She still considers the Temple Scroll as a work which originated within the Qumran community (p. 171). H. Stegemann insists that texts of the community must be related to the Teacher of Righteousness, a requirement which only very few of the community's works fulfill. See his definition in "Die Bedeutung der Qumranfunde für die Erforschung der Apokalyptik," *Apocalypticism in the Mediterranean World and the Near East* (ed. D. Hellholm; 2nd ed.; Tübingen: Mohr, 1989) 511.

17 For the purpose of the present list major terms were culled from works such as the *Rule of the Community* (1QS), *Hodayot* (1QH), the *Damascus Covenant* (CD), the *War Scroll* (1QM) and the *Pesharim*. In some cases I have indicated in the notes what led me to assign certain texts to the Qumran community. See, for instance, 4Q512-513 (Ordinances).

especially a small one, contains, or could have contained, the pertinent terms.

RESULTS

The total number of manuscripts listed in the Appendix is about 800.[18] The small discrepancy between this figure and that obtained through the serial numbering of the Qumran caves and documents is due to the loss of some numbered fragments[19] and to several alterations in the numbering.[20] The figure 800 represents, therefore, the manuscripts which are accounted for and which can at present be checked either through publication or with the help of photographs and inventory lists. With a complete list of manuscripts at hand it is now possible to assess some aspects of the collection which were not apparent before. Some of them are summarized in Tables II and III (see Appendix) and are reviewed below.

Interrelations of the Caves

An important fact to emerge from the listing is that the share of cave 4 manuscripts within the collection is larger than what is usually maintained: it represents nearly three quarters of the entire collection. This means that the composition and nature of cave 4 decide to a large extent the character of the entire Qumran collection. Moreover, the contents of most of the caves are essentially similar and interlinked. Practically all the caves with significant quantities of manuscripts contain at least one work, and usually more than one, represented by one or several other copies in cave 4. This is the case for caves 1, 2, 3, 5, 6 and 11, for both CT and NCT works. The distribution of copies of the same works in the various caves is as follows:

---

18   Cf. Table II. This number includes seven Greek manuscripts found in cave 7 and some 20 non-literary documents.
19   Thus, for instance, the photos and museum plates of 4Q229-4Q233, 4Q237-4Q240 are as yet unaccounted for (cf. the list provided by Tov, above n. 3), and were therefore not included in the list.
20   Compare, for instance, the serial numbering 4Q1-4Q127 for 4Q biblical manuscripts with the figure 158 arrived at in other lists (cf. n. 9). At the same time a number of additional manuscripts have been identified, thus compensating for the unaccounted manuscripts.

	4Q	1Q	2Q	3Q	5Q	6Q	11Q
Texts with Terminology of the Community							
Rule of the Community	+	+					
Damascus Document	+					+	+
War Rule	+	+					
Serekh Ha-Milḥama	+						+
Hodayot	+	+					
Prayers for Festivals	+	+					
Songs of Sabbath	+						+
Mysteries	+	+					
Rule of Farmer	+	+					
Texts without Terminology of the Community							
Tongues of Fire	+	+					
Joseph Apocryphon	+		+				
Jubilees	+	+	+	+			+
Apocryphal Psalms	+						+
Book of Giants	+	+	+			+	
New Jerusalem	+	+	+		+		+
Testament of Levi	+	+					
Temple Scroll[21]	+						+
Total[22]	**17**	**11**	**4**	**1**	**2**	**2**	**6**

In spite of some individual peculiarities, the overall picture emerging from the foregoing comparison clearly shows the interrelationship among the caves. Each cave contained at least one copy of a work found in cave 4. This fact suggests that all the caves housed segments of one and the same collection. This conclusion is also corroborated by the fundamental homogeneity of all the manuscript caves (1Q, 2Q, 3Q, 4Q, 5Q, 6Q, 11Q) both in their contents and in their configuration: biblical manuscripts represent approximately one third of the entire collection, a proportion found more or less in caves 4 and 5. NCT manuscripts represent about

---

21 Fragment 4Q365a 2*, originally assigned to the Reworked Pentateuch, may constitute either a copy of a different recension of the Temple Scroll, or one of its sources. Cf. n. 69.

22 A case of the same type of works housed in different caves may be offered by 6Q17. Although not an actual copy, it nevertheless belongs with the calendrical texts from cave 4 (4Q321-4Q322).

another third of the entire collection, a proportion to be observed also in caves 1 and 2. Cave 4 has a slightly larger ratio, nearly 40%. CT manuscripts form about a quarter of the entire collection; this proportion is similar to that found in caves 1 and 11. Cave 4 has nearly 30% of such manuscripts. Finally, more than a tenth of the manuscripts of the entire collection are unidentified. A similar proportion of such manuscripts is found in caves 4 and 11. In other caves it is somewhat higher.

Configuration of the Entire Collection

The collection falls into more or less three equal portions: (1) biblical texts, (2) CT works, and (3) NCT works. The nonbiblical texts are distributed among some 190 works, only nine of which were known before the discovery of the Qumran scrolls. Significantly, all of them are NCT works, and with the exception of the Book of Giants all were handed down by Christian and not by Jewish tradents (Ben Sira, Tobit, Letter of Jeremiah, Apocryphal Psalms, 1 Enoch, Jubilees, Testament of Levi, Testament of Naphtali). But none of the CT works was transmitted by other channels.

As for the differences between the CT and NCT texts, they are to be observed in their respective distinctive genres: CT works include Rules (the Rule of the Community, 1QSa, 1QSb, the War Scroll, CD, and partly the Songs of the Sabbath Sacrifice) and *pesharim* (biblical *pesharim*, Melchizedeq, Florilegium, etc.), peculiar to the community. NCT compositions include pseudepigrapha, Hebrew and Aramaic, not found among the CT works.

Notwithstanding their diversity, the Qumran manuscripts employ a limited number of styles and genres: the CT works include rules of the community, halakhic rulings, liturgical and poetical compositions, and sapiential works. The NCT texts include narrative, poetic, prophetic, and wisdom texts modelled on biblical antecedents. They also comprise pseudepigraphic Hebrew works, together with apocalyptic, aggadic and testamentary Aramaic compositions. Not only is the Qumran collection characteristic in the use it makes of a well-defined range of genres and styles, but it is also remarkable in its exclusion: none of the Jewish Greek works were found there (such as the Wisdom of Solomon), nor, for that matter, works such as the Psalms of Solomon. Nor is there any remnant of the pro-Hasmonean 1 Maccabees, or the Book of Judith. No precursor to the later tannaitic literature has surfaced at Qumran, nor to the New Testament.[23] One cannot, then, escape the

---

23   In spite of the numerous publications of J. O'Callaghan, his identification of tiny Greek fragments from cave 7 as belonging to various writings of the New

conclusion that the collection was intentional and not a haphazard assemblage of disparate works.[24]

Literary Genres

A great variety of literary forms and styles is to be observed in both CT and NCT works. The two groups show striking similarities as well as marked differences. The similarity is apparent above all in genres modelled on biblical forms and styles. Thus we find in both groups liturgical, psalmodic and wisdom compositions, all drawing to various degrees on biblical forerunners. In this connection it may be observed that whereas liturgical and psalmodic works of this type were known from the 1Q specimens long ago, the importance and size of the CT sapiential works were not sufficiently known. Their unique place within the community's literature becomes discernable only now, with preliminary publications of some of these works.[25] The detailed analysis of these texts should, I suspect, modify our understanding of the community in significant respects.

A particular problem is presented by halakhic texts. Some of them undoubtedly contain terminology related to the Qumran community (see the *halakhah* in CD, or in the 4QTohorot texts). However, other halakhic texts, although containing halakhic rules identical with the ones of the community, do not employ its terminology. Therefore, such texts were not assigned to the CT category of works but to the NCT category (e.g. 4Q251 and the

---

Testament was rejected by the great majority of scholars as unsubstantiated and fanciful. For a list of his publications see J. Fitzmyer, *The Dead Sea Scrolls, Tools*, 168-9.

24   As was argued, for instance, by N. Golb, "The Problem of Origin and Identification of the Dead Sea Scrolls," *Proceedings of the American Philosophical Society* 124 (1980) 1-24 (esp. 11). Golb disputes the view that the manuscripts, at least in part, were authored by a community of Essenes whose center was at Qumran. Golb has rightly criticized those who defend this identification with loose argumentation and insufficient evidence. In his wholesale rejection of this identification, he, however, disregards the positive evidence which led scholars to identify the Qumran community as Essene in the first place, namely, the striking similarity between the community described by 1QS and that of the Essenes according to Josephus. Golb's own solution, namely that the scrolls were brought from the Jerusalem Temple archives and were hidden in the caves at the eve of the fall of Jerusalem in 70 C.E., is disproved by the character of the collection as well as its peculiar connection to Qumran. For an acute critique of Golb's arguments cf. F. García Martínez and A.S. van der Woude, "A 'Groningen' Hypothesis of Qumran Origins and Early History," *RQ* 14 (1990) 521-41 and Newsom, "Sectually Explicit."

25   A collection of sapiential works (4Q413-4Q426) is now available in a version based on J. Strugnell's texts, as reconstructed from the concordance of 4Q texts: B.Z. Wacholder and M.G. Abegg, *A Preliminary Edition of the Unpublished Dead Sea Scrolls* (Washington: Biblical Archaeology Society, 1992) fasc. 2.40-184.

Temple Scroll[26]). The same qualifications apply also to calendrical, chronological and astrological texts. They too do not contain CT and, therefore, were assigned to the NCT category. In this way room is left for the possibility of placing their origin outside the immediate context of the community.

Works Without the Terminology of the Community (=NCT)

Perhaps the most revealing, and certainly the least known, part of the Qumran collection is that of the NCT works category.

a. Hebrew

Some works belonging to this category were known before the discovery of Qumran: Tobit[27], Ben Sira, apocryphal psalms[28] and Jubilees. Otherwise, this group contains works modelled on various biblical forms and styles: legal, narrative, prophetic, psalmodic and sapiential. Except for Jubilees and the apocryphal psalms, all the Hebrew works in this category are unknown from other sources. Halakhic and calendrical works also belong here.

b. Aramaic

Significantly, all the Aramaic texts fall into the NCT category.[29] The importance of the Aramaic texts within the entire collection is

---

26   The Temple Scroll (=11QT) presents a special case. Written as a pseudepigraphon of divine speech to Moses, it reworks and imitates the Torah throughout. It does not contain any of the specific terminology distinctive of the CT works. In subject matter it contains biblical and other legal materials, some of which are shared by the Damascus Document, 4QMMT and Jubilees. It may, therefore, have been produced by a circle close to the community but not identical to it. Additional arguments for placing the origin of 11QT outside the Qumran community are advanced by H. Stegemann, "The Origin of the Temple Scroll," *SuppVT* 40 (1988) 235-56; idem., "The Literary Composition of the Temple Scroll and its Status at Qumran," *Temple Scroll Studies* (ed. G.J. Brooke; *JSPS* 7; Sheffield: JSOT Press, 1989) 123-89; idem, "The Institutions of Israel in the *Temple Scroll*," *The Dead Sea Scrolls: Forty Years of Research*, 156-96.

27   In addition to the Aramaic manuscripts, Tobit is also represented by fragments of one Hebrew manuscript (4Q200). A Greek papyrus fragment (7Q2) of the apocryphal Letter of Jeremiah was found in cave 7.

28   Apocryphal psalms known outside Qumran are contained in 11QPs[a]: XXI, 11-17 = Ben Sira 51:13-19; XVIII, 1-39; XXIV, 3-17; Syriac Apocryphal Psalms II-III; XXVIII, 3-14 = Ps 151 (LXX Ps 151, Syriac Apoc. Ps. I).

29   Aramaic targums were not included here but with the biblical manuscripts. Some of the Aramaic texts and other NCT works were labelled as pre-Qumranic by B.Z. Wacholder, "The Ancient Judeo-Aramaic Literature (500-164 BCE): A Classification of Pre-Qumranic Texts," *Archaeology and History in the Dead Sea Scrolls* (ed. L.H. Schiffman; *JSPS* 8; Sheffield: JSOT Press, 1990) 257-81. Wacholder points to possible roots of the Qumran Aramaic texts in ancient pagan Aramaic literary tradition. A more comprehensive collection of the Aramaic apocalypses from Qumran is now available in the volume by F. García

reflected by its size: it forms 13% of the entire collection, and 38% of the NCT works. Similar ratios are to be observed in cave 4 taken by itself. Unlike the variety of forms and themes manifested in the Hebrew NCT works, the Aramaic ones are much more uniform. They contain almost exclusively visionary-pseudepigraphic compositions, testaments and narrative-aggadic works.[30] In fact, precisely these three types are to be found in the Aramaic apocryphal works known before the discovery of the scrolls: Tobit, 1 Enoch and the Testament of Levi. They raise the issue of the significance and origins of these genres and their relationship to the apocalyptic literature.

Finally, it is interesting to note the distribution and size of the various compositions in the collection. Overall, the nearly 800 manuscripts are distributed among some 200 works, and probably even more. CT works represented by the largest number of copies are the Damascus Document, the Rule of the Community, the War Rule and the Hodayot. The Sapiential Texts and the Songs of the Sabbath Sacrifice are also represented by a significant number of copies. The most popular NCT works were Jubilees, 1 Enoch and the Book of Giants. The calendrical texts are also well represented.

THE COLLECTION IN HISTORICAL PERSPECTIVE

The general implications of the lists below demand a comprehensive discussion which I hope to publish elsewhere. Here I will content myself with only a few observations. The first and most immediate impression gained from these lists is that of the uniform character of the entire collection. All the caves contain the same types of works in more or less the same proportions. In fact, on a smaller scale most of the minor caves mirror the picture of cave 4. The links between cave 4 and the minor caves are also indicated by the presence in both of copies of the same works. Being an integral part of the Qumran site, cave 4 as the center of the library also establishes a close link between the entire collection and the site.[31]

Martínez, *Qumran and Apocalyptic, Studies on the Aramaic Texts from Qumran (Studies on the Texts of the Desert of Judah* 9; Leiden: E.J. Brill, 1992).

30   The horoscope preserved in 4Q561 is also added to this group. Its possible background is discussed by J.C. Greenfield and M. Sokoloff, "Astrological and Related Omen Texts in Jewish Palestinian Aramaic," *JNES* 48 (1989) 201-14.

31   The archaeological links between the site and the caves were pointed out by the first excavators. Cf. R. de Vaux, *Archaeology and the Dead Sea Scrolls* (London: Oxford University Press, 1973) 99-106. Of special significance in this respect are lamps unearthed only at Qumran and in the caves. The peculiarity of the lamps found only in these two sites has been recently emphasized in a report on the progress in preparing for publication the material from the excavations at

Hence the site, the caves and the manuscripts must be seen as one complex. This much clearly emerges as solidly established by the facts. No less clear is the uniform and peculiar character of the collection. However, the interpretation of these facts is subject to debate. It seems to me that the numerous copies of quite a number of works found in cave 4 point to its character as a library.[32] The minor caves should be viewed, in my opinion, as adjacent smaller, 'micro-libraries,' perhaps for private use. At the same time, the Qumran library is not just any library. Its homogeneous character and its selectiveness define it as a library of a specific circle or school, a school close to but not identical with the community. Perhaps we are dealing with the parent group from which the Qumran community branched off at one time. The Qumran library would then be the specific literature produced by the community together with a body of literary works which they took over from their parent group. If this would be the case, the study of the NCT part of the library of Qumran may hold the key for uncovering the origins and nature of the Qumran community.

Qumran. See R. Donceel, "Reprise des travaux de publication des fouilles au Khirbet Qumran," *RB* 99 (1992) 557-73. Also the scrolls' jars are characteristic almost exclusively of Qumran and the caves.

32   This point was also made by C. Newsom, "Sectually Explicit," 171. With minor differences the hypothesis that the Qumran manuscripts form the library of the community was recently argued along similar lines by García Martínez and van der Woude, "A 'Groningen' Hypothesis of Qumran Origins," 521-26.

DEVORAH DIMANT

APPENDIX

Table I: List of Qumran Works and Manuscripts[33]

NAME	SIGLA	COPIES IN CAVES							TOTAL
		4Q	1Q	2Q	3Q	5Q	6Q	11Q	
I. LITERARY WORKS WITH TERMINOLOGY RELATED TO THE COMMUNITY									
RULES									
Rule of the Community (1QS=1Q28)	4Q255-4Q264;1Q28	10	1	-	-	-	-	-	11
Text related to the Rule	5Q11	-	-	-	-	1	-	-	1
Damascus Document	4Q266-4Q273;5Q12;6Q15	8[34]	-	-	-	1	1	-	10
Work related to but not identical with CD and 1QS	4Q265	1	-	-	-	-	-	-	1

---

33 In the following list manuscripts were grouped as works, wherever possible. Copies of the same work were, therefore, listed under the same entry. However, occasionally manuscripts of similar nature were grouped in the same entry, which are not necessarily copies of the same work. Such entries are marked by *. Entries marked by + were verified by photographs. To avoid confusion the names given to the fragments in Tov's list (cf. n. 3) are preserved here even though they are not always appropriate.

34 For description of all eight cf. J.M. Baumgarten, "The Laws of the *Damascus Document* in Current Research," *The Damascus Document Reconsidered* (ed. by M. Broshi; Jerusalem: Israel Exploration Society, 1992) 57-61. For previous partial descriptions as well as a list of other discussions of this work cf. F. García Martínez, "Damascus Document: A Bibliography of Studies 1970-1989," ibid., 63-83.

THE QUMRAN MANUSCRIPTS

NAME	SIGLA	COPIES IN CAVES							TOTAL
		4Q	1Q	2Q	3Q	5Q	6Q	11Q	
War Rule (1QM=1Q33)	4Q471;4Q491-4Q496;1Q33	7	1	-	-	-	-	-	8
A Polemical text	4Q471a[35]	1	-	-	-	-	-	-	1
Text Related to the War Rule	4Q497	1	-	-	-	-	-	-	1
Serekh ha-milḥamah related to the War Rule	4Q285;[36] 11Q14	1	-	-	-	-	-	1	2
Juridical Document	2Q25	-	-	1	-	-	-	-	1
Decree of Sect (?)	5Q13	-	-	-	-	1	-	-	1
A text related to the community	4Q477	1	-	-	-	-	-	-	1

---

35 Distinctive style and content set fragment 4Q471a apart from the remaining fragments of this manuscript. Containing polemical formulations, this fragment does not correspond to any known part of the War Rule, nor is it in line with the War Rule's tenor and subject-matter. It was therefore suggested that this fragment does not belong with the copy of the War Rule. Cf. E. Eshel and M. Kister, "A Polemical Qumran Fragment," *JJS* 43 (1992) 277-81. This fragment may well come from a different manuscript. Its polemical character suggests the classification with CT works.

36 4Q285 has been partially published in a preliminary form by G. Vermes, "The Oxford Forum for Qumran Research Seminar on the Rule of War from Cave 4 (4Q285)," *JJS* 43 (1992) 86-90. J.T. Milik noted the similarity in tenor between this scroll and the work preserved in 1QM, and therefore thought that it constituted another copy of the same composition. Cf. his remarks in "Milkî-ṣedeq et Milkî-reša' dans les écrits juifs et chrétiens," *JJS* 23 (1972) 143. But Milik himself admits that there is no actual overlapping between the two, whereas there is some between 4Q285 and 11Q14. I have therefore arranged them together, but separated them from 1QM. For 11Q14 cf. A.S. van der Woude, "Ein neuer Segenspruch aus Qumran (11QBer)," *Bibel und Qumran—Hans Bardtke zum 22.9.1966* (Berlin: Evangelische Haupt-Bibelgesellschaft, 1968) 253-58. This work is not related to 4QBerakhot (4Q286-4Q290).

NAME	SIGLA	COPIES IN CAVES							TOTAL
		4Q	1Q	2Q	3Q	5Q	6Q	11Q	
HALAKHIC WORKS*									
4QMMT (Polemical with parenetic passages)	4Q394-4Q399	6	-	-	-	-	-	-	6
Ritual of Purifications	4Q512[37]	1	-	-	-	-	-	-	1
*Ordinances	4Q159;4Q513[38]-4Q514	3	-	-	-	-	-	-	3
POETICAL AND HYMNIC WORKS									
Hodayot (1QH=1Q35)	4Q427-4Q432;1Q35	6	1	-	-	-	-	-	7
Hodayot-like fragment	4Q433;4Q440	2	-	-	-	-	-	-	2
Hymns-Barkhi Nafshi	4Q434-4Q438	5	-	-	-	-	-	-	5
Text similar to Barkhi Nafshi	4Q439	1	-	-	-	-	-	-	1
*Miscellaneous poetic frags	4Q369,[39] 1Q36-1Q40;3Q6; 6Q16;6Q18;11Q15-11Q16	1	5	-	1	-	2	2	11

---

*   See addition on p. 56.

37   Note the typical community terms such as שׁוּב יֵשׁע (4Q512 70-1 2; cf. e.g. 1QS 10:20; 1QH 2:9; CD 2:5).

38   This work is considered here as belonging to the community's literature due to the occurrence in 4Q513 3+4 4 of the term מִצְוַת עֲרָיוֹת (cf. 1QH 2:5; 1QS 4:11; CD 16:2).

39   Included now in Wacholder and Abbeg, *Preliminary Edition*, 2.233-6.

40

THE QUMRAN MANUSCRIPTS

NAME	SIGLA	COPIES IN CAVES							
		4Q	1Q	2Q	3Q	5Q	6Q	11Q	TOTAL
LITURGICAL WORKS									
Berakhot	4Q286-4Q290	5	-	-	-	-	-	-	5
Text related to Berakhot	4Q280[40]	1	-	-	-	-	-	-	1
Prayers for Festivals	4Q507-4Q509;1Q34;1Q34bis	3	1	-	-	-	-	-	4
Prayer of Michael(?)[41]	4Q471b	1	-	-	-	-	-	-	1
Words of the Luminaries[42]	4Q504-4Q506	3	-	-	-	-	-	-	3

---

40 Originally labelled by Milik as 4QTohorot[d] and assigned by him to the Tohorot manuscripts. See his comments in "Milkî-ṣedeq et Milkî-reša'," 126-30. In the list recently published by Tov in *BA* 55 it is still presented in this way. But content and style place it with the Berakhot texts (4Q286-4Q290).

41 This fragment has close textual affinities with 4Q277 and 4Q491 11.

42 The character of these prayers is difficult to define. On the one hand they do not employ the most explicit terms connected with the Qumran community. This is why, for instance, Stegemann excludes them from the literature of the community. Cf. his definition in "Die Bedeutung der Qumranfunde für die Erforschung der Apokalyptik," 511. However, some terms used occur in typical CT works. See, for instance, 4Q504 1-2 ii 17 להתנחם (compare use and context of both the same verb and noun in 1QS 3:13-16). Also the formulation of the suffering experienced by the group in 4Q504 1-2 vi 6-8 is reminiscent of similar formulations in CT works (cf. 1QS 1:13). The first editor, M. Baillet, concluded that the prayers go back to an Assidean circle which he considered as the parent group of the Essene (i.e. Qumran) community. Cf. his comments in *Qumran Grotte 4, III; DJD* VII (Oxford: Clarendon Press, 1982) 137. E. G. Chazon, who has recently reedited these texts, has reached a similar conclusion, suggesting that the prayers originated in a proto-Qumranic group. Cf. her Jerusalem dissertation, *A Liturgical Document from Qumran and its Implications: "Words of the Luminaries"* (4QDibHam) (Jerusalem: Hebrew University, 1991) 89. See also her arguments in the article cited above in n. 14, pp. 15-17.

NAME	SIGLA	COPIES IN CAVES							
		4Q	1Q	2Q	3Q	5Q	6Q	11Q	TOTAL
*Canticle of the Maskil	4Q510-4Q511; (8Q5 [43])	2	-	-	-	-	-	-	3
Exorcist psalms	11Q11 [44]	-	-	-	-	-	-	1	1
Songs of Sabbath Sacrifice	4Q400-4Q407;11Q17 [45]	8	-	-	-	-	-	1	9
*Daily prayers	4Q503	1	-	-	-	-	-	-	1
Lamentation	4Q501	1	-	-	-	-	-	-	1

---

[43] Texts from cave 8 were not included in a separate count because they contained biblical texts, a phylactery and a mezuza, which are included in the overall number of biblical manuscripts (cf. n. 9). The only identifiable non-biblical fragment is that of 8Q5. Written in a poetic style, it contains the formula בשמכה אל [ג]בור אני מפחד ("In Your name, I [po]werful One, I instill fear..."), which is the exorcism formula employed by the Canticles of the Maskil against demons. This fragment must therefore have belonged to the same type of canticle. This was noted also by J.M. Baumgarten, "On the Nature of the Seductress in 4Q184," *RQ* 15 (1991) 135-6.

[44] For the classification of this fragment as a canticle of the Maskil cf. É. Puech, "11QPsAp^a: un rituel d'exorcisme, Essai de Reconstruction," *RQ* 14 (1990) 377-408.

[45] Fragments of another copy of this work were found at Masada. This work is of distinct CT character, as is evident from various terms employed by it. See for instance, שׁבע שׁיר (4Q400 1 i 16; compare 1QS 10:20; CD 2:5; 1QH 2:9, 14:34); נכבדה (4Q401 17 4 ; MasŠŠ i 1; compare 1QS 5:11; CD 3:14; 4Q508 2 4). I therefore do not understand the hesitations of C. Newsom in ascribing this work to the Qumran community. See, for instance, her formulation in "Sectually Explicit," 181-2.

THE QUMRAN MANUSCRIPTS

NAME	SIGLA	COPIES IN CAVES							
		4 Q	1Q	2 Q	3 Q	5 Q	6 Q	11Q	TOTAL
*Miscellaneous Liturgical pieces	4Q392-4Q393;4Q409;4Q457 4Q441-4Q442;4Q444;[46] 4Q499;1Q30	8	1	-	-	-	-	-	9
+Prayers	4Q291-4Q293	3	-	-	-	-	-	-	3
Prayer ("Ritual of Marriage")	4Q502[47]	1	-	-	-	-	-	-	1
EXEGETICAL WORKS									
*Continuous Pesharim	4Q161-4Q173;1QpHab; 1Q14;1Q15;1Q16;3Q4	13	4	-	1	-	-	-	18
*Thematic Pesharim	4Q174-4Q178;4Q180;4Q182; 11Q13	7	-	-	-	-	-	1	8
Pesher on Genesis	4Q252-4Q254	3	-	-	-	-	-	-	3

46 This is a group of tiny fragments belonging to various manuscripts. Information on these fragments and on 4Q443 and 4Q457 was given by their editor, E.G. Chazon, in a paper read at the SBL Annual Meeting, San Francisco, November 1992. I thank Esther Chazon for placing the manuscript at my disposal.

47 Terms such as ברית אמת (4Q502 I 2 6), לכה ברכה (4Q502 I 1 10), or אשר צדק (4Q502 I 9 9), as well as others, point to the CT character of this text.

DEVORAH DIMANT

NAME	SIGLA	COPIES IN CAVES							
		4 Q	1 Q	2 Q	3 Q	5 Q	6 Q	11 Q	TOTAL
SAPIENTIAL WORKS									
Sapiential Work A	4Q416-4Q418	3	-	-	-	-	-	-	3
Sapiential Work B	4Q413;4Q415	2	-	-	-	-	-	-	2
Wisdom Texts	4Q419;[48] 4Q408[49]	2	-	-	-	-	-	-	2
Book of Mysteries	4Q299-4Q301;1Q27	3	1	-	-	-	-	-	4
Various Sapiential Fragments	4Q410;4Q423-4Q426; 4Q474-4Q481;[50] 4Q487	9	-	-	-	-	-	-	9
Two Ways	4Q473	1	-	-	-	-	-	-	1
Parable of the Tree	4Q302a	1	-	-	-	-	-	-	1

---

48 In a conference in New York in December 1992, T. Elgvin reviewed some of these sapiential texts. Among the CT sapiential works he distinguishes two distinct groups: (1) 4Q416–4Q418; 4Q413; 4Q415; 4Q420–4Q421; 4Q419, and (2) 4Q410; 4Q424.

49 Included in the publication of Wacholder and Abegg *Preliminary Edition* 2.240-3.

50 These small fragments seem to belong to a CT work. Note the expression ב[ ]ני שבת (4Q476 2 5), reminiscent of the community's preoccupation with the correct observance of the Sabbath.

THE QUMRAN MANUSCRIPTS

NAME	SIGLA	COPIES IN CAVES							
		4Q	1Q	2Q	3Q	5Q	6Q	11Q	TOTAL
+Wisdom Text with Beatitudes	4Q525[51]	1	-	-	-	-	-	-	1
Meditation on Creation[52]	4Q303-4Q305	3	-	-	-	-	-	-	3
*Way of Righteousness	4Q420-4Q421	2	-	-	-	-	-	-	2
Rule for the Farmer	4Q423;1Q26	1	1	-	-	-	-	-	2
+Rule?	4Q524	1	-	-	-	-	-	-	1
VARIA									
*Various fragments	4Q181[53] 4Q183;4Q306; 4Q464a,[54] 1Q31;3Q9	4	1	-	1	-	-	-	6

51 This work has survived in several large fragments from a Herodian manuscript (three museum plates; PAM nos. 43.600, 43.595, 43.596). For details see S.A. Reed, *Qumran Cave 4 (4Q521-4Q575) Starcky, Dead Sea Scrolls Inventory Project* 8.10. É. Puech has published some fragments of 4Q525 in "Un hymne essénien en partie retrouvé et les Béatitudes," *RQ* 13 (1988) 83-8 and in "4Q525 et la péricope des Béatitudes en Ben Sira et Matthieu," *RB* 98 (1991) 80-106. The text established by Starcky is reproduced by Wacholder and Abegg, *Preliminary Edition*, 2.186-203. The fragments employ terminology distinctive of the community. See for instance, 4Q525 19 4 היכמחה; 4Q525 22 8 ליהוד לאשר.

52 Note 4Q303 1 1: משכל שמוע, a characteristic wisdom-address formula, which may indicate the general character of the work. Therefore, this work belongs together with the sapiential texts. The reference to the addressees as "possessing understanding" may indicate a connection to the Qumran community.

53 J.T. Milik assumes that this fragment and 4Q180 are copies of the work preserved in 11Q13(Melch). See his analysis in "Milkî-ṣedeq," 109-24. Differences of style, structure and subject matter argue against such an assumption. See my arguments in "The Pesher on the Periods (4Q180) and 4Q181," *IOS* 9 (1979) 77-102.

54 The occurrence of the terms ברית, קץ עד (4Q464a 1 3,5) suggests CT character. For a preliminary edition cf. M.E. Stone and E. Eshel, "An Exposition on the Patriarchs (4Q464) and Two Other Documents (4Q464a and 4Q464b)," *Le Muséon* 105 (1992) 243-64.

NAME	SIGLA	COPIES IN CAVES							TOTAL
		4 Q	1 Q	2 Q	3 Q	5 Q	6 Q	11 Q	
CRYPTIC									
Texts in cryptic writing[55]	4Q298;4Q249;4Q250;[56] 4Q313; 4Q317;4Q362; 4Q363;4Q363a	8	-	-	-		-	-	8
II. LITERARY WORKS WITHOUT TERMINOLOGY CONNECTED TO THE COMMUNITY									
A. HEBREW									
NARRATIVES									
Tobit	4Q200;4Q478(?)	2	-	-	-	-	-	-	2
*Noachic literature[57]	1Q19;1Q19bis	-	1	-	-	-	-	-	1
Flood Apocryphon	4Q370	1	-	-	-	-	-	-	1
Three Tongues of Fire	4Q376;1Q29	1	1	-	-	-	-	-	2
*Miscellaneous Torah-like frags.	4Q374-4Q375;4Q377;4Q368	4	-	-	-	-	-	-	4
Joseph Apocryphon	4Q371-4Q373;2Q22	3	-	1	-	-	-	-	4

55   I assume that texts written in cryptic script belong to the community. One such text, 4Q298, contains the title in normal script, which reads, "Words of the Sage to the Sons of Dawn." Both the term Sage (משכיל) and the term Sons of Dawn (בני שחר) are typical of the community.

56   This text is copied on the verso of 4Q249.

57   These fragments are often seen as remnants of a lost apocryphon of Noah, traces of which are to be observed also in 1 Enoch (cf. n. 77). The most recent discussion of this topic is that of García Martínez, Qumran and Apocalyptic, 1-44.

THE QUMRAN MANUSCRIPTS

NAME	SIGLA	COPIES IN CAVES							TOTAL
		4 Q	1 Q	2 Q	3 Q	5 Q	6 Q	11 Q	
Psalms of Joshua	4Q378-4Q379	2	-	-	-	-	-	-	2
Vision of Samuel	4Q160	1	-	-	-	-	-	-	1
+Tehillot Haavot[58]	4Q382	1	-	-	-	-	-	-	1
Jeremiah Apocryphon	4Q385b;4Q387b;4Q389a; 4Q383;4Q384(?)	5	-	-	-	-	-	-	5
Text mentioning Zedekiah	4Q470	1	-	-	-	-	-	-	1
*Miscellaneous narrative texts	4Q458;4Q461-4Q462;[59] 4Q463;3Q7;6Q9;6Q12-6Q13	4	-	-	1	-	3	-	8

58 The fragments assigned to this manuscript are not of the same character; they contain both narrative and poetical portions and may therefore belong to two different works.

59 4Q462 1 was recently edited in a preliminary form by M. Smith, "4Q462 (Narrative) Fragment 1: A Preliminary Edition," RQ 15 (1991) 55-77. This text offers an intriguing specimen of an apocryphal narrative and is difficult to classify. It contains references to "light" and "darkness" but nothing else which may be described as distinctive of the community's literature.

NAME	SIGLA	COPIES IN CAVES							
		4Q	1Q	2Q	3Q	5Q	6Q	11Q	TOTAL
Exodus Paraphrase (An apocryphon ?[60])	4Q127	1	-	-	-	-	-	-	1
POETIC AND LITURGICAL WORKS									
Apocryphal and non-canonical Psalms	4Q380-4Q381;4Q448;[61] 4Q88; 11Q5 (11QPs ^{a}); 11Q6 (11QPs^b)[62]	4	-	-	-	-	-	2	6
Lamentations	4Q179	1	-	-	-	-	-	-	1
Grace after Meals[63]	4Q434a	1	-	-	-	-	-	-	1
Benediction	4Q500	1	-	-	-	-	-	-	1

---

60 This is a Greek papyrus which has survived in several small fragments, the largest of which were published by E. Ulrich, "A Greek Paraphrase of Exodus on Papyrus from Qumran Cave 4," *Studien zur Septuaginta: Robert Hanhart zu Ehren* (eds. D. Fraenkel, U. Quast, J.W. Wevers; *MSU* 20; Göttingen: Vandenhoeck & Ruprecht, 1990) 287-98. In a forthcoming paper I have pointed out that the context and vocabulary are actually non-biblical and, therefore, have suggested that the papyrus contains in fact an apocryphon written in a biblicizing style. Cf. my discussion in "4Q127—An Unknown Jewish Apocryphal Work? *Al Shule Ha-Me‘il*: Studies in Biblical, Jewish and Near Eastern Ritual, Law and Literature in Honor of Jacob Milgrom (in press).

61 This is a poetic text with a mention of "King Jonathan." Cf. H. and E. Eshel and A. Yardeni, "A Scroll from Qumran which Includes Part of Psalm 154 and a Prayer for King Jonathan and his Kingdom," *Tarbiz* 60 (1991) 295-324 (Hebrew).

62 These two 11Q manuscripts and 4Q88 are Psalms collections with apocryphal psalms. They were, therefore, taken into account also in the group of biblical manuscripts. 11Q5 (11QPs^a) and 4Q88 (4QPs^f) contain the apocryphal Apostrophe to Zion. Cf. J. Starcky, "Psaumes Apocryphes de la Grotte 4 de Qumrân (4QPs^f vii-x)," RB 73 (1966) 353-71.

63 Published by M. Weinfeld, "Grace after Meals in Qumran," *JBL* 111 (1992) 427-40.

THE QUMRAN MANUSCRIPTS

NAME	SIGLA	COPIES IN CAVES							TOTAL
		4Q	1Q	2Q	3Q	5Q	6Q	11Q	
Various Liturgical fragments	4Q443;4Q449-4Q457	10	-	-	-	-	-	-	10
Poetical Fragment	4Q521	1	-	-	-	-	-	-	1
PSEUDEPIGRAPHA									
Jubilees	4Q176 19-20;[64] 4Q216; 4Q218-4Q224;1Q17-1Q18; 2Q19-2Q20;3Q5;11Q12	9	2	2	1	-	-	1	15
Text close to Jubilees	4Q482-4Q483	2	-	-	-	-	-	-	2
Pseudo-Jubilees	4Q217;[65] 4Q225-4Q227	4	-	-	-	-	-	-	4
Test. Naphtali	4Q215	1	-	-	-	-	-	-	1
Words of Moses	1Q22	-	1	-	-	-	-	-	1
Moses Apocryphon	2Q21	-	-	1	-	-	-	-	1
Pseudo-Ezekiel	4Q385-4Q388;4Q391	5	-	-	-	-	-	-	5

64 Identified by M. Kister, "Newly-Identified Fragments of the Book of Jubilees: Jub 23:21-23, 30-31," *RQ* 12 (1985-87) 529-36.
65 Unlike J.T. Milik, the present editor of these fragments, J. VanderKam, considers this manuscript to belong to a pseudo-Jubilees work. See his review of the 4Q Jubilees manuscripts, "The Jubilees Fragments from Qumran Cave 4," *The Madrid Qumran Congress* (eds. J. Trebolle Barrera and L. Vegas Montaner; *Studies on the Texts of the Desert of Judah* 11,2; Leiden–Madrid: E. J. Brill–Editorial Complutense, 1992) 2.635-48.

DEVORAH DIMANT

NAME	SIGLA	COPIES IN CAVES							TOTAL
		4 Q	1 Q	2 Q	3 Q	5 Q	6 Q	11Q	
Pseudo-Moses	4Q385a;4Q387a;4Q388a; 4Q389;4Q390[66]	5	-	-	-	-	-	-	5
Pseudepigraphic Work	4Q459-4Q460	2	-	-	-	-	-	-	2
*Prophetical fragments	4Q522;[67] 1Q25;2Q23;6Q10	1	1	1	-	-	1	-	4
Maledictions	5Q14	-	-	-	-	1	-	-	1
EXEGETICAL WORKS									
Pentateuch Reworked	4Q364-4Q367;4Q158	5	-	-	-	-	-	-	5
Joshua Paraphrase	4Q123	1	-	-	-	-	-	-	1
Genesis Paraphrase	4Q422	1	-	-	-	-	-	-	1
Exodus	4Q422a	1	-	-	-	-	-	-	1

66 Published by me in "New Light from Qumran on the Jewish Pseudepigrapha—4Q390," *The Madrid Qumran Congress* 2.1-44.

67 Labelled as "work with place names," this text is now partly published by É. Puech, "La pierre de Sion et l'autel des holocaustes d'après un manuscrit hébreu de la grotte 4 (4Q522)," *RB* 99 (1992) 676-96. See also his comments in "Fragments du Psaume 122 dans un manuscrit hébreu de la grotte IV," *RQ* 9 (1978) 547-50. Puech speculates about the possibility of a Qumranic origin, but in the absence of any CT elements in the text it was grouped here together with NCT works. It can be classified as poetic as well.

50

NAME	SIGLA	COPIES IN CAVES							
		4 Q	1 Q	2 Q	3 Q	5 Q	6 Q	11 Q	TOTAL
Exposition on Patriarchs	4Q464[68]	1	-	-	-	-	-	-	1
SAPIENTIAL TEXTS									
Ben-Sira	2Q18	-	-	1	-	-	-	-	1
Wicked Woman	4Q184	1	-	-	-	-	-	-	1
Sapiential Texts	4Q411; 4Q412	2	-	-	-	-	-	-	2
Wisdom text?	4Q185	1	-	-	-	-	-	-	1
HALAKHIC TEXTS									
Tohorot	4Q274-4Q279;4Q281-4Q283	9	-	-	-	-	-	-	9
Purification Rulings	4Q414	1	-	-	-	-	-	-	1
Temple Scroll	11Q19(=11QT);11Q20; (4Q365a)[69]	1	-	-	-	-	-	2	3

68 This is an expository text, as is indicated by the occurrence of the term מעשי של in 4Q464 2 7. But without the presence of the exegetical method and contents peculiar to the CT works, it is difficult to assign this fragment to the CT texts on the basis of this term alone. For this reason, and considering the subject matter, it was classified with NCT fragments. For an edition see Stone and Eshel, "Exposition on the Patriarchs" (see, n. 53).

69 Fragment 4Q365a 2* contains a list of the twelve tribes overlapping with 11QT[a]44. Yadin thought that this manuscript constitutes another copy of the Temple Scroll. Cf. idem, *The Temple Scroll* (Jerusalem: Israel Exploration Society, 1983), 1.8-9; 3, pl. 38* (no. 5). If this is the case, it would present another instance where a copy of a work known from cave 11 was found also in cave 4. However, originally assigned to the Reworked Pentateuch, this 4Q fragment was considered by the first editor John Strugnell as being one of the sources of the Temple Scroll rather than an actual copy of it. Cf. his opinion as quoted by B.Z. Wacholder, *The Dawn of Qumran* (Cincinnati: Hebrew Union College Press, 1983) 205-6. The present editors of the 4QPentReworked, Emanuel Tov and Sidnie A. White, agree that the fragment does not belong with the Reworked Pentateuch and may form a different recension or source of the Temple Scroll.

		COPIES IN CAVES							
NAME	SIGLA	4 Q	1 Q	2 Q	3 Q	5 Q	6 Q	11Q	TOTAL
Legal Commentary on Torah	4Q251	1	-	-	-	-	-	-	1
CALENDRICAL AND CHRONOLOGICAL TEXTS									
*Mishmarot Texts[70]	4Q320;4Q321;4Q321a	3	-	-	-	-	-	-	3
*Calendrical texts	4Q322-4Q330;[71] 6Q17	9	-	-	-	-	1	-	10
Horoscope	4Q186	1	-	-	-	-	-	-	1
Otot	4Q319	1	-	-	-	-	-	-	1
*+Lists and calendars	4Q334;4Q337	2	-	-	-	-	-	-	2
Astronomical Fragments(?)	4Q335-4Q336	2	-	-	-	-	-	-	2
+Historical Work	4Q331-4Q333	3	-	-	-	-	-	-	3
MISCELLANEA									
*Various pieces	4Q228;4Q247;[72] 4Q248; 4Q294-4Q297	7	-	-	-	-	-	-	7

70 In the opinion of the present editor of these texts, Shemaryahu Talmon, the Mishmarot texts form a distinct group, different from other calendrical texts (private communication). In the absence of overlapping it is impossible to know whether all these manuscripts are copies of one and the same work.

71 The number of manuscripts is larger than the serial numbering of the manuscripts due to the identification of four additional ones: 4Q324a, 4Q324b; 4Q324c; 4Q329a. In the opinion of Talmon, fragment 6Q17, published in DJD 3.132, also belongs here. It was classified accordingly.

72 This is a small piece published by J.T. Milik, *The Books of Enoch* (Oxford: Clarendon Press, 1976) 256.

THE QUMRAN MANUSCRIPTS

NAME	SIGLA	COPIES IN CAVES							
		4Q	1Q	2Q	3Q	5Q	6Q	11Q	TOTAL
Lists	4Q338-4Q341	3	-	-	-	-	-	-	3
Copper Scroll	3Q15	-	-	-	1	-	-	-	1
B. ARAMAIC									
Tobit	4Q196-4Q199	4	-	-	-	-	-	-	4
Genesis Apocryphon	1Q20	-	1	-	-	-	-	-	1
1 Enoch	Enoch-4Q201-4Q202; 4Q204-4Q207;4Q212; Astronomical Book- 4Q208-4Q211	11	-	-	-	-	-	-	11
Book of Giants	4Q203;4Q530-4Q532; 4Q533(?);1Q23;1Q24(?); 2Q26(?);6Q873	5	2	1	-	-	1	-	9

73 This work is represented by the following manuscripts: 4Q203 (=Giants[a]) is published by Milik, *The Books of Enoch*, 310-17; 4Q530 (=Giants[b]) and 4Q531 (=Giants[c]) are partly published by Milik, ibid., 230, 304-8; 4Q532 (=Giants[d]) is still unpublished. As copies are considered here also, the more doubtful identifications of 1Q24 and 2Q26 (by Milik, *Enoch*, 309). Milik refers (ibid., 309) to two other "groups of fragments" in the lot of Starcky without further information. Is one of them identical with what is now designated as 4Q533 (Giants or Pseudo-Enoch)? In any case, it is included in the above list. I have, however, omitted another supposed copy, Giants[e] identified by Milik, ibid., 236-7 (pl. XIX) as part of an Enochic manuscript, i.e. 4Q206 fragments 2-3, because this identification rests on Milik's attribution of the Book of Giants to the Enochic collection. Some ten years ago I pointed out that this hypothesis is untenable, given the distinctive literary character of the Book of Giants (third person narrative in the Book of Giants in contrast to first person pseudepigraphic framework in 1 Enoch). See my comments in "The Biography of Enoch and the Books of Enoch," *VT* 33 (1983) 16 n. 8.

DEVORAH DIMANT

NAME	SIGLA	4Q	1Q	2Q	3Q	5Q	6Q	11Q	TOTAL
					COPIES IN CAVES				
New Jerusalem	4Q554-4Q555;1Q32;2Q24; 5Q15;11Q18	2	1	1	-	1	-	1	6
Visions of Amram	4Q543-4Q548	6	-	-	-	-	-	-	6
Testament of Levi	4Q213-4Q214; 1Q21	2	1	-	-	-	-	-	3
Apocryphon of Levi[74]	4Q537;4Q540-4Q541	3	-	-	-	-	-	-	3
Testament of Qahat	4Q542	1	-	-	-	-	-	-	1
*Various Patriarchal Pseudepigrapha	4Q538-4Q539	2	-	-	-	-	-	-	2
Pseudo-Daniel	4Q243-4Q245	3	-	-	-	-	-	-	3
Aramaic Apocalypse	4Q246[75]	1	-	-	-	-	-	-	1
The Prayer of Nabonidus	4Q242	1	-	-	-	-	-	-	1

Similar observations were made by K. Beyer, *Die aramäischen Texte vom Toten Meer* (Göttingen: Vandenhoeck & Ruprecht, 1984) 259, J. VanderKam, "Enoch Traditions in Jubilees and Other Second-Century Sources," *SBL Seminar Papers 1978* (Missoula: Scholars Press, 1978) 1.229-51, and J.C. Reeves, *Jewish Lore in Manichaean Cosmology (Monographs of the Hebrew Union College* 14; Cincinnati: Hebrew Union College Press, 1992) 55.

74 The editor, É. Puech, now considers this group of manuscripts as a distinctive work. See "Fragments d'un apocryphe de Levi et le personnage eschatologique, 4QTestLevi c-d (?) et 4QAJa," *The Madrid Qumran Congress* 2.449-502.

75 Recently edited by É. Puech, "Fragment d'une apocalypse en araméen (4Q246=pseudo-Dan^d) et le royaume de Dieu," *RB* 99 (1992) 98-131. Cf. also the comments of G. Vermes, "Qumran Forum Miscellanea I," *JJS* 43 (1992) 301-3.

THE QUMRAN MANUSCRIPTS

NAME	SIGLA	COPIES IN CAVES							
		4Q	1Q	2Q	3Q	5Q	6Q	11Q	TOTAL
Proto-Esther(?)	4Q550[76]	1	-	-	-	-	-	-	1
Daniel-Susanna(?)	4Q551[77]	1	-	-	-	-	-	-	1
Elect of God	4Q534[78]	1	-	-	-	-	-	-	1
+Apocalypse - Four kingdoms	4Q552;4Q553	2	-	-	-	-	-	-	2
*+Vision(?)	4Q556-4Q558	3	-	-	-	-	-	-	3
+Words of Michael	4Q529	1	-	-	-	-	-	-	1
*+Miscellaneous narrative texts	4Q535-4Q536;[79] 4Q549	3	-	-	-	-	-	-	3
*+Miscellaneous texts	4Q562-4Q575	14	-	-	-	-	-	-	14
+Magical Text	4Q560	1	-	-	-	-	-	-	1
+Biblical Chronology	4Q559	1	-	-	-	-	-	-	1

76 Published by J.T. Milik, "Les modèles araméens du livre d'Esther dans la grotte 4 de Qumrân," *RQ* 15 (1992) 321-406.
77 Published by J.T. Milik, "Daniel et Susanne à Qumran?" *De la Tôrah du Messie: Études d'exégèse et d'herméneutique bibliques offertes à Henri Cazelles* (ed. M. Carrez et al.; Paris: Desclée, 1981) 337-59.
78 Milik thinks that this manuscript is a copy of the same work represented also by 4Q535 and 4Q536, labelled by him as the Birth of Noah. In his opinion also the horoscope preserved in 4Q561 is a copy of the same work. Cf. idem, *The Books of Enoch*, 56, where he quotes from 4Q535 3 3. In a recent article Milik quotes 4Q536 2 ii 10-13. Cf. idem, "Les modèles araméens," 357. He mentions there five copies of this work, without providing any information on the additional copy. His thesis is not substantiated by the data published to date.
79 Cf. previous note.

DEVORAH DIMANT

NAME	SIGLA	COPIES IN CAVES							
		4 Q	1 Q	2 Q	3 Q	5 Q	6 Q	11 Q	TOTAL
Horoscope	4Q561[80] (cf. 4Q186)	1	-	-	-	-	-	-	1
Zodiology and Brontology	4Q318	1	-	-	-	-	-	-	1
*Unidentified Aramaic fragments[81]	4Q309-4Q310;4Q488-4Q490;1Q63-1Q68;2Q33;6Q14;6Q19;6Q23	5	6	1	-	-	3	-	15
NON-LITERARY DOCUMENTS									
*Varia[82]	4Q341-4Q361;6Q26	21	-	-	-	-	1	-	22
UNIDENTIFIED FRAGMENTS[83]									

---

80 This text was initially labelled by its first editor a messianic aramaic text. Cf. J. Starcky, "Un texte messianique araméen de la grotte 4 de Qumrân," *École des langues orientales anciennes de l'Institut Catholique de Paris: Mémorial du cinquantenaire 1914-1964* (Paris: Bloud et Gay, 1964) 31-66. J.A. Fitzmyer later suggested that the text refers to Noah rather than to a messianic figure. See idem, "The Aramaic 'Elect of God' Text from Qumran Cave 4," *Essays on the Semitic Background of the New Testament* (Missoula: Scholars Press, 1974) 158-9.

81 Assuming these fragments to originate from non-community works, they were all counted together with the remaining Aramaic manuscripts, whereas the unidentified Hebrew manuscripts were considered as a separate group (cf. below).

82 Including five documents in Aramaic. This group contains, among other, accounts of money, lists of names and acts of purchase.

83 This group contains all the Hebrew fragments too tiny to be either read or classified in one of the three main categories. Illegible Aramaic fragments are listed separately with the Aramaic manuscripts.

THE QUMRAN MANUSCRIPTS

NAME	SIGLA	COPIES IN CAVES							TOTAL
		4Q	1Q	2Q	3Q	5Q	6Q	11Q	
*+small fragments	4Q124-4Q126; 4Q302; 4Q307;[84] 4Q308; 4Q311-4Q312; 4Q445- 4Q447;4Q464b; 4Q469; 4Q479- 4Q481; 4Q481^{a-f};4Q484-4Q486; 4Q498; 4Q515-4Q520; 4Q523; 4Q526-4Q528; 1Q41-1Q62;1Q69; 1Q70; 1Q70^{bis}; 2Q27-2Q32; 3Q8; 3Q10-3Q11; 5Q9-5Q10; 5Q16- 5Q25; 6Q25; 6Q20-6Q25; 6Q27- 6Q31; 6QX1; 6QX2; 11Q21-11Q23	35	24	6	3	12	13	3	96
HALAKHIC WORKS (Addition)									
Serekh ha-niddot	4Q284	1	-	-	-	-	-	-	1
Leqet	4Q284a[85]	1	-	-	-	-	-	-	1

---

84 Two fragments containing some words from Psalm 122 were published by É. Puech, "Fragments du Psaume 122 dans un manuscrit hébreu de la grotte IV," *RQ* 9 (1978) 547-54. Since other fragments assigned to the same manuscript do not contain biblical text, Puech believes that the two fragments published by him contain a Psalm quotation from a non-biblical manuscript.

85 The editor of this fragment, J.M. Baumgarten, informs me that the term משקה הרבים ("the drink of the Many"), peculiar to the community, occurs in one of the fragments. This is why the text is included in the CT texts section. Other fragments originally assigned to the same manuscript are considered now as belonging to a different work—serekh ha-niddot (=4Q284), classified under NCT halakhic works.

Table II: Cave Distribution

Cave	Biblical MSS	MSS with Terminology of the Community	MSS without Terminology of the Community			Undentified Mss.	Total literary documents
			Heb.	Aram.	Total		
4Q	158[a]	158	127	76	203	35	554
1Q	15[b]	17	6	11	17	24	73
2Q	17	1	6	3	9	6	33
3Q	3	3	3	-	3	3	12
5Q	8[c]	3	1	1	2	12	25
6Q	7	3	5	4	9	13	32
8Q	4[d]	1	-	-	-	-	5
11Q	11[e]	6	5[f]	1	6	3	26
Total[g]	223	192 ~ 115 works	153 ~ 45 works	96 ~ 25 works	249 ~ 70 works	96	760

a   Including 35 other manuscripts (phylacteries, mezuzot, Aramaic targums).

b.   Including 1 phylactery.

c   Including 1 phylactery

d.   Including 1 phylactery and 1 mezuza.

e   Including 1 Aramaic targum and 11QPs[a], 11QPs[b].

f.   Including 2 copies of Apocryphal Psalms (11QPs[a], 11QPs[b]).

g.   Together with 7 Greek manuscripts of Cave 7 and 22 non-literary documents (not included in the above table) the total number of manuscripts is 789.

THE QUMRAN MANUSCRIPTS

Table III: Types of Works and their Distribution

Cave	Biblical MSS	MSS with Terminology of the Community	MSS without Terminology of the Community	Unidentified MSS	Total
Total	223 30%	190 25%	259 33%	96 12%	768 100%

Cave	Biblical MSS	MSS with Terminology of the Community	MSS without Terminology of the Community	Unidentified MSS	Total
4 Q	158 28%	156 28%	213 38%	35 6%	562 100%
1 Q	15 21%	17 23%	17 23%	24 33%	73 100%
2 Q	17 52%	1 3%	9 27%	6 18%	33 100%
5 Q	8 32%	3 12%	2 8%	12 48%	25 100%
6 Q	7 22%	3 10%	9 28%	13 40%	32 100%
11 Q	11 44%	6 23%	6 23%	3 12%	26 100%

4QTOHORAa: AN UNPUBLISHED QUMRAN TEXT ON PURITIES*

Jacob Milgrom

One of the distinguishing traits of the rabbinic dialectic in the Talmud is that every possible contingency is considered. The unpublished Qumran text 4Q Toha mars this distinction, for not a single one of its halakhic cases is mentioned anywhere in rabbinic literature. The extant text of Frag. 1 consists of nine broken lines; its beginning and end are missing, thus necessitating reconstructions galore. The text and translation which follow should therefore be regarded as tentative:[1]

1 יחל להפיל את תח[נו]נו [מ]שכב יגון ישכב [ומושב] אנחה ישב
בדד לכול הטמאים ישב ורחוק מן

2 הטהרה שתים עשרה אמה בדברו אליו ומערב צפון לכול בית מושב ישב
רחוק כמידה הזות

3 איש מכול הטמאים [אש]ר י[נגע] בֿו ורחץ במים ויכבס בגדיו ואחר יאכל בו
הוא אשר אמר טמא טמא

4 יקרא כול ימי היֹו[ת בו] ה[נ]גֿע והזובה דם לשבעת הימים אל תגע בזב
ובכול כלי [א]שר יגע בו הזב וש[כב]

5 עליו אוֹ אשר ישב עליו [ואם] נגעה תכבס בגדיה ורחצה ואחר תוכל ובכול
מודה [אל] תתערב בשבעת

6 ימיה בעבור אשר ל[ו]א תֿגֿאֿל את מ[ח]נֿי קד[ושי] ישראל וגם אל תגע בכול
אשה [זבה] דם לימים רב[ים]

7 והסופר אם זכר ואם נקבה אל י[נ]גע בזב זו]בֿו בדוה בנדתה כי אם טהרה
מ[נד]תה כי הנה ד[ם]

8 הנדה כזוב ואש[ר] נוגע בו ואם [תצא ממנו ש]כבת הזרע מגעו יטמא [וכו]לֿ
נֹוגע באדם מכול

9 הטמאים האלה בשבעת ימי טה[רתם א]ל יוכל כאשר יטמא לנפ[ש] ורחץ
וכבס ואח]ר יוכל

---

*   I am indebted to the following colleagues: Joseph Baumgarten who shared his photographs of this text, Émile Puech and Elisha Qimron for sharing their epigraphic and caligraphic expertise, and Lawrence H. Schiffman for providing a willing and able sounding board for some of the ideas developed here.

1   The text accompanied by full apparatus will be published by J.M. Baumgarten in a future volume of DJD. A preliminary edition by him appears above, 1-8.

1. he shall begin to lay down his pl[ea]. He shall lie in a [b]ed of sorrow and reside in [a dwelling of] sighs. He shall reside apart from all impure persons. He shall be distant from

2. the (food of) purity by twelve cubits while speaking with him (an impure person?). He shall reside northwest of any inhabited dwelling distant by the same measure.

3. [Whoev]er of the impure persons to[uches} him shall bathe in water, launder his clothes, and afterwards he may eat of it (the common food). This is what is meant by "'impure' (to the) impure

4. he shall call out" all the days the [aff]liction is [in him]. As for the woman who is discharging blood, for seven days she shall not touch a male with a genital flux, or any object [th]at he has either touched, l[ain]

5. upon, or sat upon. [And if] she has touched, she shall launder her clothes, bathe, and afterwards she may eat. However, she should (strive) with all her might [not] to intermingle (with pure persons) during her seven

6. days in order n[o]t to defile the c[a]mps of the ho[ly ones of] Israel. She must not touch any woman who [is discharging] blood for ma[ny] days.

7. Whoever is counting off (the seven days of purification), whether male or female, must not tou[ch a male during (?)] his fl[ux] (or) a woman during her menstrual infirmity unless she is purified from her me[nses]. For behold the blo[od of]

8. the menstruant is equivalent to the genital flux; so (too) the one who touches it (the blood). And if he (the male during his seven purificatory days) [has an e]mission of semen, his touch transmits impurity.

9. [Any]one who touches any of these impure persons during the seven days of [their] purif[ication may n]ot eat, just like one who has become defiled by a corp[se, but must bathe,] launder, and afterwa[rds he may eat.

COMMENTS

L.1

יחל להפיל את תח[נונ]ו. This reconstruction is based on אנחנו מפילים תחנונינו (Dan 9:18) and החלותה לנפל לפניו (Est 6:13). Does the latter citation indicate the possibility that the book of Esther was known at Qumran?

The מצרע is the subject of ll.1-4. He is not mentioned by name but the scriptural allusions and description render the identification unmistakable. These few opening words suffice to indicate—in conformance with biblical, Mesopotamian, and later rabbinic tradition—that צרעת ("scale-disease") was regarded as a divine punishment for various egregious sins.[2] Qumran adds a new element, that the afflicted person should be penitent (so too rabbinic literature, e.g., t. Neg. 6:7), presumably admit his wrongdoing, and upon recovery from his illness, should recite the fixed blessings of thanksgiving of 4Q512.[3]

He shall lie in a [b]ed of sorrow and reside in [a dwelling] of sighs. The hendiadys יגון ואנחה (e.g., Isa 35:10; 51:11) has been split, as often happens in biblical poetry (e.g., Ps 31:11) and has been aptly applied to the מצרע who, according to the Torah, should adopt the pose of a mourner: "His clothes shall be rent, his head shall be disheveled, and he shall cover his upper lip" (Lev 13:45). Note should also be taken of the poetic, elegiac quality of this line.

He shall reside apart from all impure persons. To the biblical בדד ישב, "he shall reside apart" (Lev 15:46), Qumran adds "from all impure persons." The significance of this interpretation is investigated below.

L.2

twelve cubits. The rabbis, however, fix no limits. "R. Yohanan said: It is prohibited to go four cubits to the east of a leper. R. Simeon b. Laqish said: even a hundred cubits. They really did not differ: the one who said four cubits referred to a time when there was no wind blowing, whereas the one who said a hundred cubits referred to a time when a wind is blowing" (*Leviticus Rabbah* 16:3).

The (food of) purity, הטהרה. This term (also CD 9:21, 23) and its more usual form טהרת הרבים (e.g. 1QS 6:16-17; 7:3, 16, 19) refer to the solid food of the community prepared and consumed in a state of purity. I admit, however, that this meaning makes no sense to me in this context. How could pure food come within 12 cubits distance from the banished leper? Considering the following expression, "while speaking with him," one would have expected the word to read הטהור, "a pure person."

while speaking with him, בדברו עליו. The only possible antecedent is הטמאים, "impure persons" (l.1), though the lack of

---

2   E.g., Num 12:9; 2 Sam 3:25; 2 Kgs 5:27; 2 Chr 26:18-21; *CAD* A 234-35; b. Arakh. 15b-16b; and for further references and discussion, cf. J. Milgrom, *Leviticus,* vol. I (AB3; New York: Doubleday, 1991), Chap. 13, Comment B.

3   Cf. M. Baillet, DJD 7 (Oxford: Clarendon Press, 1982) 265-278.

agreement in number is jarring. The text would make more sense if the prior word הטהרה would be regarded as an error for הטהור, "a pure person;" cf. the previous note.

Northwest. This contradicts the explicit statement of the *Temple Scroll* that all impurity bearers must dwell in the east (11QT 46:16-18). However, it should be noted that this latter statement refers only to the Temple-city, whereas in the discussion of residences for banished impurity bearers in other cities no directions are given (11QT 48:14-16). Yet the specification of northwest is surprising since that is the source of the prevailing winds in the land of Israel. Hence, the *Temple Scroll* locates the impurity bearers in precisely the opposite direction—the east.

For the same reason, the rabbis ordain that a tannery may be set up only on the east side of a town (Mishnah, B. Meṣ. 2:9) On the other hand, the *Temple Scroll* places the latrines "to the northwest of the (Temple-)city" (11QT 46:14) which, being enclosed by structures, were not affected by the wind.[4] If Qumran intended the same northwest location for latrines in cities other than Jerusalem, was its purpose to locate impurity bearers in the most undesirable and least frequented area and thereby to enforce their isolation?

inhabited dwelling, בית מושב. A term borrowed from Lev 25:29 and employed by Qumran to specify Scripture's vaguer designation, "his dwelling (מושבו) shall be outside the camp" (Lev 13:36). Cf. also the term בית מושבת (CD 11:10-11).

L.3

The prohibition against eating before purificatory ablutions and Qumran's exegesis of the biblical verse are discussed below.

L.4

כול ימי היו[ת בו] הנ[נ]גע. The reconstruction is based on כל ימי אשר הנגע בו (Lev 13:46) and כל ימי היות (1 Sam 22:4; cf. Judg 18:31; 1 Sam 25:16).

והזבה דם לשבעת הימים. "As for the woman who is discharging blood." This phrase does not refer to the זבה but to the menstruant who is described in Scripture with similar terms: זבה דם... שבעת ימים (Lev 15:19).

touched. One of the text's innovations. A *zāb* and his couch and seat defile, i.e., transmit impurity (Lev 15:5-7), but not objects he has touched. Indeed, these objects are not even defiled if he washes beforehand (v 11). The additional severity of her impurity is prob-

---

4   See Y. Yadin's discussion in *The Temple Scroll*, vol. I (Jerusalem: Israel Exploration Society, 1983) 296-98.

ably due to her being a menstruant, i.e., impure to begin with; see the discussion of this innovation below.

L.5

intermingle, תתערב. I have rendered this term according to its meaning in all its occurrences in the Qumranic documents. Without exception they fall in a ritual context, namely, a forbidden mixture of pure and impure or profane and holy persons or substances (1QS 6:17; 7:24-25; 8:23; 9:8; 1QH 16:14; 11QT 32:15; 37:11-12; 45:4-5). The one doubtful attestation is אל יתערב איש מרצונו בשבת (CD 11:4-5 and cf. the unpublished Dᶜ 3 i 1) which S. Schechter, followed by C. Rabin, renders, "Let no man starve himself voluntarily on the Sabbath" by emending יתערב to יתרעב[5] or by rendering it "have sexual intercourse," in keeping with the subsequent teaching of the Karaites that it was forbidden on the Sabbath.[6] However, neither the emendation nor the sexual interpretation is warranted here. The latter, in particular, is vitiated by the adverbial modifier "with all her might." The only plausible effort that a menstruant need exert is to avoid contact with others and thereby defile them.

L.6

The language is based on Lev 15:31 and Num 5:2. For other Qumran attestations of the root גאל meaning "defile," see 1QM 9:8; CD 12:16.

a woman who [is discharging] blood for ma[ny] days, אשה [זו]ב[ה] דם [לימים רב]ים. The prolix language is that of Scripture, ואשה כי יזוב זוב דמה ימים רבים (Lev 15:25). Scripture also is the model for assuming that all the rules obtaining for the *zāb* (vv 3-13) apply equally to the *Zābâ* (vv 25-27).

L.7

Whoever is counting off, והסופר. This verb is used in Scripture exclusively for the *zāb* (Lev 15:13) and *zābâ* (v 28) to designate their seven-day purificatory period.

tou[ch a male during] his fl[ux], יג[ע בזוב זו]בו. This is Milik's reconstruction in the concordance of unpublished Qumran texts (privately issued) which I find doubtful since the alleged subject, the *zāb*, is not discussed. I have, however, no alternative to offer.

---

5   Cf. S. Schechter, *Documents of Jewish Sectaries* I (Cambridge: Cambridge University Press, 1910) XLIX; C. Rabin, *The Zadokite Documents* (Oxford: Clarendon Press, 1954) 54.

6   Cf. E. Qimron, "'אל יתערב איש מרצונו בשבת' (ברית דמשק יא: 5-4)," *Proceedings of the Ninth World Congress of Jewish Studies*, vol. I, section D (Jerusalem: World Union of Jewish Studies, 1986) 9-15.

בדוה בנדתה. Language which describes the menstrual state in Lev 12:26.

Ll.7-8

For behold the blo[od of] the menstruant is equivalent to the genital flux, so (too) the one who touches it (the blood). This text lays down the rule that the impurity of the *zāb* and the menstruant are of equal magnitude. Hence, the person in his purification stage is contaminated to the same degree—requiring immediate ablutions— if he or she touches the menstruant or the *zāb* or any object which they have touched. Since the menstruant is only required to undergo ablutions whereas the *zāb* is also required to offer sacrifices on the following morning (Lev 15:14-15, 29-30), it would be logical to assume that the impurity of the former is not as severe as that of the latter, a notion that this text denies. Paradoxically, the reverse is true: blood is a severer contaminant than semen as shown by the fact that it is capable of tertiary transmission (Lev 15:23).[7] Qumran is certainly on the right biblical track; it just does not go far enough.

L.8

And if he [has an e]mission of semen, his touch transmits impurity. A seminal emission defiles only that on which it impinges (Lev 15:16-18). However, if it is emitted during one's purification period, the combined impurity is now severe enough to defile by touch; see the discussion below.

Ll.8-9

A general rule: All who become impure, whether they bear the least impurity—touching someone during his purification period— or bear the severest impurity—touching a corpse, may not eat until they have purified themselves by means of ablutions; see the discussion below.

CONCLUSIONS

For this paper I will touch only on the text's main theme: an impure person touching another impure person. As indicated, this problem is not raised by the rabbis. One obvious reason is that the subject is academic (a more cogent reason is presented below). With the destruction of the Temple the incurrence of impurity no longer

---

7   See my exegesis on this verse in *Leviticus* (n. 2), ad loc.

results in penalties (with the exception of sexual congress with a menstruant). For Qumran, however, which maintains that every command of the Torah has eternal validity and that, in particular, the Torah's laws of purity must be rigorously followed, the problem of impurity is existentially pertinent. Since Qumran banishes or isolates the major carriers of impurity, it is both logical and realistic that impure persons are able to contact one another.

Moreover, as is their wont, the Qumran materials find a scriptural warrant for their ultimate ruling. The banished scale-diseased person (מצורע), in accosting another person, must "call out 'impure, impure'" טמא טמא יקרא (Lev 13:45b). 4QToh[a], indeed, cites this phrase (ll.3-4) but clearly reads it as follows: "'impure' (to the) impure he (the מצורע) shall call out".[8] If then Qumran argues that Scripture insists on impure persons keeping apart from one another (already implied by 11QT 46:16-18), it clearly has to have sanctions in mind. What are they?

4QToh[a] cites three cases: (1) Any impure person touching a מצרע (l.3); (2) a menstruant touching a zāb or zābâ (one suffering with a chronic genital flux) or the objects he or she has touched, lain upon, or sat on (ll.4-5); and (3) any (pure) person touching anyone during the seven day purificatory period (ll.8-9). In all three cases the procedure is the same: the one making the contact with the severer impurity must undergo ablutions and laundering before he or she may eat (ll.3, 5, 9).

In view of biblical and rabbinic law, the innovation is total both in regard to cases and consequences. The problem of impure persons touching other impure persons (case 1) is raised by this text for the first time.[9] The bedding and seat of the zāb and zābâ do indeed defile according to the Torah (Lev 15:5, 6, 10) but not the objects they touch (case 2). In fact, if they wash their hands, their touch does not even defile (Lev 15:11)! Finally, though the person touch-

---

8　This insight is not mine but that of my son, Jeremy J. Milgrom. The rabbis also came to this conclusion, interpreting בדד (Lev 13:46) as בלבד "alone," i.e., that scale-diseased persons must dwell apart from other impurity bearers (Tgs; Sifra Nega'im, Tazria' 12:13; Sifre Num. 1; Leviticus Rabbah 16:3) but not from each other. Qumran probably had this in mind since the biblical evidence points to the fact that scale-diseased persons lived in groups (2 Kgs 7:3-10; cf. Luke 17:11-19). Moreover, the Temple Scroll states explicitly: "You shall make three places to the east of the (Temple-) city, separated one from another (emphasis mine), into which shall come the mĕṣōrāʿîm, zābîm and the men who have had a (nocturnal) emission" (11QT 46:16-18). The inference can only be that each group of impurity bearers was expected to reside together.

9　The rabbis do discuss the problems of impure objects touching each other (e.g., b. Pes. 14a). Even then they invoke the principle of "the impurity is satiated" (e.g., b. Men. 24a) which indicates their reluctance to ascribe "life" to impurity. But strikingly, they never even raise the issue of impure persons touching each other.

ing someone during the purificatory period (case 3) probably incurs a minor impurity,[10] he needs to purify himself just as if he contacted a corpse-contaminated person (1.9). The consequence, as noted above, is the same in all three cases: the person who touches must fast until he or she undergoes immersion and laundering.

All three cases are characterized by three innovative teachings. The first is that any existing impurity is increased by contact with impurity that is greater in strength. Thus, an impure person touching the *měṣōrāᶜ* (case 1), the menstruant touching the *zāb* or *zābâ* (case 2), and a pure person touching someone in his purificatory period (case 3) are all instances of a lesser (or no) impurity contacting a greater impurity. The operative principle seems to be that the weaker impurity will absorb some of the stronger impurity or, more correctly stated, that some of the stronger impurity will transmit itself to the weaker one. Thus, one can readily understand Qumran's explicit prescription that impure persons must be segregated from impure persons of a different category (e.g., the *měṣōrāᶜ* from the *zāb*; cf. 11QT 46:16-18; cf. 48:14-17) lest they increase their impurity by contact with one another.

Clearly, at work here is a conception of impurity that is vital and active. Moreover, since Qumran espouses a cosmogonic doctrine akin to dualism—ascribing impurity to the forces of Belial—its concept of impurity is more than dynamic; it is demonic. Perhaps it was mainly this reason that accounts for the absence in rabbinic writings of any consideration of the case of impure persons touching each other.[11] For the rabbis, impurity was solely an inert and powerless state. Qumran's concept, on the other hand, held impurity to be autonomous and dangerous, a concept that for the rabbis bordered on heresy. The purpose of the ablution, then, would be the elimination of the impurity increment, to restore the impurity to its prior and lesser status quo, a status that could effectively be controlled and eliminated by the prescribed purificatory rites ordained in Scripture.

A second innovation of 4Q Tohᵃ derives indirectly from a clause in case 3: if a man (presumably a *zāb*) has a seminal emission during his purificatory period his touch defiles (1.8). The implication is that if his present impurity is not increased by contact with another impurity, then his touch does not defile. Here, to our surprise,

---

10 Demonstrated in outline form in J. Milgrom, "The Priestly Impurity System," *Proceedings of the Ninth World Congress of Jewish Studies*, vol. I (Jerusalem: World Union of Jewish Studies, 1986) 121-27 and more amply in idem, *Leviticus* (n. 2), chap. 15, Comment F.

11 See note 9.

Qumran is apparently more lenient than the rule which can be deduced from Scripture that the *zāb* does indeed defile during his purificatory period.[12] The key to Qumran's leniency lies in another of its documents, the *Temple Scroll*. There we learn that the corpse-contaminated persons or objects must undergo immersion and laundering on the first of a seven-day purificatory period (11 QT 49:16-17). This teaching is now confirmed by the recently published 4Q Ord[c],[13] which stipulates that first-day ablutions are required for all those whose impurity (and hence, whose purification) lasts more than one day. The reason for this requirement becomes apparent from the fact, stated above, that the ablution functions to reduce a level of impurity. In 4QOrd[c] the first-day ablution allows the person to eat from the common food of the community. In 4Q Toh[a] we must conclude that though the person is still impure (but only to sancta)[14] his ablution allows him to contact profane things or persons. Here, then, Qumran is more lenient than the priestly Torah (as mentioned above)—all because Qumran prescribes ablutions at the commencement of purification.

The third innovation introduced by 4QToh[a] is its insistence that the newly or augmented impure person may not eat before undergoing his or her ablutions (cf. also 4QOrd[c]). This rule is the leitmotif of the text, the refrain that occurs with each impurity bearer (ll.3, 5, 8-9).[15] A striking parallel is recorded in Philo: "A husband and wife, who have intercourse in accordance with the legitimate usages of married life, are not allowed, when they leave their bed, *to touch anything* [emphasis mine] until they have made their ablutions and purged themselves with water" (Laws 3.63). Clearly, Philo records a tradition that sexual intercourse not only defiles the participants for the following day, as stipulated by the Torah (Lev 15:18), but the defiled participants in turn defile everything they contact until they perform their ablutions (which further proves that the ablution functions to reduce the level of impurity).

Nonetheless, the imposition of a fast prior to the ablution, as demanded by our text, is *sui generis*.[16] Indeed, it is totally unrelated

---

12 The absence of an ablution requirement for the *zāb* and *zābâ* at the beginning of their purificatory period implies that their impurity continues in force. For details, see the references in n. 10.

13 Cf. M. Baillet, DJD 7 (Oxford: Clarendon Press, 1982) 295-98.

14 See the comparative table in Milgrom, *Leviticus* (n. 2), chap. 15, Comment F.

15 L. H. Schiffman has kindly pointed out to me that Rock. 43.976 cited by Y. Yadin (n. 4), 188-89, may be reconstructed: ‎"לוא יבוא אל המקדש/]וכבס ורחץ‎", ‎"ואחר י[אכל ואל המקדש]יבוא‎", "he may not enter the sanctuary. [But if he launders and washes, then he may e]at and [enter] the sanctuary" (ll.9-10).

16 It may have influenced the later practice, attested among the Falashas, that "one who touches a person of another religion or any defiling object (or person)

to the problem of impurity. After all, before the person who was already impure actually touched the *mĕṣōrāᶜ* or *zāb* (cases 1 and 2), he or she most certainly could eat! The innovation, then, is not a matter of impurity but of sanctions. It is Qumran's method of forcing the impure individual to undergo ablutions.

Why the urgency for the ablutions? And why impose the drastic penalty of an enforced fast until the ablutions are performed? Once again, we are confronted with the phenomenon of impurity conceived as an active, malevolent force, but this time revealed in a different dimension: it grows in strength unless checked and reduced through ablutions. This view is entirely rooted in Scripture. He who neglects to purify himself must bring a purification offering if his neglect is accidental (e.g., due to amnesia, as stipulated in Lev 5:1-3) and is subject to *kārēt* (excision by divine agency) if his neglect is deliberate (Num 19:13, 20). The fact that he brings a purification offering means that his impurity, originally of a minor nature—having contacted an impure carcass or person (vv 2-3)—has now burgeoned into major proportions, capable of polluting the sanctuary really.[17] Qumran clearly champions this biblical doctrine, one rendered even more dangerous in Qumran's dualistic theology which, as stated above, assigns impurity to the autonomous and demonic powers of Belial.[18] Thus, the comparison of the person touching the purifying person to the person touching a corpse (1.9) proves apt. The former contracts the slightest impurity which defiles the sacred but not the profane.[19] The latter contracts the gravest impurity: a corpse-contaminated person defiles all objects and persons (Num 19:14-16). 4QTohᵃ insists, nonetheless, that all impurity bearers, greater and lesser alike, must undergo ablutions at once, and until they do so they may not eat.

---

may not eat anything until evening but must be quarantined in the (above-) mentioned tent for the entire day. In the evening he immerses himself in water and becomes pure" (*Sefer Eldad Hadani*, in *Kitbe R. Abraham Epstein*, vol. I [Jerusalem: Mosad Harav Kook, 1950] 173). I owe this reference to Dr. Tirzah Meacham.

17   For details, see Milgrom (n. 2), chap. 4, Comments B and C.
18   E.g., 1QS 1:23-24; CD 4:12-19.
19   See Milgrom (n. 2), chap. 15, Comment E.

SACRAL AND NON-SACRAL SLAUGHTER ACCORDING TO THE *TEMPLE SCROLL*

Lawrence H. Schiffman

In columns 52-53 of the *Temple Scroll* (11QT), among other things, the text deals with a number of laws which relate to the slaughter of animals, either in regard to sacrifices (קדשים) or in regard to non-sacral slaughter (שחיטת חולין):

1. The prohibition of sacrificing a blemished animal (11QT 52:3-5);
2. The prohibition of slaughtering a pregnant animal (11QT 52:5-7);
3. The law of the first born of a pure (kosher) animal, including the prohibition of sacrificing a blemished first born animal (11QT 52:5-12);
4. The prohibition of non-sacral slaughter within a boundary of three days' journey from the Temple (11QT 52:14-16);
5. The obligation to slaughter blemished animals only at a distance of 30 *ris* from the Temple (11QT 52:16-19);
6. The prohibition of eating animals slaughtered outside of the Temple in the City of the Sanctuary (11QT 52:19-21);
7. The law of non-sacral slaughter (11QT 53:07-8).

In general, these laws deal with two things: sacral and non-sacral slaughter on the one hand, and blemished and disqualified animals on the other hand. In this paper we will deal with the first matter. Some of the other issues have already been dealt with by us elsewhere.[1]

THE TEMPLE SCROLL: THE LITERARY FRAMEWORK

Before entering the subject of slaughter itself, it is necessary to make some introductory remarks regarding the *Temple Scroll* in general and the specific passages to be treated here. The scroll in its entirety is a reworking of biblical material with a number of

---

1   See L.H. Schiffman, "The Deuteronomic Paraphrase of the Temple Scroll," *RQ* 15 (1992) 543-67.

additions, most of which are short.[2] The most prominent and longest of these additions, as is well known, is the Law of the King which is found in cols. 56-59.[3]

Besides these additions, the scroll is built on the reworking which we mentioned. Some of these modifications constitute only minor variations or changes in the order of the prescriptions, and some of them represent an attempt to harmonize one passage in the Torah with another and to derive legal rulings from them. There are only a small number of quotations with no tendentious (intentional) adaptations or such harmonizations. The more we study the scroll in detail, the fewer such examples of unmodified quotation seem to exist.

Scholars have already pointed out that this scroll is not a unity. Rather, if we may borrow an expression from the Rabbis, מגילות מגילות ניתנה, "it was given in a series of scrolls."[4] The scroll was originally composed as separate documents which have been put together to constitute the whole. We may recognize a number of sources which were available to the author/redactor who apparently made use of them when he composed his scroll.[5]

One of these sources was the Festival Calendar (cols. 13-29); a second was perhaps the series of laws on matters of ritual purity and impurity (cols. 55-57); and a third was definitely the Law of the King. Nonetheless, the relationships between these sections, as well as the process of harmonization and reworking, testify to an author who controlled all the material and left his own stamp firmly on it.

When did he do his work? Based on numerous studies which I have conducted of aspects of this scroll, I have come to agree fully with Professor Yadin who fixed the date of the text in the days of John Hyrcanus (135/4-104 BCE) or Alexander Janneus (103-76 BCE).[6]

---

2   See Y. Yadin, *The Temple Scroll* (Jerusalem: Israel Exploration Society, 1983) 1.71-88. On the genuine textual variants in the scroll's rendering of the biblical text, see E. Tov, "מגילת המקדש' וביקורת נוסח המקרא," *Eretz-Israel* 15 (1981/2) 100-111.

3   L.H. Schiffman, "The King, His Guard and the Royal Council in the *Temple Scroll*," *PAAJR* 54 (1987) 237-59.

4   B. Giṭ. 60a.

5   A.M. Wilson, L. Wills, "Literary Sources in the *Temple Scroll*," *HTR* 75 (1982) 275-88; H. Stegemann, "The Literary Composition of the Temple Scroll and its Status at Qumran," *Temple Scroll Studies* (ed. G.J. Brooke; Sheffield: JSOT Press, 1989) 123-45, although we cannot accept his conclusions; M.O. Wise, *A Critical Study of the Temple Scroll from Qumran Cave 11*, Studies in Ancient Oriental Civilization 49 (Chicago: The Oriental Institute of the University of Chicago, 1990); F. García Martínez, "Sources et rédaction du *Rouleau du Temple*," *Henoch* 13 (1991) 219-32.

6   Yadin, 1.386-90; M. Hengel, J.H. Charlesworth, D. Mendels, "The Polemical Character of 'On Kingship' in the Temple Scroll: An Attempt at Dating 11QTemple," *JJS* 37 (1986) 28-38.

There is no doubt, in my view, that in this period the scroll was composed and redacted from its component sources. Today, however, the date of the sources of the *Temple Scroll* has become an important question.

This importance stems from the significance of the exceedingly important text 4QMMT, מקצת מעשי התורה, known also as the "Halakhic Letter."[7] The parallels between this text and the *Temple Scroll*[8] lead to the unquestionable conclusion that the *Temple Scroll* was influenced by Sadducean law and exegesis and, in fact, even by written Sadducean sources.[9] Such sources would explain the parallels between the new text (MMT) and the *Temple Scroll*.

When the author/redactor of the scroll came to arrange the sources which were available to him, and after he had dealt with the major issues, i.e. his polemic against the present order of affairs in the Jerusalem Temple and the architecture of the Temple itself, as well as against the Hasmonean political order, he saw that his "Torah" remained incomplete. Therefore, the author/redactor of the scroll took upon himself the task of composing the last section, the paraphrase of large parts of the legal section of the book of Deuteronomy.[10] For this reason he dealt with numerous issues in Deuteronomy. Nevertheless, even without the desire to present his text as a complete Torah, he would have included in his scroll the material to be discussed here dealing with sacral and non-sacral slaughter.

Before turning to the subject of this paper, we should remember that this scroll, as it came from the hands of the author/redactor, does not intend to reflect any actual Temple, sacrificial order, or political regime. On the contrary, the scroll in its entirety is the fruit of the dreams and aspirations of the author and his sources for

---

7   See E. Qimron, J. Strugnell, "An Unpublished Halakhic Letter from Qumran," *Biblical Archaeology Today* (ed. J. Amitai; Jerusalem: Israel Exploration Society, 1985) 400-407; another article by the same title, *Israel Museum Journal* 4 (1985) 9-12 and plate I; and L.H. Schiffman, "The New Halakhic Letter (4QMMT) and the Origins of the Dead Sea Sect," BA 55 (1990) 64-73. A full bibliography is available in Z.J. Kapera, *Qumran Cave Four, Special Report* (Krakow: Enigma Press, 1991) 75-80.

8   L.H. Schiffman, "*Miqṣat Ma'aseh Ha-Torah* and the *Temple Scroll*," RQ 14 (1990) 435-57.

9   M. Lehmann, "The Temple Scroll as a Source of Sectarian Halakha," RQ 9 (1978) 579-87, esp. 579; J.M. Baumgarten, "The Pharisaic-Sadducean Controversies about Purity and the Qumran Texts," *JJS* 31 (1980) 157-70; L.H. Schiffman, "The Temple Scroll and the Systems of Jewish Law of the Second Temple Period," *Temple Scroll Studies* (ed. G.J. Brooke; Sheffield: JSOT Press, 1989) 239-55; and the important article of Y. Sussman, "חקר תולדות ההלכה ומגילות מדבר יהודה, הרהורים תלמודיים ראשונים לאור מגילת 'מקצת מעשי התורה'", *Tarbiz* 59 (1989/90) 11-76.

10   See above, n. 1.

a life of sanctity, purity and uprightness, in accordance with his interpretation of the canonical Torah. In the view of the author, his entire Torah, the material taken from the canonical Torah as well as his new Torah, was itself the result of God's revelation to the Jewish people, without the intermediacy of Moses, at Mt. Sinai.[11] Only in this literary and historical framework is it possible to understand the legal materials which he included in his work.

The study that follows will present first the laws from the *Temple Scroll*. Then the biblical material which lies behind these prescriptions will be examined. We will then explain how these laws relate to their biblical sources. Finally, general conclusions regarding the nature of the scroll will be drawn.

THE LAWS OF SLAUGHTER

In 11QT 52:13-16 there is a law relating to non-sacral slaughter in the vicinity of the Temple:

לוא תזבח שור ושה ועז טהורים בכל שעריכה, קרוב למקדשי דרך שלושה ימים.
כי אם בתוך מקדשי תזבחנו לעשות אותו עולה או זבח שלמים. ואכלתה ושמחתה
לפני במקום אשר אבחר לשום שמי עליו.

You may not slaughter an ox, sheep or goat which are pure (i.e. kosher) animals in any of your gates, within three days' proximity of My Temple. Rather, you must slaughter it (such an animal) in My Temple so as to make it a burnt offering or a whole-offering sacrifice. Then you shall eat and rejoice before Me in the place upon which I shall choose to place My name.[12]

According to this passage, it is forbidden to slaughter a pure, kosher animal within a boundary of three days' journey of the Temple. Within this area, only sacral slaughter is permitted.

This passage appears in the scroll immediately after sections almost directly quoted from Deut 25:4 and 22:10 (11QT 52:12-13). The common element uniting all the matters dealt with on col. 52 (after line 3) is the connection to the slaughter of animals. With our law, the scroll turns to Deut 12 which it then follows all along until

---

11   Yadin 1.71-3, cf. 406-7; B.A. Levine, "The Temple Scroll: Aspects of its Historical Provenance and Literary Character," *BASOR* 232 (1978) 17-21. Cf. B.Z. Wacholder, *The Dawn of Qumran* (Cincinnati: Hebrew Union College, 1983) 13-17; L.H. Schiffman, *Sectarian Law in the Dead Sea Scrolls, Courts, Testimony and the Penal Code* (Chico, CA: Scholars Press, 1983) 14-17.
12   All translations in this article are mine.

verse 26. There is no doubt, therefore, that our passage is based on Deut 12:5-7 with reference to Leviticus 17.[13]

The second law regarding this matter is that which forbids eating in the City of the Sanctuary any meat from an animal which was slaughtered outside of the Temple. Thus 11QT 52:19-21 provides:

לוא תואכל בשר שור ושה ועז בתוך עירי אשר אנוכי מקדש לשום שמי בתוכה אשר לו
יבוא לתוך מקדשי וזבחו שמה, וזרקו את דמו על יסוד מזבח העולה, ואת חלבו יקטירו.

You may not eat the meat of an ox, sheep or goat within My city, which I sanctify in order to place My name there, which does not come into My Temple (so that) they slaughtered (it) there, and sprinkled its blood on the base of the altar of burnt offering(s) and offered its fat(s).

Here, it is forbidden to eat in the City of the Sanctuary of meat which was slaughtered outside the Temple, and the blood and fats of which were not properly offered there. What emerges from this passage is that in order to be permitted to eat of an animal in the city of the sanctuary the animal must be slaughtered as a שלמים (whole-offering).

An additional law which deals with this topic is 11QT 53:07-8 which permits non-sacral slaughter at a distance from the Temple:

[כי ארחיב את גבולכה כאשר דברתי לכה וכי ירח]ק [ממכה המקום אשר בחרתי לשם
שמי שמה, ואמרתה אוכלה בשר כי א]ותה נפשכה לאכול ב]שר. בכול אות נפשכה]
תואכל בש]ר. וז]ב]חת]ה מצואנכה ומבקריכה כברכתי אשר אתן לכה ואכלתה
בשעריכה, והטהור והטמא בכה יחדיו כצבי וכאיל. רק חזק לבלתי אכול הדם; על
הארץ תשופכנו כמים וכסיתו בעפר. כי הדם הוא הנפש ולוא תואכל את הנפש עם
הבשר. למען ייטב לכה ולבניכה אחריכה עד עולם, ועשיתה הישר והטוב לפני אני ה'
אלוהיכה.

[When I enlarge your territory as I promised you, and if the place which I have chosen there to place My name is too fa]r [from you, and you say, "I should (like to) eat meat," for you] desire to eat m[eat, you may] eat as much m[eat as you desire. [You may] s[laughter] any of your sheep and goats or cattle, according to My blessing which I will give to you. You shall (or: must) eat it in your gates, (it may be eaten by both) the pure and impure among you together (or: alike), as though it were a gazelle or a hart. Only be certain (lit. strong) that you do not eat the blood. You must spill it on the ground like water and you must cover (it) with dirt. For the blood is the life-essence, and you may not eat the life-essence with the meat. (All this you must do) in order that it should be good for

13   Yadin 2.231-2.

you and for your children after you forever. For you shall do what
is right and good before Me; I am the Lord your God.[14]

In this passage there are a number of prescriptions. First, based
on a midrashic exegesis which we will discuss below, the scroll
rules that non-sacral slaughter is permitted at a distance from the
Temple, i.e. in the cities of Israel beyond the boundary of three
days' journey. Second, the scroll prescribes that it is permissible to
eat the meat of non-sacral slaughter even if one is ritually impure.
Third, the eating of blood is forbidden, and, therefore, there is an
obligation to cover the blood.

The Biblical Background

The problem with which these texts deal is the contradiction
which emerges from the legislation of the Torah regarding the
slaughter of animals.[15] In Lev 17:1-9 the Torah forbids all
slaughter, whether במחנה ("in the camp") or מחוץ למחנה ("outside of
the camp"), which is not connected with the bringing of a שלמים
sacrifice. The punishment for this transgression is excision (כרת).
There the Torah says that this ruling is intended to force the
bringing of the sacrifice, its slaughter, the sprinkling of the blood,
and the offering of the fats before the Tent of Meeting, in order to
prevent idolatrous worship, i.e. sacrifice to the satyrs (שעירים). It is
important to emphasize that in verse 7 this law is said to apply for
eternity.

Leviticus continues with a prescription regarding the spilling of
the blood in verses 10-13. Although it appears that this section
repeats the general prohibition of eating blood, actually the
positioning of this passage raises the possibility that the text here
supplies a second reason for the prohibition of slaughter outside the
sanctuary. These verses say that if an animal is slaughtered not in
accordance with the procedures for a שלמים sacrifice, and if its blood
is not sprinkled on the altar as required, eating that meat itself
constitutes the eating of blood which is prohibited by the Torah.

---

14   For detailed commentary, see Yadin 2.237-8. This passage has been studied in E.
      Tov, "*Deut*. 12 and *11QTemple* LII-LIII, A Contrastive Analysis," *RQ* 15
      (Mémorial Jean Starcky I; 1991) 169-73.
15   Cf. B.A. Levine, *Leviticus* (Philadelphia and New York: Jewish Publication
      Society, 1989) 112-14; M. Weinfeld, *Deuteronomy and the Deuteronomic School*
      (Oxford: Oxford University Press, 1972) 213-14; M. Haran, בתפיסת ריכוז הפולחן"
      "המקור הכוהני, *Beer Sheva* 1 (1972/3) 114-21; Y. Aloni, מקום הפולחן ומקום השחיטה"
      "לפי ויקרא יז ו-ט, *Shnaton* 7-8 (1983) 21-49; A. Rofé, מבוא לספר דברים (Jerusalem:
      Academon, 1988) 14-18.

In verses 13-14 Leviticus deals with the slaughter of wild beasts and fowl. Since these animals are not suitable for offering as שלמים, the Torah rules that it is permissible to "hunt" them. The require-ment of covering the blood of such animals makes clear that according to Leviticus, the killing of these animals was intended to be by slaughter which enabled the blood to flow out. Here the Torah provides us with the reason for covering the blood. The blood which requires covering is the blood of the life-essence (דם הנפש), the blood which flows as a result of the slaughtering during the time in which the animal passes from life to death. It is this blood which one may not eat, and, therefore, it must be covered.

When we look at the chapter in its entirety, it is clear that the slaughter of beasts and fowl requires the covering of the blood, while the same blood in the slaughter of domesticated animals is that which is sprinkled on the altar in the sacrifice of שלמים. In other words, the covering of the blood of beasts and fowl is a substitute for the sprinkling of the blood of שלמים. This fact strengthens the view of most scholars that non-sacral slaughter, of cattle, sheep or goats, was totally forbidden according to Leviticus 17.

Deuteronomy 12 also deals with the subject of slaughter. The chapter begins with a general commandment regarding the centralization of the sacrificial worship of the Lord (verses 1-5). In verses 6-7 it appears that there is a general commandment to bring all sacrifices to this central shrine, and there to eat and drink in the presence of the Lord. Verse 7 emphasizes the novelty of these arrangements by comparison with the old order which the author wishes to uproot. But immediately thereafter, in verses 10-14, there is a sort of repetition, a doublet, which goes back over all those matters already dealt with at the beginning of the chapter. All this material, which is reviewed twice, deals on the surface with the slaughter of sacrifices in the Temple.

Beginning with verse 15, there occurs what appears to be a description of non-sacral slaughter which requires the spilling of the blood upon the earth (and not its covering), unless this passage refers to what came before and we wish to interpret it as permitting the offering of as many שלמים as is desired. However, from the apposition of this command with that requiring the bringing of voluntary offerings for which vows were made and other sacral gifts in verse 17, it·appears that indeed verses 15-16 are a shorter version of the law of non-sacral slaughter.

In verses 20-28 we find an explicit law which establishes the legitimacy of non-sacral slaughter. But in this formulation there is a condition. According to verses 20 and 21, non-sacral slaughter outside of the sanctuary is permitted only at a distance from the Temple. This passage permits non-sacral slaughter for cattle and animals of the flock, and prescribes that it is permitted to slaughter these animals exactly as beasts are slaughtered (the gazelle and hart—verse 22). Further, since the subject is non-sacral animals, not sacrifices, our passage rules that it is permitted even for those who are impure to eat of these animals after slaughter. Deuteronomy emphasizes here the prohibition of eating the blood of the life-essence and requires that it be spilled upon the earth. To avoid any misunderstanding, the text reminds us in verses 26-27 that even at a distance it is forbidden to slaughter sacrificial animals outside of the Temple.[16]

THE INTERPRETATION OF THE LAWS IN THE *TEMPLE SCROLL*

The author/redactor of the *Temple Scroll* entered this maze of difficulties and repetitions in order to bring about order, according to his method and the method of his sources, by weaving together everything into one unified and new whole. We will attempt here to see how he interpreted these biblical passages. The only approach which will enable us to make a determination in this regard is the detailed analysis of each text in comparison with the biblical material which we have just surveyed.

11QT 52:13-16

This passage is not a direct quotation from the Torah but rather a free reworking based on Deut 12:5-7, in relation to other texts, including Leviticus 17.[17] The words לוא תזבח שור ושה ועז, "you may not slaughter an ox, sheep or goat," are based on Deut 17:1, ...לא תזבח. שור ושה, except that the scroll removed the divine name (instead of replacing the third person with the first as is usual) and added the goat, according to שור או כשב או עז in Lev 17:3. Even this small word ועז in the text of the scroll hints at a halakhic midrash according to which the author (or his source) determined that Deut 12:5-7 deals with the prohibition of Leviticus 17, that of non-sacral slaughter.

---

16   Tov, 170 sees these disparities and duplications as resulting from the internal history of Deuteronomy 12. He sees the *Temple Scroll* as attempting to solve the literary problems posed in this chapter and, therefore, eliminating the same duplications and difficulties modern scholars have noted. Yet it must be remembered that the author of our scroll sought to establish the law in his new "Torah." For that reason, as we will see below, his rewriting of the canonical Torah was intended to clarify the law and harmonize what appeared on the surface to be conflicting passages.

17   Yadin 1.315-7, 2.231-2.

We will see below how the author/redactor of the scroll softened, nonetheless, this prohibition in Leviticus by means of an analogy between these passages.

The word הטהורים was added by the author/redactor of the scroll himself to stress that this law refers actually to every pure (kosher) domesticated animal even if its name is not mentioned here. בכול שעריכה in the scroll comes from Deut 12:17 which the scroll took to be a repetition of the prohibition of non-sacral slaughter.

קרוב למקדשי כי אם שלושת ימים is an invention of the author, according to whom this is the definition of the distance mentioned in Deuteronomy. Since he interpreted Deut 12:20-28 as permitting non-sacral slaughter but only at a distance from the central sanctuary, he had to determine the boundary. That boundary served him also for the law of tithes. 11QT 43:12-17 permits the redemption of tithes for those who live במרחק מן המקדש דרך שלושת ימים (lines 12-13).[18]

In the case of tithes also we are dealing with the exegesis of the words וכי ירבה ממך הדרך... כי ירחק ממך המקום (Deut 14:24). But how did the author know that three days' journey constitute a "far distance?" This he learned from Exod. 8:23-24 where Moses asked: דרך שלשת ימים נלך, "Let us go three days' journey," and Pharoah answered: רק הרחק לא תרחיקו ללכת, "Just do not go too far," i.e. do not go further than the distance of three days' journey. From this the author/redactor of the scroll learned by a sort of גזירה שוה that a far distance is more than three days' journey.

The words of the scroll, כי אם בתוך מקדשי תזבחנו לעשות אותו עולה או זבח שלמים, are based on Deut 12:5-6 and Lev 17:9. כי אם בתוך מקדשי is an abbreviated form of the entire Deut 12:5. Instead of והבאתם שמה in verse 6, which is not sufficiently unambiguous and which fits the context in Deuteronomy which discusses also gifts which are not slaughtered but simply presented, the scroll uses תזבחנו לעשות אותו since there the subject is sacrifices which are prepared (עשה) by slaughtering. עולה או זבח שלמים comes from the words of verse 6, עלתיכם וזבחיכם. The author of the scroll added the word שלמים which already in his time had replaced the more general and less exact term זבה. Furthermore, in Lev 17:5 the expression וזבחי שלמים appears. The author of the scroll added the word שלמים from there, again basing himself on Leviticus 17 in accord with his view that the text in Leviticus deals with the prohibition of non-sacral slaughter not everywhere, but only in close proximity to the Temple. It is possible

---

18 See Yadin 2.183-4; J.M. Baumgarten, "The First and Second Tithes in the *Temple Scroll*," *Biblical and Related Studies Presented to Samuel Iwry* (Winona Lake, Indiana: Eisenbrauns, 1985) 5-15.

also that the use of תזבחנו in the scroll has been conditioned by וזבחו in Lev 17:5.

The scroll concludes this section with a pronouncement: ואכלתה ושמחתה לפני במקום אשר אבחר לשום שמי עליו. Here the author has adapted parts of Deut 12:7 and then 5. The words ואכלתה ושמחתה are based upon ואכלתם...ושמחתם in verse 7. From there the author returned to verse 5 and drew from it כי אם אל המקום אשר יבחר ה׳ אלהיך, which he adapted into לפני במקום אשר אבחר by switching from the third to first person and making other changes as well. He skipped מכל שבטיכם, and in place of לשום את שמו שם wrote לשום את שמי עליו, with the usual change in person from third to first. It should be noted that he interpreted the biblical שם as עליו. This may be an attempt to avoid anthropomorphism which would result from the notion that God could be located in any place.

From the examination of this passage it emerges that the scroll interpreted Deut 12:5-7 as forbidding non-sacral slaughter within three days' journey of the Temple, and as requiring that all slaughter within this boundary must be in the form of שלמים sacrifices. But at the same time, by means of midrashic exegesis, the scroll reached the conclusion that the prohibition in Lev 17:1-9 refers to the same question. Therefore, the author greatly softened this prohibition in Leviticus, transforming it from a general prohibition of all non-sacral slaughter into a prohibition of such slaughter only within three days' journey of the Temple.

Even though from the point of view of style the main text here is Deut 12:5-7, it is possible to maintain, correctly I think, that the law before us uses these verses in Deuteronomy to interpret and to mitigate the law of Leviticus 17. From a logical point of view, it appears that the author of the scroll began with the problem raised by the prohibition of Leviticus 17 and from it arrived at the solution based on his exegesis (or eisegesis) of Deut 12. In any case, for him, Lev 17:1-9 dealt only with non-sacral slaughter within the three day limit, and Deut 12:5-7 dealt with the same issue.

11QT 52:19-21

Despite the fact that within the three day limit it was considered by the scroll to be obligatory to offer all domesicated animals as שלמים sacrifices, we do not hear of any prohibition of eating the meat slaughtered beyond this boundary. But regarding the City of the Sanctuary itself, the *Temple Scroll* in 52:19-21 prohibited eating any meat that was not slaughtered there, the blood of which had not been sprinkled on the altar and the fat of which had not been burned there. In other words, the scroll forbade eating any meat except sacrifices in the City of the Sanctuary.[19]

How did the author of the scroll know to forbid the meat of non-sacral slaughter in the City of the Sanctuary? This law certainly results from interpretation of Deut 12:26-29. As we have already established, this passage appears to be a repetition of matters already covered in Deuteronomy 12. But there, in verse 27, it is said: ועשית עלתיך הבשר והדם על מזבח ה׳ אלהיך... והבשר תאכל. According to this verse, he established that it was forbidden to eat meat במקום אשר יבחר ה׳ (verse 26), that is, in the City of the Sanctuary, which had not been sacrificed according to the law on the altar of the Lord as שלמים. The author/redactor formulated this verse according to the style of his larger work and changed it from a positive commandment (from which in his view one could learn a negative commandment) into an absolute negative commandment. In this way he ruled לוא תואכל בשר based on Deut 12:27 והבשר תאכל with the change from positive to negative.

The phrase שור ושה ועז brings the text back to Deut 17:1 and Lev 17:3. But more importantly, it returns explicitly to line 13 in the scroll which is related, as we have already seen, to the same subject. As a replacement for המקום אשר יבחר ה׳ in verse 26, the scroll puts in עירי אשר אנוכי מקדש לשום שמי בתוכה, and with this formulation there is a second transition back to Deut 12:5 and to the words of the scroll, above in line 16.   The words of the scroll אשר לוא יבוא לתוך מקדשי וזבחו שמה are intended to explain verse 27, הבשר והדם על מזבח, ה׳ אלהיך. The scroll's וזרקו את דמו על יסוד מזבח העולה is an exegesis of על מזבח ה׳ אלהיך ודם זבחיך ישפך in Deuteronomy.

One more detail still must be explained, namely the scroll's command, ואת חלבו יקטירו. Even though the continutation of this sentence is in the lacuna at the top of col. 53 of the scroll, it is possible to locate the source of this detail. It is derived from Lev 17:6 where it appears along with the obligation that the blood be sprinkled by a priest for שלמים sacrifices intended to be eaten. Even though the scroll understood this passage in Leviticus as referring to the law for areas within three days' journey of Jerusalem, the author/redactor learned from here that for all sacrifices of שלמים in the sanctuary it is an obligation to burn the fats, even when the purpose of the sacrifice is only to secure meat for human consumption. That such an obligation exists in general for שלמים sacrifices is known from Lev 7:30, a passage to which the scroll does not relate in this context. But it appears that this obligation did

---

19   Yadin 1.318-20.

exist in the view of the author of our scroll. It is also possible that in the lacuna the scroll set aside an emolument for the priest who offered the שלמים, but it is impossible to know for certain.

The author of the scroll interpreted Deut 12:26-28 as requiring that no meat which was not sacrificed as a שלמים offering could be eaten in the City of the Sanctuary. This passage from the book of Deuteronomy, which appears at first glance to be extra, served for the *Temple Scroll* as the source of this law.

11QT 53:07-08

The last law regarding this subject is 11QT 53:07-8. From a distance this law appears to be an almost verbatim quotation from the Torah, but we will see that the matter is much more complex.

The author apparently changed from the third to the first person in the restored section in lines 07-1. It is most probable that the scroll combined כי ירחיב... and כי ירחק... (Deut 12:20-21) into one introductory sentence.[20] The author included in this sentence all the material from these two verses, thus creating out of it one unit.

Here the scroll created a midrashic harmonization between verses 21 and 15. From verse 21 the author drew the command to slaughter cattle and sheep and goats (with a change in the order—מצואנכה ומבקריכה). Then he turned to verse 15 from which he took כברכתי אשר אתן אליכה which is an adaptation of Deut 12:15, כברכת ה׳, אלהיך אשר נתן לך, with a change to the first person as is usual. The transition from verse 21 to 15 was aided by the words אשר נתן... לך which appear in both these verses. This common element served to provide a bridge back to verse 21 from which the scroll drew the words ואכלתה בשעריכה. Then the author wove together the end of verse 22 and verse 15 into one text. First, he dealt with the matter of the pure and impure (with a reversal of the order in both verses). In accord with the LXX and the Samaritan his text reads בכה in verse 22. From verse 22 he took יחדיו. The occurence of יאכלנו in both verses (although it does not appear here in the scroll) serves as a transition to verse 15 from which the author drew כצבי וכאיל.

The creation of this text led the author to omit a number of unnecessary phrases which were in the book of Deuteronomy which was before him. Otherwise, the text would have come out unreadable. Then the scroll continued with verse 23, from which it took רק חזק לבלתי אכול את הדם, except that it immediately switched to verse 24 and wrote על הארץ תשופכנו כמים.

---

20   Contrast Tov, "Deut 12," 172-3 who is of the view that the scroll presented only the first introductory formula.

Here the scroll adds the words וכסיתו בעפר following Lev 17:13, וכסהו בעפר. This addition is entirely for the purpose of clarifying the law. According to Lev 17:13 the obligation of covering the blood would appear to apply only to beasts and fowl. Nevertheless, the author/redactor of the scroll understood this law to refer also to domesticated animals.

The author then explains to us that the reason for the requirement of covering the blood, according to Deut 12:23, is כי הדם הוא הנפש ולוא תואכל את הנפש עם הבשר, "for the blood is the life-essence, and you may not eat the life-essence with the meat." The change in the order (in Deuteronomy the spilling of the blood appears in verse 24 and the warning against eating blood appears before it in verse 23) is intended to create a harmonization with verse 16 in which the order is the same as that in the *Temple Scroll*. This law in the scroll comes to a conclusion with a blessing which is derived from verse 28, with small changes and the switch from third person to first as is common throughout the scroll.

We have already said that this law reflects a midrashic harmonization of material from Deut 12:20-25, the main text at this point in the scroll, with commands from Deut 12:15-16. But we must explain why the author of the scroll (or his source) had to invest so much effort to create this new text.

As we saw above, Deut 12:15-16 appears to duplicate 12:20-25. The tannaim understood 12:15 as ruling that it is permissible to redeem sacrificial animals which are unfit.[21] However, according to our author, these two texts deal with the same issue, non-sacral slaughter at a distance from the Temple. Our scroll wanted to remove any possibility of another understanding and, therefore, wove the entirety into a unified whole which provides for the permissibility of non-sacral slaughter at a distance of three days' travel from Jerusalem.

We can summarize now the relationship of this law to the biblical material we have surveyed. The author understood Deut 12:20-28 to refer to non-sacral slaughter at a distance of three days' journey from the Temple. Deut 12:15-16 was understood by him to deal with the same subject. Therefore, by effecting a midrashic harmonization and reediting the material, the scroll effectively deleted this unit, so to speak, from the Torah. Lev 17:13, dealing with covering of the blood, was understood by the scroll to fix the law not only for beasts and fowl, but for all non-sacral slaughter at

---

21 ספרי דברים, 71 (ed. L. Finkelstein [New York: Jewish Theological Seminary, 1969] p. 134).

a distance, an interpretation which it is very difficult to square with the verse itself.

In examining this law in the *Temple Scroll* we have seen how much the author went out of his way to derive from the material in Deut 12 and Leviticus 17 a unified, unambiguous series of laws. This subject was clearly of great importance to the author/redactor of the scroll. In 11QT 47:7-18 there appear specific laws regarding the bringing of skins into the City of the Sanctuary.[22] It is clear that these laws in connection with the skins are based on the laws of slaughter we have discussed here, although discussion of this matter must remain beyond the scope of this study. Furthermore, in 4QMMT, soon to be published by E. Qimron and J. Strugnell, there was a similar set of laws on this topic to those in the *Temple Scroll*, and one of the laws reads as follows: ‏[והם שוחטים] מחוץ למחנה שור‎ ‏וכש[ב ועז‎, "[and they slaughter] outside of the camp cattle, sh[eep] and goats" (as restored by Qimron and Strugnell). The camp here is a reference to "the camp of Israel," identical with the City of the Sanctuary (the Temple precincts) in the view of the author(s).[23] This law certainly deals with non-sacral slaughter within the three day boundary. Like the author of our scroll, the authors of the "Halakhic Letter," apparently of Sadducean origin, opposed non-sacral slaughter in this area, and required that slaughter be accomplished only through the offering of ‏שלמים‎ sacrifices. The presence of laws pertaining to the skins of animals in 4QMMT points to the importance of this issue to the founders of the Dead Sea sect.

It appears that the Pharisees and those who followed them, including the Hasmoneans in this period, did perform non-sacral slaughter in this area, and it was against this practice that the authors of both the "Halakhic Letter" and the *Temple Scroll* polemicized. The polemic against such slaughter, and against the bringing of the skins of animals slaughtered in this way into the Temple, or the bringing of the meat of animals slaughtered at a distance of more than three days' journey, was a central issue for the *Temple Scroll*.

Against this background it is possible to understand why the author of the scroll emphasized that Deut 12:20-28 and 15-16 dealt with the same thing. Twice in 20-25 Deuteronomy says that the

---

22   See L.H. Schiffman, "*Miqṣat Maᶜaseh Ha-Torah* and the *Temple Scroll*," *RQ* 14 (1990) 442-48; idem, "The Prohibition of the Skins of Animals in the *Temple Scroll* and "*Miqṣat Maᶜaseh Ha-Torah*," *Proceedings of the Tenth World Congress of Jewish Studies*, Division A, The Bible and its World (Jerusalem: World Union of Jewish Studies, 1990) 191-8.

23   Cf. L.H. Schiffman, "Exclusion from the Sanctuary and the City of the Sanctuary in the Temple Scroll," *Hebrew Annual Review* 9 (1985) 307-8, 315.

permission to slaughter non-sacrally is dependent on being at a distance from the central shrine. But in 15-16 the context is entirely different. In verses 13-14 the subject is the slaughter of sacrificial offerings and the obligation to perform it only in the Temple precincts. Immediately thereafter we find 15-16, which present no limitation regarding distance. It was theoretically possible to conclude from these passages that non-sacral slaughter was indeed permissible anywhere, and that the requirement of distance applied only to that discussed in 20-25. Therefore, it would have been possible to conceive of three areas as follows: (1) Jerusalem, where only the slaughter of sacrifices was permitted; (2) locations in close proximity, within three days' journey, where it would be permissible to perform either sacral or non-sacral slaughter; and (3) areas distant from Jerusalem where only non-sacral slaughter was possible from a practical point of view.

The author/redactor of the *Temple Scroll* wanted to ensure that there would not remain the slightest hint or possibility of non-sacral slaughter within the three day limit from the Temple. Therefore, he had to understand these verses (15-16) as duplicating 20-25, and for this reason he executed the harmonization we have described.

SUMMARY AND CONCLUSIONS

It is worthwhile to summarize the approach of the author of the *Temple Scroll* to the biblical material in Lev 17 and Deut 12. Lev 17:1-9 was understood by the scroll as forbidding non-sacral slaughter within the distance of three days' journey of the Temple. Deut 12:5-7 was understood in the same way. The remainder of the material in Lev 17, especially verses 13-14, was interpreted as requiring the covering of the blood in all cases of non-sacral slaughter (at a distance of more than three days' journey from the Temple), including even that of domesticated animals—cattle, sheep and goats. Deut 12:15-16 was understood as an unnecessary repetition of the law of non-sacral slaughter which, in the author's view, was also the subject of Deut 12:20-26. Verse 27 was taken as prohibiting the eating of the meat of non-sacral slaughter in the City of the Sanctuary.

These interpretations led the author/redactor of the *Temple Scroll* to a three-fold division regarding matters of slaughter. He recognized three areas, each with its own regulations. In the City of the Sanctuary it was forbidden to eat any meat which had been slaughtered outside. Within the boundary of three days' journey from the Temple it was forbidden to slaughter animals except in the context of שלמים sacrifices in the Temple. Beyond this boundary it was permitted to perform non-sacral slaughter, which included the covering of the blood even for domesticated animals.

Whose laws were these? From our studies of the מקצת מעשי התורה it is clear that this text expresses the Sadducean approach, while the opponents of the founders of the sect, apparently the Pharisees and the Hasmoneans in this period, followed an approach similar to that known to us from rabbinic literature as Pharisaic. If so, since we have found support for and parallels to the views of the *Temple Scroll* on matters of slaughter in this "Halakhic Letter," it appears that here, as in many other areas as well, we may hope that finally we are able to recover Sadducean material from the Second Temple period. If, indeed, the author of the *Temple Scroll* transmitted to us the exegetical basis on which this three-fold division we have described was based, it may be possible to conclude that everything we have studied here is the result of the exegetical method of the Sadducees. But in these matters, as in so many questions relating to the study of the Dead Sea Scrolls, we are only at the beginning of the journey. Final conclusions will have to await the full publication of all the texts and their study by other scholars.

GROUPS OF BIBLICAL TEXTS FOUND AT QUMRAN[*]

Emanuel Tov

The issue under investigation is that of the possible existence of groups of biblical texts among the Qumran finds. Under this heading several questions ought to be asked, but only one of them is relevant under the circumstances:

1. Are there any pairs of texts of which one has been copied from the other, and is the study of such pairs of texts instructive in any way? The answer to this question can be brief: scholars have not recognized any fragments that can be proven to be copies of another known text. There probably is one exception, but the case is not clear enough. According to E. Ulrich, 4QDan^b has been copied from 4QDan^a.[1] The two texts share only a few exclusive readings, but their common base is supported by the identical layout of the column. My own research has led me to believe that 4QTest (4Q175), a collection of biblical and other texts, has been copied from 4QDeut^h in the quotation from Deuteronomy 33.[2] But, on the whole, we are not likely to find many instances of pairs of texts relating to each other as prototype and copy. In itself it would not be unusual to find such pairs, since some texts found in Qumran must have been copied from other texts that were once extant at Qumran and which are among the known scrolls. But much depends on the vicissitudes of what has been preserved, and a close relationship can usually not be proven.

2. Are there any overlapping Qumran texts and what can we learn from them concerning the textual relation between the Qumran texts? Here, too, we can be brief: a surprisingly small number of

---

[*]   In this article the customary abbreviations for biblical scrolls are used. For lists and exact bibliographical references, see J.A. Fitzmyer, *The Dead Sea Scrolls, Major Publications and Tools for Study* (Revised edition; Atlanta: Scholars Press, 1990); F. García Martínez, "Lista de MSS procedentes de Qumran," *Henoch* 11 (1989) 149-232. Asterisks are used to denote texts still to be published.

[1]   E. Ulrich, "Daniel Manuscripts from Qumran. Part I: A Preliminary Edition of 4QDan^a," BASOR 268 (1987) 17-37; "... Part 2: Preliminary Editions of 4QDan^b and 4QDan^c," BASOR 274 (1989) 3-26; "Orthography and Text in 4QDan^a and 4QDan^b and in the Received Massoretic Text," *Of Scribes and Scrolls, Studies on the Hebrew Bible, Intertestamental Judaism, and Christian Origins* (ed. H.W. Attridge, J.J. Collins, T.H. Tobin; Lanham, New York/London: University Press of America, 1990) 29-42.

[2]   For the text of this Deuteronomy scroll, see the dissertation of Duncan mentioned in n. 3.

texts overlap, and even when they do, they do not contain many words that can be compared.

Since the amount of information on both issues is rather limited, we turn to a third question, which will preoccupy us more, namely:

3. Can we recognize at Qumran any *groups* or *clusters* of texts? And if so, what is the nature and background of these groups and which textual situation is reflected in them? Such groups are found in Qumran, we believe, but the principles that hold them together differ in each instance.

Our investigation does not disregard definitions that have been made in the past with regard to clusters of texts defined as either textual families, groups, recensions, or streams, but it is probably preferable to turn to these definitions only at a later stage in the investigation. Abstract formulations are of limited use as a point of departure, and it may be better not to superimpose our definitions on the evidence, but rather to let the material speak for itself.

For the purpose of the present research, all the available editions of the Qumran biblical texts have been reviewed, both in the DJD series and elsewhere. At this stage most of the Qumran biblical texts are known in some form or another, especially with the recent completion of five Harvard dissertations providing most of the texts of Genesis, Deuteronomy and the Minor Prophets from cave 4.[3] To these I added the texts of Leviticus, Joshua and Jeremiah on which I myself am working,[4] all the texts of Isaiah, and the manuscripts written in the palaeo-Hebrew script to be published by Professor Ulrich. I am grateful to Professor Ulrich for allowing me to examine his future editions of these texts. I have not yet studied the large group of Psalms texts and a smaller group of Exodus texts to be published by him. In the meantime, one has to content himself with a list of the variants of the Psalms texts published by P.W. Skehan.[5]

The search for *groups* of Qumran biblical texts is not new in research. Many scholars have stressed that the Qumran finds yielded groups of texts that have been described as proto-

---

3   R. E. Fuller, *The Minor Prophets Manuscripts from Qumran, Cave IV* (1988); J.R. Davila, *Unpublished Pentateuch Manuscripts from Cave IV, Qumran: 4QGen-Ex^a, 4QGen$^{b-h, j-k}$* (1988); S.A. White, *A Critical Edition of Seven Manuscripts of Deuteronomy: 4QDt^a, 4QDt^c, 4QDt^d, 4QDt^f, 4QDt^g, 4QDt^i, and 4QDt^n* (1988); J. A. Duncan, *A Critical Edition of Deuteronomy Manuscripts from Qumran, Cave IV: 4QDt^b, 4QDt^e, 4QDt^h, 4QDt^j, 4QDt^k, 4QDt^l* (1989); N. R. Jastram, *The Book of Numbers from Qumrân Cave IV (4QNum^b)* (1990).

4   That is 4QLev^{c,d}, 4QJos^b, 4QJer^{a-e}.

5   P. W. Skehan, "Qumran and Old Testament Criticism," *Qumrân, Sa piété, sa théologie et son milieu* (ed. M. Delcor; BETL 46; Paris: Duculot, 1978) 173-82.

Massoretic, pre-Samaritan and Septuagintal, while sometimes slightly different terms have been used. Other texts have been described as independent—a qualification introduced by my own publications.[6] These so-called non-aligned texts, however, do not reflect a group of texts in the same sense as the others. So far the descriptions of all these groups have been only very general, and they have not taken into consideration all the available evidence, or even most of it, as will be done in the present paper. Nor has the nature, background and size of these groups been described in the past.

This paper deals with the possible existence of textual groups among the biblical manuscripts found at Qumran and their nature. In view of the fragmentary nature of the material we are not likely to find two or more overlapping texts covering exactly the same chapters. At most we will find groups of texts sharing *common textual characteristics*. Under this rubric various kinds of groupings come to mind, relating to the closeness of the Qumran scrolls to either 𝕸, 𝕲 or 𝖆𝖆. At the same time, we should also be open to new types of clusters, that is, groups of texts reflecting characteristics not known previously. In principle, any number of texts may be called a group, if they are closely related internally and differ from other textual entities. The biblical texts sharing the so-called Qumran practice of orthography and linguistic features compose such a group, not known beforehand. Other possibilities should be examined as well.

Let us turn first to the grouping of the texts according to the criterion of a close relationship with sources outside of Qumran. The rationale for such a comparison of the scrolls with 𝕸, 𝖆𝖆 and 𝕲 is problematical at one level. For why should the Qumran texts be compared at all with these three textual entities? On various occasions I have tried to show that these entities are not the "main" texts of the OT, as they have often been called in the past, nor do they represent three text-types or recensions, as is usually claimed.[7] In my view they represent just three texts of the OT, the main importance of which is in their being fostered and preserved by religious groups. The choice of these three texts by religious groups makes them more prominent and better preserved than they would have been, had they not been fostered by these groups. However, at one point there may have been other texts, possibly

---

6   "A Modern Textual Outlook Based on the Qumran Scrolls," *HUCA* 53 (1982) 429-48.

7   For the arguments and counter arguments, see the article mentioned in the previous note.

"better" or "more original" than the known ones. But we cannot compare the Qumran texts with these as yet unknown texts. We will therefore have to content ourselves with a comparison of the Qumran scrolls with the three mentioned texts. But there is more at stake. It so happens—and this is no coincidence—that many of the Qumran texts *are* actually close to 𝔐, a small number to 𝔪, and a few to 𝔊, so that also post factum the comparison with these texts is actually justified. But, as remarked, there are other groups of texts as well.

Our analysis of the degree of proximity between texts is based on the recognition of agreements between any two or more texts. These agreements need to be significant enough to set the two texts apart from other texts, either in their content or orthography.

As for orthography, if one adheres to the view, as I do,[8] that *grosso modo* the Hebrew Qumran scrolls display two main systems of orthography, this recognition allows us to ascribe each scroll to one of those two groups. These two systems are on the one hand the so-called Qumran practice and on the other the texts not written in this system. But this is merely one criterion for subdividing texts, since within each orthographic group biblical texts are further subdivided according to their textual character. Among the texts not written in the Qumran practice, the group of 𝔐 is the largest one, reflecting more or less the orthography and content of the medieval biblical manuscripts.

Having said this, we must make one further step. If a text has been recognized as more or less reflecting the orthography of 𝔐, *how many* deviations from that orthography do we allow and still assign it to the group of 𝔐? There is no simple answer to this question. However, the problem is not very grave, as the number of such differences in spelling is never excessive; actually it is unusually low.

The analysis of the content differences proceeds similarly. If as a rule a Qumran text agrees with the medieval 𝔐, and usually or often disagrees with other textual witnesses, that text is considered to be close to 𝔐, and its occasional deviations from the medieval text do not alter the picture. Such a text will therefore be considered as belonging to the Massoretic group. If, on the other hand, the text differs here and there from 𝔐, while often agreeing with 𝔊 and/or 𝔪 against 𝔐, it should be considered non-aligned or independent. This theoretical description thus allows for a reasonably objective description of the relation between texts. The

---

8   "The Orthography and Language of the Hebrew Scrolls Found at Qumran and the Origin of These Scrolls," *Textus* 13 (1986) 31-57.

description of the relation between texts is actually more complicated than is implied by the above remarks, since often there is no clear opposition between 𝔐, 𝔪 or 𝔊, and in such cases the textual nature of a Qumran text cannot be described well. A Qumran text can be equally close to 𝔐 and 𝔊 if they do not differ much in a certain section or book, such as is the case with many sections of Isaiah.

Reference has been made in the past, also in my own writings, to the relevance of the quality of the variants to matters of textual relation. More specifically, if two texts exclusively share one or more errors, termed "Leitfehler" or "indicative errors" by P. Maas,[9] they must be closely related. Because of the fragmentary status of the preserved evidence it is hard to evaluate these Leitfehler, but if the two texts exclusively share several such errors, the conclusion of a close relation is nevertheless possible. (Note, however, that many other texts, which could have shared those readings, may have been lost.) On the other hand, if the two texts share a reading which probably is original, while the corrupted reading is found in the other source(s), the closeness expressed by the shared reading is less significant, since it is natural for any two texts to share original readings. However, in many cases in which the nature of variants is taken into consideration much weight is placed on one's judgment on the originality of the reading. Since scholars do not usually agree in such evaluations, these judgments should not be used, in my view, when the overall relation between texts is determined.

Faute de mieux, in the analysis of the relation between texts, statistics are used, but the aforementioned caveats should be borne in mind. Such statistics are of special significance when the texts diverge substantially. Thus in Jeremiah one can easily decide whether the Qumran fragments agree with either 𝔐 or 𝔊. Likewise, in the Torah it is often easy to discern whether or not a fragment agrees with either 𝔐 or 𝔪. We will not provide the numbers on which the statistics are based, but it should be realized that these statistics are based on both positive and negative evidence as described above.

---

9   P. Maas, *Textual Criticism* (trans. B. Flower; Oxford: Clarendon, 1958) 42 = *Textkritik*, in: A. Gercke, E. Norden, *Einleitung in die Altertumswissenschaft*, I, VII (3rd ed.; Leipzig, 1957).

I. THE FAMILY OF THE PROTO-MASSORETIC TEXTS

In our search for groups of Qumran texts we first turn to the texts which resemble the medieval form of 𝔐 as extant, for example, in codex L. The fact that the character of 𝔐 cannot be determined in *textual* terms is not relevant to the present discussion. A large segment of the Qumran scrolls reflects the textual tradition of 𝔐. Now that most of the biblical scrolls are known in some way or another, this situation has become increasingly clear. According to our statistics, some *forty* percent of the Qumran texts reflect the tradition of 𝔐 with regard to orthography and content, though not in paragraphing. For example, the text of the rather extensive 4QJer[a] and 4QJer[c][10] is almost identical with codex L, although the paragraphing differs much, usually with paragraph divisions added or expanded in the Qumran scrolls.

There is no doubt that the medieval Massoretic Text and many of the Qumran texts reflect the same consonantal framework. In other words, the predecessors of the medieval 𝔐 were already extant at Qumran, and therefore also elsewhere in ancient Israel. As for details, when one compares 1QIsa[b] [11] dating from the first century BCE with codex L, written one thousand years later, one easily recognizes the close relation between the two texts which sometimes are almost identical. Thus on p. 7 = plate 9 (Isa 50:7-51:10 [13 verses]) of this scroll, one finds only four differences in minor details and two differences in orthography (our reading differs from that of Sukenik), as illustrated below:

Differences Between 1QIsa[b] and MS L in 50:7-51:10 (p. 7 = plate 9)

		1QIsa[b]	MS L
Isa	50:11	ומאזרי	מאזרי
	51:1	ע[ל]	אל
		[ו]על	ואל
	4	ולאמי	ולאומי
	7	יודעי	ידעי
		וממגדפתם	ומגדפתם

---

10   See E. Tov, "The Jeremiah Scrolls from Qumran," *RQ* 14 (1989) 189-206 (with plates).

11   See E.L. Sukenik, אוצר המגילות הגנוזות (Jerusalem: Bialik Institute and the Hebrew University, 1955).

On p. 6 = plate 8 (Isa 48:17-49:15 [likewise 13 verses]), one finds 16 differences all of which concern only minutiae: 7 differences in orthography and 9 minor differences, mainly linguistic:

Differences between 1QIsa^b and MS L in 48:17-49:15 (p. 6 = plate 8)

	1QIsa^b	MS L
48:17	מדרכיך	מדריכך
18	ולא	לוא
	שלמך	שלומך
21	צר	צור
49:3	הת[פאר]	אתפאר
4	כלתי	כליתי
	אך	אכן
5	כה	—
	יוצרי	יצרי
6	הנקל	נקל
	ארץ	הארץ
7	**אדני** יהוה	יהוה
	גואל	גאל
	יקומו	וקמו
	קדוש	קדש
8	[ש]ממת	שממות

In accordance with the above remarks concerning the textual status of the witnesses of Isaiah it should be remembered that the mentioned fragments, ₥ and the reconstructed *Vorlage* of ₲ usually differ only slightly. Hence, the Qumran texts which are closely related to ₥ are also close to ₲, though to a smaller degree, and if orthography is brought to bear on the issue as well (an area that usually cannot be examined with regard to ₲), the resemblance between the Qumran scrolls (especially 1QIsa^b) and ₥ is prominent.

The above tables refer to one column only. When examining all the fragments of 1QIsa^b, which comprises segments of 46 chapters, we find the following types of features in the scroll which represent differences from codex L, all of which concern minutiae:

Types of Differences Between Codex L and 1QIsa[b][12]

Orthography	107
Addition of conjunctive *waw*	16
Lack of conjunctive *waw*	13
Article	4
Differences in letters	10
Missing letters	5
Differences in number	14
Differences in pronouns	6
Different grammatical forms	24
Different prepositions	9
Different words	11
Minuses of words	5
Pluses of words	6
Different sequence	4

The close relationship between L and 1QIsa[b] is matched by other texts. In the sections in which 1QIsa[b] overlaps with 4QIsa[d*] both of them are close to codex L. This situation needs to be examined for other texts as well, especially for long texts. Two such long texts are 4QJer[a] and 4QJer[c]. 4QJer[a] is very close to codex L, with only 15 differences in the chapters preserved as well as 11 differences in orthography, none of them in important matters. There are, however, quite substantial differences in the indication of paragraphs.[13] 4QJer[c] is further removed from codex L, but still very close, with some 19 differences in content and 18 differences in orthography.[14] The closest any long text from the Judean Desert comes to codex L is probably the Minor Prophets scroll from

---

12   According to M. Cohen, "האידאה בדבר קדושת הנוסח לאותיותיו וביקורת הטקסט," *Deoth* 47 (1978) 83-101, esp. 86, n. 4.

13   This text has also been corrected extensively, almost always towards the text that is also contained in the medieval tradition of 𝔐. However, this fact is probably irrelevant to the present discussion, as these corrections were made not towards an external, different, source, but on the basis of the text from which 4QJer[a] was copied, and that text happened to be close to the medieval Massoretic text. For a more extensive discussion of this issue, see the article quoted in n. 10 and further E. Tov, "The Textual Base of the Corrections in the Biblical Texts Found in Qumran," *The Dead Sea Scrolls, Forty Years of Research* (eds. D. Dimant, U. Rappaport; Leiden–Jerusalem: E.J. Brill–Magnes–Yad Izhak Ben-Zvi, 1992) 299-314.

14   In the case of these texts their closeness to 𝔐 is exclusive, as their common text differs much from 𝔊, and no other text is known for Jeremiah (the other versions have been made from a text close to 𝔐).

Murabba'at, but this text is a little younger than the Qumran texts, and it does not come from Qumran.

So far we have mentioned four scrolls only, 1QIsa[b], 4QIsa[d*], 4QJer[a] and 4QJer[c], all of them closely related to the medieval text of 𝔐. Together with other texts, they form a small group sharing one feature, namely, their close relation to 𝔐. This group is well-represented among the Qumran scrolls, reflected in some *forty* percent of the texts of which a considerable portion has been preserved, significant enough in order to determine their textual character. The recognition that a certain Qumran text is closely related to 𝔐 follows the principles applied above with regard to 1QIsa[b], 4QIsa[d*] and 4QJer[a,c]. That is, a small number of deviations from codex L (as in the case of 1QIsa[b]), together with the lack of major agreements with the other textual witnesses and the existence of the orthography of 𝔐.

Below, the number of the texts closely agreeing with codex L will be mentioned. At this point a remark on the coherence of the Massoretic group is in order, especially with regard to matters of spelling. The close agreement with regard to orthography is the more noteworthy when we realize that the Massoretic spelling does not follow a clearly recognizable system. In 𝔐 certain tendencies, idiosyncracies, and preferences in early and late books are recognized, but on the whole inconsistency rather than consistency is the rule.[15] It is therefore the more significant that many of the Qumran scrolls reflect the spelling practice also known from the medieval codices, with all its idiosyncracies. Already at the period of the Qumran scrolls these texts formed a closely connected group which should probably be named a family. The texts belonging to this family were copied from each other with the utmost care and precision, with room for individuality left mainly in the matter of paragraphing.

At the same time, the Qumran texts differ here and there from codex L, and it is in order to investigate whether patterns of differentiation between the majority text from the Middle Ages and certain Qumran scrolls can be detected. To mention just one example, in the proto-Massoretic 4QJer[c] one usually finds the spelling יעקוב as opposed to the defective spelling in the medieval manuscripts.

The Qumran proto-Massoretic group ought to be investigated also with regard to possible clusters within this group regarding

---

15   For recent discussions, see F.I. Andersen, A.D. Forbes, *Spelling in the Hebrew Bible* (Biblica et Orientalia 41; Rome, 1986); James Barr, *The Variable Spellings of the Hebrew Bible, The Schweich Lectures of the British Academy* 1986 (Oxford: University Press, 1989).

spelling and content. Because of the paucity of overlapping Qumran texts,[16] this investigation is very limited. A possible clustering of 1QIsa^{a,b} and 4QIsa^{c*,d*} (of which 1QIsa^a and 4QIsa^{c*} reflect the Qumran orthography), against the medieval text, is visible. Such clusters, if detected, could show how 𝔐 has developed after the Qumran period. It should thus be possible to pinpoint readings in which the medieval text reflects a later development.

Thus, in the well-known text in Isa 53:11 the shorter reading in 𝔐 יראה נפשו (מעמל) contains the minority reading. On the other hand, two proto-Masoretic Qumran texts, 1QIsa^b and 4QIsa^{d*}, as well as 1QIsa^a (written in the Qumran orthography) and 𝔊 (δεῖξαι αὐτῷ φῶς) add אור. This is a mere external description, not referring to the intrinsic value of the readings. In a now classic article, Seeligmann suggested that the minority reading of the medieval text reflects the original text.[17]

II. Texts Written in the "Qumran Practice" of Orthography and Morphology

The close connection between the proto-Masoretic Qumran texts derives from their common text or tradition shared with the medieval tradition. A second cluster of Qumran texts is linked by a different feature, viz., idiosyncracies in orthography and morphology, visible, for example, in 1QIsa^a. According to the view developed in two articles,[18] these texts reflect a system of idiosyncratic spelling and language which sets them apart from the other Qumran texts, though not necessarily from all other texts, since individual features are spotted elsewhere. *Faute de mieux*, we call the system of these texts the "Qumran practice," but this system could have been in vogue in other places in ancient Israel. We could therefore call this orthography "Palestinian" or "contemporary," but those terms are less neutral. The notion that these texts are intimately connected with the Qumran covenanters derives from the fact that virtually *all* the Qumran sectarian writings are written in this system. We are inclined to ascribe these texts to a Qumran scribal school, since in addition to the mentioned

---

16   The following overlapping texts—often short—more or less agree with each other: 4QGen^b and 4QGen^g; 4QDeut^{d,e}; 4QDeut^{e,f} and 5QDeut; 4QDeut^{c,e,f}; 4QDeut^{a,f}; 4QDeut^{f,g} and 1QDeut; 4QDeut^{c,f,g}; 1QIsa^b and 4QIsa^d; 4QJer^a and 4QJer^c; 4QPs^b and 11QPs^a.

17   I.L. Seeligmann, "δεῖξαι αὐτῷ φῶς," *Tarbiz* 27 (1958) 127-41.

18   See my article quoted in n. 6 as well as "Hebrew Biblical Manuscripts from the Judaean Desert: Their Contribution to Textual Criticism," *JJS* 39 (1988) 5-37, esp. 10-16.

characteristics, these texts also share certain scribal habits.[19] Scribes employing this system copied from a variety of texts. It is, however, not easy to characterize the textual character of the *Vorlagen* of these texts; the scribes took so many liberties that their *Vorlagen* cannot easily be identified. This pertains, e.g., to contextual harmonizations, frequently occurring in 1QIsa[a]. Possibly that text was copied from a text that did not differ much from the Isaiah scrolls from cave 4, or from 1QIsa[b], most of which are rather close to 𝕸, but we cannot be certain. Likewise, the *Vorlage* of 2QJer may have been close to 𝕸.

The fact that these texts have been created by a scribal school, and thus share peculiarities in the areas of orthography, morphology, and scribal habits thus determines the textual character of these texts only to a certain extent. Some of these texts may have been copied from texts of the proto-Massoretic group. 4QSam[c] is equally close to 𝕸 and the Lucianic text of 2 Samuel 14-15 which in that section probably reflects the Old Greek translation.[20] 4QNum[b], containing a rather lengthy text, is very close to 𝖒, and secondarily also to 𝕲. Other texts were copied from sources of a different nature. 2QExod[b] contains an unusual text, especially with regard to its sequence of verses. This applies also to 4QDeut[j], a Deuteronomy text which also incorporates sections of Exodus. 4QDeut[k] and 4QXII[c,e] reflect non-aligned texts differing in small details from the other sources. As for other texts written in the "Qumran practice," the textual character of 1QDeut[a], 2QExod[a], 2QNum[b], 2QDeut[c], 3QLam, 4QLam, and 4QQoh[a] is not clear. On the whole this group is relatively small. It stands to reason that the texts under consideration were copied from other texts once found in Qumran and possibly some of them are known to us. However, so far such exclusive connections have not yet been established, with the

---

19 See especially the article mentioned in the previous note: (1) With the exception of the "parenthesis" in 11QpaleoLev, one instance of cancellation dots in 4QJer[a], and the paragraphos in the Aramaic 4QTestLev[a], as far as the Hebrew and Aramaic Qumran texts are concerned, scribal marks of any kind are found only in the Hebrew manuscripts written in the "Qumran practice," especially in the scrolls from cave 1. (2) The use of initial-medial letters in final position is another characteristic of these texts. (3) The writing of the divine names יהוה and אל(הים) in palaeo-Hebrew characters in texts written in the Assyrian script occurs only in the texts written in the "Qumran" orthography and morphology.

20 See my own analysis, "Determining the Relationship between the Qumran Scrolls and the LXX: Some Methodological Issues," in E. Tov (ed.), *The Hebrew and Greek Texts of Samuel, 1980 Proceedings IOSCS, Vienna* (Jerusalem: Academon, 1980) 45-67, esp. 58-61. Ulrich, on the other hand, stresses especially the links with the Lucianic tradition: "4QSam[c]: A Fragmentary Manuscript of 2 Samuel 14-15 from the Scribe of the Serek Hay-yaḥad (1QS)," *BASOR* 235 (1979) 1-25.

exception of the aforementioned 4QDan[b] which may have been copied from 4QDan[a].

Of special interest is the comparison of two or more overlapping texts written in the "Qumran practice." Such research can be performed on several sectarian non-biblical manuscripts such as 4QDibre Hameorot, 4QMMT, 4QM[a-f] // 1QM. For the biblical texts, however, such material is very scarce. The main evidence pertains to 4QIsa[c*] and 1QIsa[a]. These two texts reflect the same orthographical and linguistic system, but differ in details. These differences are not surprising since both texts are also internally inconsistent[21] with regard to orthography and morphology.[22] This comparison shows that scribes belonging to this school adhered to a general system, but there was room for individuality. According to our statistics, some *twenty-five* percent of the Qumran biblical texts we have were produced by the Qumran scribal school.

In addition to the texts belonging to the Massoretic group and texts produced by the Qumran school of scribes, we find a few scattered texts not belonging to these groups. Some of them form small groups, while others should be taken as individual texts.

III. Texts that Are Closely Related to the LXX

Of great importance for scholarship are Hebrew texts from Qumran reflecting a close relationship to 𝕲, or phrased more carefully, to its Hebrew parent text. It has, however, always been difficult to formulate rules for calculating the amount of closeness between a Qumran text and 𝕲.[23] Statistics and counting of agreements alone do not suffice for establishing such a close relationship. In our view, what counts beyond mere statistics is establishing a close relation between 𝕲 and a Qumran scroll in significant, characteristic, or even "recensional" readings (variants). At that level important links between 𝕲 and the Qumran scrolls can be established, at this stage, only with 4QJer[b,d], and to a lesser degree also with 4QDeut[q] and

---

21 The second part of 1QIsa[a] is more *plene* than the first part. In the first part the 4Q text usually is more *plene* than 1QIsa[a], while in the second part of the scroll (col. XXVII ff. of 1QIsa[a]) the two are closer to each other.

22 The overlapping section in Deuteronomy 11 in Deut[j,kl], both written in the "Qumran practice," is not substantial enough to support significant conclusions. Note further the biblical and non-biblical material in 4QPs[f] // 11QPs[a,b].

23 For a detailed analysis, see the present author's article, "The Contribution of the Qumran Scrolls to the Understanding of the Septuagint," in: G.J. Brooke and B. Lindars, eds., *Septuagint, Scrolls and Cognate Writings: Papers Presented to the International Symposium on the Septuagint and its Relation to the Dead Sea Scrolls and Other Writings* (Manchester, 1990) (SCS 33; Atlanta: Scholars Press, GA 1992) 11-47.

4QLev^{d*}. At a second level, 4QSam^a shares many important readings with 𝔊, but several of these agreements pertain to presumably "original" readings, which are less significant for establishing a close relation between sources. At a third level, close relations are recognized with the following sources, mainly on the basis of statistics: 4QDeut^{c,h,j} (these texts actually belong to group V). Other texts for which a close relation has mistakenly been mentioned in the scholarly literature are: 1QIsa^a, 2QDeut^c, 4QSam^c, 5QDeut, and 5QKings.

Had we found more texts of this kind, we would have called them a small group, but at this stage there are just a few scattered texts. We cannot speculate too much on the relation between these texts, since there is simply not enough evidence. They are not in the nature of a closely-knit textual family like the 𝔐 group, nor a scribal school like the texts written in the "Qumran practice," but they represent individual copies that in the putative stemma of the biblical texts happened to be close to the Hebrew text from which 𝔊 was translated. Since 𝔊 was merely a single copy of the biblical text, and not a family, recension, or revision, the recognition of Hebrew scrolls that were close to the *Vorlage* of 𝔊 is of limited importance.

IV. PRE-SAMARITAN TEXTS

Again a different type of internal relationship between closely connected texts is found in the texts which are often named "pre-Samaritan."[24] These texts share certain characteristic features, also extant in 𝔪 which was to be created at a later date on the basis of one of the pre-Samaritan texts. The common characteristics of these texts pertain to textual-editorial changes. They remove grammatical and contextual problems by deleting, adding or changing details. Characteristic of these texts are the frequent additions from Deuteronomy in the parallel sections in the earlier books of the Torah. Equally characteristic are internal additions in the narratives based on other parts of the story. The latter two types of additions are usually termed "harmonizing," and even if the term is not exact, it is clear what is meant. In addition to these characteristic readings the pre-Samaritan texts and 𝔪 also share content variants not related to the aforementioned features. 4QNum^b stands out from this group since it is written in the Qumran orthography and morphology. The following texts belong to this

---

24   See the present author, "Proto-Samaritan Texts and the Samaritan Penta-
        teuch," *The Samaritans* (ed. A. D. Crown; Tübingen: J. C. B. Mohr, 1988) 399-407.

group: 4QpaleoExod^m, 4QNum^b, and 4QDeut^n. This text was also used in 4Q Rewritten Pentateuch a,b (4Q158, 4Q364). Of the characteristic Qumran writings, 4QTest (175) was based on such a text in the Exodus section. The features which these texts have in common render it a textual recension, if a recension is taken as a group of texts sharing textual-editorial characteristics in identical or different texts. Since the texts share typological features, the term "text-type" also applies to them. This is a special group since ₥, not found at Qumran, belongs to the same group. The difference between ₥ and the Qumran texts is that the former also contains a few sectarian readings, the major one referring to Shechem as the central place of worship, while such readings are lacking in the Qumran texts. This special situation was created when the Samaritans took one of the non-sectarian—now named pre-Samaritan—texts and made it the basis for the new, sectarian text. The nature of this group of texts is thus determined by its common typological, recensional characteristics. The exact place where these texts were created or used is not known, but for one thing they are not known outside Palestine.

V. Non-Aligned (Independent) Texts

Finally, at Qumran we also find evidence of texts that we have named non-aligned or independent (see n. 6). This term is probably important only for the history of scholarship, since it says very little about the nature of the text itself. The use of this term implies that the text does not stand in any specifically close relation to either ₥, ₥ or ₲. It agrees with each one of these texts, though not exclusively, and by the same token it also differs from these texts. At the same time it also contains many readings not found in the other texts. But this notion is only important as against the once prevalent understanding that all Qumran texts, or actually all texts, are expected to conform with one of these three textual traditions. This view is now abandoned.

Several such non-aligned texts have been recognized at Qumran. Usually the employment of this term merely means that the texts under consideration follow an inconsistent pattern of agreements and disagreements with ₥, ₥ and ₲, as in the case of 4QDeut^{b,c,h,k}, 4QIsa^{c*}, 4QXII^{c,e}, 4QDan^a and 11QpaleoLev^a. But the really independent texts are the ones which contain readings that significantly diverge from the other texts, such as 4QDeut^{j,n}, 4QJosh^{a*}, 4QJud^{a*}, 4QSam^a, 5QDeut. According to our statistics these texts comprise some *twenty-five* percent of the evidence.

We now turn to the list describing the textual character of the Qumran texts examined. The first part of the list refers to all the caves except for cave 4. Texts which are equally close to 𝔐 and 𝔰𝔪 are referred to as 𝔐/𝔰𝔪.

Cave 1: Several texts (6) reflect 𝔐/𝔰𝔪 (numbers 2, 3, 5) or 𝔐 (7, 8b, 71). Different are 1QDeut[a] (1Q4) and 1QIsa[a] (both "Qumran practice"), and probably also 1QPs[b] (based on the tetragrammaton in palaeo-Hebrew) and 1QPs[c], both written in the "Qumran practice." The character of texts 1, 6, 9, 72 cannot be determined.

Cave 2: Two texts (16, 17) reflect 𝔐. Different are 2QEx[a,b], 2QNum[b], 2QDeut[c], 2QJer (all: "Qumran practice"). The nature of texts 1, 4, 5, 6, 8, 9, 10, 11, 14, 15 cannot be determined.

Cave 3: 3QLam reflects the "Qumran practice" (based on the use of the tetragrammaton in palaeo-Hebrew). Two texts (1, 2) are too small to be considered.

Cave 5: Three texts reflect 𝔐 (2, 5, 6). 5QDeut (5Q1) is of a different nature (independent). The nature of texts 3, 4, 7 cannot be determined.

Cave 6: Two texts reflect 𝔐 (4, 6). The nature of the other texts (1, 2, 3, 5, 7) cannot be determined.

Cave 8: The nature of the texts from this cave (1, 2) cannot be determined.

Cave 11: 11QEzek and 11QPs[c] reflect 𝔐. 11QpaleoLev[a] is non-aligned. The "Qumran practice" is reflected in 11QPs[a,b], both textually independent, and probably also in 11QLev[b] (note the tetragrammaton in palaeo-Hebrew).

When limiting the analysis to the binary question of whether or not a particular text reflects 𝔐, we conclude that, disregarding cave 4, 15 texts reflect 𝔐 (three scrolls from cave 1 are equally close to 𝔰𝔪), while 15 texts do not reflect that tradition. The number of proto-Massoretic texts was probably much higher, since many of the fragmentary texts, the nature of which cannot be decided, make the impression of containing such a text.

The texts from **cave 4** are discussed book by book. Much of the relevant material is available in the dissertations mentioned in n. 3. Many of the Torah texts are equally close to 𝔐 and 𝔰𝔪.

Of the Genesis fragments, four texts are equally close to 𝔐 and 𝔰𝔪: c, e, g, j. Three reflect 𝔐: a, b, f. The text of d, h, k is too fragmentary to be analyzed.

Of the Exodus fragments, three reflect 𝔐 (4QpaleoGen-Exod[l], 4QGen-Exod[a], 4QExod[f] [apparently]), and one is pre-Samaritan

(4QpaleoExod^m). Eight of the Exodus texts, however, have not been consulted.

Of the Leviticus texts, c is equally close to 𝔐 and 𝔪 and d is equally close to 𝔪 and 𝔊. The two other texts have not been consulted.

4QNum^b is pre-Samaritan, and secondarily also close to 𝔊.

Of the Deuteronomy fragments, the following manuscripts agree equally with 𝔐 and 𝔪: d, f, g, i, paleo-r. The following texts are of a different nature: b, c, h, n (non-aligned), q (close to 𝔊). j, k (both textually non-aligned), and m are written in the "Qumran practice." The nature of a, e, l, paleo-s cannot be determined. I have not seen o and p.

Of the texts of Joshua, b is close to 𝔐 (in its preserved readings; there is uncertainty with regard to some reconstructions). 4QJosh^a* contains a non-aligned text.

In Judges, a may well reflect a non-aligned text. I have not seen b.

In Samuel, b reflects 𝔐, while a is non-aligned and c is written in the "Qumran practice."

I have not seen the one text of Kings.

Most of the Isaiah texts are close to 𝔐 and secondarily also to 𝔊: a, b, d, e, f, h, k, l. The "Qumran practice" is reflected in c (textually non-aligned). The nature of the text of j, m, n, o, pap-p, q, r cannot be determined.

Two of the texts of Jeremiah reflect 𝔐 (a, c), while two other ones (b, d) reflect 𝔊. The nature of e cannot be determined.

Two texts of Ezekiel (a, b) follow 𝔐; the nature of c cannot be determined.

In the Minor Prophets, the text of a is non-aligned. The following texts are written in the "Qumran practice:" c, e (both textually non-aligned). The nature of b, d, f cannot be determined.

Psalms: I have not seen most of the texts. Several of them are reportedly written in the "Qumran practice."

The nature of 4QpaleoJob^c cannot be determined.

The two texts of Proverbs reportedly reflect 𝔐.

I have not seen the texts of Ruth, Canticles and Chronicles.

4QQoh^a is written in the "Qumran practice" (textually unclear).

Daniel: The text of d and e cannot be determined, while a is non-aligned and b is written in the "Qumran practice" (textually undetermined).

The text of Ezra reportedly reflects 𝔐.

The statistics for the texts from cave 4 are as follows:

Of the cave 4 texts, 33 texts follow 𝔐 (10 of these are equally close to 𝔐 and 𝔰𝔪 and 8 are equally close to 𝔐 and 𝔊); 32 texts are of a different nature (non-aligned, pre-Samaritan, 𝔊-like, "Qumran practice"), but because of the partial overlapping one cannot present exact numbers.

The overall statistical picture is as follows: of the 84-89 texts studied some *forty* percent could be said to be closely related to 𝔐, while *sixty* percent are of a different nature. More precisely, some *twenty-five* percent reflect the Qumran orthography, some *ten* percent are close to either 𝔊 or 𝔰𝔪, and some *twenty-five* percent are non-aligned. But, as noted, these figures may be somewhat misleading, since several of the Torah texts are equally close to 𝔰𝔪 and several of the Isaiah texts are equally close to 𝔊. Moreover, there is a slight overlap between the different groups, since a few of the texts are written in the "Qumran practice" and at the same time are textually non-aligned. It should also be remembered that not all the texts have been studied. Not covered by our survey are seven of the Exodus texts, 17 texts of Psalms, as well as 10 other ones; in other words, 34 texts have been excluded, while almost ninety texts have been covered.

Conclusions

Our main purpose was to examine whether within the large group of Qumran biblical texts clusters of texts could be found. Such evidence has been found, but the principle which holds these groups together differs greatly, so that any generalizations on the nature of the collection of the Qumran texts may be misleading.

To find evidence at Qumran of a special scribal school is not surprising. In fact, the number of such texts is smaller than could be expected, namely some twenty percent for the biblical texts.

Of the texts not written in the "Qumran" orthography and morphology, the largest segment (some *forty* percent) belongs to the closely-knit proto-Massoretic family, with a smaller group belonging to a textual-editorial pre-Samaritan recension, reflected outside Qumran in 𝔰𝔪. Again, other texts reflect a stage in the literary development of the Hebrew Bible, reflected in both 𝔊 and some of the Qumran texts. Not all texts belong to groups, however. A relatively large number of the texts should be considered non-aligned, that is not linked with any of the other texts or groups.

As for negative evidence, no proof was found that the scrolls written in the palaeo-Hebrew script reflect a separate textual group, since these texts are not uniform from a textual point of view:

most of them reflect 𝕸, or 𝕸 as well as 𝔀, while 4QpaleoExod^m is pre-Samaritan, and 11QpaleoLev and 4QpaleoGen-Exod^l are non-aligned.

We did not speculate on the question of the coexistence, peaceful or not, of these groups in the Qumran community, nor on the proportions of the different groups. We merely want to establish that there existed different groups in addition to a number of texts that have been described as non-aligned.

At an earlier stage of my research (see the article quoted in n. 6), I stressed the almost infinite number of texts existing for the individual biblical books. Because of the existence of the so-called non-aligned texts this is still true. But at the same time, the present study has shown that within the textual jungle, the majority of texts belonged to textual groups or blocks, and within these groups 𝕸 formed the largest one. As long as there is no reason to assume that the Qumran biblical evidence is sectarian in any way, with all due caution and until further notice we accept this evidence as representative for Israel in the Greco-Roman period as a whole.[25]

---

25   Thanks are due to Prof. David Carr for helpful criticisms.

THE PALAEO-HEBREW BIBLICAL MANUSCRIPTS FROM QUMRAN CAVE 4*

Eugene Ulrich

In 1955, Patrick W. Skehan published a preliminary report on a fragmentary Qumran manuscript which can claim a place as one of the most significant biblical manuscripts in this already spectacular collection of scrolls.[1] It was inscribed in the palaeo-Hebrew script, which made one automatically think that it might be connected with the Samaritan Pentateuch, and in fact Skehan initially presented it as such. But already by 1959 he had refined his view as he studied it in relation to other manuscripts in the palaeo-Hebrew script.[2]

Fragments from 13 (or 14?) biblical manuscripts in the palaeo-Hebrew script were found in the eleven caves at Qumran, plus three other manuscripts which are possibly biblical or biblically related. Three (or four?) were in cave 1, one in cave 2, two in cave 6, and one in cave 11,[3] while cave 4 held fragments from an additional six biblical manuscripts and three others which resist identification:

---

*   It is a pleasure to thank the Institute for Advanced Studies at the Hebrew University, Jerusalem, whose invitation, efficiency, and cordiality made possible a serious advance in the publication of the scrolls, and also the University of Notre Dame and the National Endowment for the Humanities for their support of the long-term work which this paper represents.
    The editions of the manuscripts treated below have been published in P.W. Skehan, E. Ulrich, J.E. Sanderson, *Qumran Cave IV, Palaeo-Hebrew and Greek Biblical Manuscripts* (DJD 9) (Oxford: Clarendon Press, 1992). As a service to scholars interested in these texts, generous amounts of the descriptions of these scrolls have been excerpted or digested from those editions.

1   P.W. Skehan, "Exodus in the Samaritan Recension from Qumran," *JBL* 74 (1955) 182-7 [=col. XXXVIII, Exod 32:10-30]. For a detailed analysis of the significance of this scroll, see J.E. Sanderson, *An Exodus Scroll from Qumran: 4QpaleoExodᵐ and the Samaritan Tradition* (HSS 30; Atlanta: Scholars Press, 1986). I wish to acknowledge the part that both Skehan and Sanderson have played in the editions and by extension in this article. The work is truly one of homogenized collaboration by now, and a number of the ideas and formulations contained in this article are theirs. I also thank Emanuel Tov and Esti Eshel for a number of helpful corrections and clarifications in this article and in the editions of the palaeo-Hebrew manuscripts.

2   P. W. Skehan, "Qumran and the Present State of Old Testament Text Studies: The Masoretic Text," *JBL* 78 (1959) 21-5.

3   The publications of the biblical scrolls in the palaeo-Hebrew script from the other caves are as follows:
    1Q3 = 1QpaleoLevᵃ, 1QpaleoLevᵇ, 1QpaleoNum: Barthélemy in D. Barthélemy and J.T. Milik, *Qumrân Cave 1* (DJD 1; Oxford: Clarendon, 1955) 51-4

1Q3	1QpaleoLev[a]	4QpaleoGen-Exod[l]
1Q3	1QpaleoLev[b]	4QpaleoGen[m]
1Q3	1QpaleoNum	4QpaleoExod[m]
2Q5	2QpaleoLev	4QpaleoDeut[r]
6Q1	6QpaleoGen	4QpaleoDeut[s]
6Q2	6QpaleoLev	4QpaleoJob[c]
11Q1	11QpaleoLev[a]	4Q123 (paraphrase of Joshua?)
		4Q124 (unidentified)
		4Q125 (unidentified)

The manuscripts from all but cave 4 had been published before 1992, and those from cave 4 appeared in *Discoveries in the Judaean Desert* (DJD), vol. 9. Skehan had prepared an edition of each of the six biblical (but not the nonbiblical) manuscripts prior to his death on September 9, 1980. Some he had prepared noticeably earlier than that date, and for several reasons Judith Sanderson and I have revised and augmented them, approximately doubling their size. One reason, of course, is that Skehan himself would have done a final revision and proofreading of his editions before he would have sent them to the press. A second reason is that with the deepening and broadening of Qumran scholarship over the past decade or two, a richer battery of questions is being asked of the material. The detailed consideration of these questions is important not only for the eventual reader but also for the editor, in order to understand the document more thoroughly and thus be able to present it to scholars more intelligibly, and to offer them greater potential for their own use of the scrolls. Moreover, the vast

and pls. VIII-IX [it is unclear whether 1Q3 is the remains of 3 or 4 manu-scripts];
2Q5 = 2QpaleoLev: Baillet in M. Baillet, J.T. Milik, and R. de Vaux, *Les 'petites grottes' de Qumrân* (DJD 3; Oxford: Clarendon, 1962) 56-7 and pl. XII;
6Q1 = 6QpaleoLev: Baillet, DJD 3.106 and pl. XX;
11Q1 = 11QpaleoLev[a]: D.N. Freedman and K.A. Mathews, *The Paleo-Hebrew Leviticus Scroll (11QpaleoLev)* (Winona Lake, IN: ASOR/ Eisenbrauns, 1985); see also D.N. Freedman, "Variant Readings in the Leviticus Scroll from Qumran Cave 11," *CBQ* 36 (1974) 525-34; E. Tov, "The Textual Character of 11QpaleoLev," *Shnaton* 3 (1978-79) 238-44 (Hebrew); F. García Martínez, "Texts from Cave 11," *The Dead Sea Scrolls, Forty Years of Research* (eds. D. Dimant and U. Rappaport; Leiden-Jerusalem: E.J. Brill-Magnes-Yad Izhak Ben-Zvi, 1992) 18-26; and especially É. Puech, "Notes en marge de 11QPaléoLévitique. Le Fragment L, des fragments inédits et une jarre de la grotte 11," *RB* 92 (1989) 161-83 et planches I-III.

majority of those who will use the DJD volumes cannot come to Jerusalem to consult the original manuscripts for a resolution of the ambiguities in the photographs; it is the duty of the editor to inform those who will work from the photographs whether, for example, a dark line is the ink of a letter or a meaningless shadow or defect.

The original extent of these six manuscripts cannot be determined with certainty. The first probably contained both Genesis and Exodus and conceivably contained the entire Torah. The second survives in only one fragment from Genesis. The third—one of the two most extensively preserved biblical manuscripts from Qumran—contains fragments of Exodus from all but the first five and last three chapters. The fourth has a modest sampling of fragments from much of Deuteronomy. The fifth has only one fragment of Deuteronomy, and the sixth preserves but three small fragments from the book of Job. It will be observed that with the exception of the last, they are all from the Books of Moses, as is the case for the other seven manuscripts in palaeo-Hebrew from the other Qumran caves. The appearance of Job in this script may well be due to an ancient tradition, later recorded in b. B. Bat. 14b, 15a, that attributed the book of Job to Moses.

There are three more palaeo-Hebrew manuscripts from cave 4, but they will not be treated here. They are not clearly identifiable as "biblical" in the traditional sense. The third is merely a single small scrap with at most a single letter identifiable on each of two lines and a couple unidentifiable letters on two other lines. The second is more extensive but yields no intelligible, connected text. The first, however, though surviving only in four small fragments, finds its closest identity to known texts in Joshua 21. This suggests, of course, that the palaeo-Hebrew script may well have been reserved for, or used especially for, what was considered the writings of Moses and his contemporaries. This, in turn, may help focus the work toward identification of the second, as yet unidentified, palaeo-Hebrew manuscript.

The purpose of this paper is to study the six biblical manuscripts from cave 4 in the palaeo-Hebrew script together,[4] in order to learn what we can from the similarities and contrasts and to see whether these manuscripts form a distinctive group of texts or are simply varied samples of the biblical scrolls in general, not to be distinguished from the other biblical manuscripts except for their

---

4   See also the earlier article by K.A. Mathews, "The Background of the Paleo-Hebrew Texts at Qumran," *The Word of the Lord Shall Go Forth* (ed. C. Meyers and M. O'Connor; Winona Lake, IN: Eisenbrauns, 1983) 549-68.

script. Full treatments of these scrolls are provided in the editions; here we must limit our focus to selected features of the manuscripts, the palaeography and date, the orthography, and the textual character of the manuscripts.

I. THE INDIVIDUAL MANUSCRIPTS

4QpaleoGen-Exod[l]

Features of the Manuscript

The extant fragments of 4QpaleoGen-Exod[l] (previously designated as 4QpaleoExod[l] or as 4QpaleoExod[n]) preserve letters from what is probably the final verse of Genesis and portions of text from Exodus 1–4; 8–12; 14; 16–20; 22; 25–28; 36; and 40(?).[5] Thus, the original scroll probably contained the entire book of Exodus and quite possibly the entire book of Genesis as well.

The first fragment preserves a right margin with holes from stitching, two letters on the first line followed by almost four blank but ruled lines, and then the beginning of the book of Exodus (Exod 1:1-5). The holes show that this was not the first column of the original scroll, despite the fact that the text is from the beginning of Exodus. The four ruled lines show that this was not the top margin of the column—significantly, no fragments from the top margin have been preserved, and the two fragments which preserve a bottom margin show, as expected, an unruled margin. The second to fourth lines have presumably been left completely blank. At the right margin of the first line of the fragment are visible parts of two letters that perfectly match the final word of Genesis, and given Qumran practices such as lack of colophons, it is difficult to imagine what this would be if not from the end of Genesis. If the analysis is correct, the format comes within one word of matching the rule found in later rabbinic sources (b. B. Bat. 13b; *Sof.* 2:2; y. Meg. 1,9[8]), calling for four blank lines between books of the Torah. Confirming evidence, however, is available from even closer sources. Another scroll from cave 4 in the Jewish script, 4QGen-Exod[a], also contains this pair of books, and both Leviticus and Numbers are included on 4QLev-Num[a]. Moreover, although the transition from the end of one book to the beginning of the next is not preserved for either

---

5   See P.W. Skehan, "The Biblical Scrolls from Qumran and the Text of the Old Testament," *BA* 28 (1965) 88, 99 [repr. in *Qumran and the History of the Biblical Text* (ed. F.M. Cross and S. Talmon; Cambridge, MA: Harvard University Press, 1975) 265, 276].

4QGen-Exod[a] or 4QLev-Num[a], the practice of leaving a number of blank lines between books on the same scroll is documented at Murabba'at (in the Minor Prophets Scroll) and Naḥal Ḥever (in the Greek Minor Prophets Scroll).[6]

The height of the scroll on which 4QpaleoGen-Exod[l] was copied can only be estimated. No column has been preserved from top to bottom, but two factors provide a reasonable estimate. The distance between the horizontal rulings for lines of script is fairly regular, at ca. 0.5 cm, and larger fragments preserving text from two contiguous columns allow an estimation of ca. 55-60 lines of text per column. Thus, the height of the inscribed part of a column was 28-30 cm, and, allowing about 4 cm each for top and bottom margins, the height of the scroll can be estimated at about 36-38 cm.

The full width of only one column is preserved, and it contains 50-56 letters per line, measuring ca. 10 cm. In columns where measurement is not possible but letters per line can be estimated, the number varies considerably, e.g., from 46-53 in one column to 66-73 in others. Only two letters are missing from the width of another column, but there the end of the skin forced the scribe to make the column narrow. That column has only 38-44 letters per line, and its estimated width is only 8.1 cm; for purposes of calculation of the size of the scroll, this column should be considered an exception.

The height of this scroll and the width of its columns are not unusual in comparison with other biblical scrolls. But the very large number of lines per column is unusual, and that large number of lines plus the small, compact size of the letters makes it fully plausible that the scroll contained both Genesis and Exodus. It is not inconceivable that it contained the entire Torah, though there seems to be no way to ascertain that.

It is customary, in manuscripts inscribed in the palaeo-Hebrew script, as also often in inscriptions in the Phoenician script, to use dots or small vertical or diagonal strokes to serve as word dividers. Similarly, one finds occasionally that a word at the end of a line is divided and the second part of the word starts the next line. Neither the word division dots nor the divisions of words between lines is normally found in biblical scrolls in the Jewish script.[7]

---

6   See Mur XII in DJD 2.182, 192, 197, 200, 202, 205; pls. LXI, LXVI, LXIX, LXXI, LXXII; and 8ḤevXII gr in DJD 8.3; pls. I, IV.

7   The Aramaic script used for international correspondence during the Persian period developed into various national scripts after the fall of the Persian empire. These included the Nabataean, Palmyrene, and Jewish scripts, the last being the form of the Aramaic script adapted and developed within Jewish scribal traditions. See F.M. Cross, "The Development of the Jewish Scripts," *The Bible and the Ancient Near East: Essays in Honor of William Foxwell Albright* (ed.

The scribe signaled divisions between paragraphs in four ways. Ten times the remainder of a line is left blank at the close of one section, and the new section is begun at the right margin of the next line. Six times that same pattern is followed plus the addition of another completely blank line, whereas eight times simply one blank line is left. Finally, six times a short interval is left within the line.[8] It is probably legitimate to consider the first three types as various equivalents to the divisions in Massoretic manuscripts classified as "open" (פתוחה, sometimes marked פ), and the fourth type as equivalent to that classified as "closed" (סתומה, sometimes marked ס). 4QpaleoGen-Exod[l], however, shows no particularly strong relationship between its divisions and the open and closed divisions as handed down in Massoretic manuscripts. Of the 24 long intervals in the scroll, only 7 correspond to the open divisions recorded in the Massoretic Text (=𝔐).[9] Of the scroll's 6 short intervals, only one (or possibly two) corresponds to the closed division in 𝔐. Furthermore, the Samaritan (=𝔖) manuscripts, which generally seem to have only one main type of division (קצה), frequently do, but often do not, correspond to those recorded in Massoretic manuscripts. The scroll's divisions are also at variance with those of 𝔖 9 times.

Thus, it would probably be illegitimate to envision an ancient ideal of a fixed pattern of divisions between sections. Rather, the ancient scribes simply appear to have made or handed on logical divisions between sections to help the reader, not to have been tradents of a pattern of standardized divisions which were viewed as a part of the text as were the words themselves.

Palaeography and Date

The palaeography of the palaeo-Hebrew manuscripts from Qumran has been described by Mark D. McLean in a 1982 Harvard dissertation written under the direction of Frank Moore Cross. McLean provides a palaeographic chart of the script of 4QpaleoGen-Exod[l]

G.E. Wright; Garden City, NY: Doubleday, 1961) 133-202, esp. 189-90, n. 5; and J. Naveh, *Early History of the Alphabet: An Introduction to West Semitic Epigraphy and Palaeography* (2d rev. ed.; Jerusalem: Magnes, 1987) 9-11.

8   In these statistics, and occasionally elsewhere in this article, the attempt is to provide a useful impression of the features of the scrolls. A few examples are sometimes omitted due to ambiguous evidence or to the disproportionate length required for descriptions of tortuous but pointless complications.

9   Both in the editions and in this article, the data concerning 𝔐 are calculated from the representation in *BHS*, and the data concerning 𝔖 are calculated from the von Gall edition.

and a discussion of the features of the script, suggesting a date in "the first half or first three-quarters of the first century BCE."[10]

Orthography

The orthography of a number of the books as they appear in the Massoretic collection and in the manuscripts of the Samaritan Pentateuch is inconsistent.[11] It is helpful to begin by noting that 𝔐 in Exodus uses both short and *plene* forms of the same words: אלכם (5:4; 7:9) and אליכם (11:9); אלהן (1:19) and אליהן (1:17); לשחת (17:1) and לשתות (7:21); קלת (9:23, 28) and הקלות (9:29). Even within the same verse 𝔐 has both הכנים and הכנם (8:14).

The orthography of many of the biblical scrolls from Qumran is also inconsistent, though—as also in the case of 𝔐 and 𝔴—there are certain tendencies observable in the orthographic practice. So it is for 4QpaleoGen-Exod[l], which strikes a moderate balance between conservative and full orthography, whereas 𝔐 in Exodus tends to be somewhat more conservative. In common with 𝔐 and 𝔴 it spells כל, אהרן, אלהים, and לא without *waw*. On the other hand, it is apparent, just as in the Massoretic texts, that the scribe is not attempting to put into practice a grammatically standardized orthography. A few examples of divergent spellings are presented here to illustrate the inconsistency in orthography in the various texts:

Exodus	Gen-Exod[l]	𝔐	𝔐[q]	𝔴[ed]	𝔴[mss]
16:2	(var.?) ו[י]לנו	וילינו	וילונו	וילנו	
16:7	(var.?) תלינו	תלונו	תלינו	תלנו	תלינו
16:30	הש[ביעי	השבעי		השביעי	
23:11	והשביעית	והשביעת		והשבעית, והשביעית והשביעית	
25:18	כרובים	כרבים		כרובים	

---

10 M.D. McLean, "The Use and Development of Palaeo-Hebrew in the Hellenistic and Roman Periods" (Ph.D. dissertation, Harvard University [University Microfilms], 1982) plate 3, lines 8-10, and pp. 66-71, 78, esp. 66 [designated 4QpaleoExod[n]].

11 See my discussion of "Orthography and Text in 4QDan[a] and 4QDan[b] and in the Received Masoretic Text," *Of Scribes and Scrolls: Studies on the Hebrew Bible, Intertestamental Judaism, and Christian Origins Presented to John Strugnell* (ed. H.W. Attridge, J.J. Collins, and T.H. Tobin; Lanham, MD: University Press of America, 1990) 29-42.

25:19   וכרב   וכרוב   וכרוב

But more typical patterns are illustrated in these examples:

Exodus	Gen-Exod[l]	𝔐	𝔐 q	𝔴 ed	𝔴 mss
9:28	קלות	קלת	קולות	
11:6	גדולה	גדלה	גדלה	
12:4	מהיות	מהית	מהיות	
12:4	נפשות	נפשת	נפשות	
12:7	המזוזת	המזוזת	המזוזת	המזוזת, המזוזות
16:30	הש[ב]יעי	השבעי	השביעי	
18:21	עליהם	עלהם	עליהם	

Textual Character and Affiliation

4QpaleoGen-Exod[l] appears, on the basis not of preserved evidence but of probable reconstruction, not to have the typological features of the Exod[m] 𝔴 tradition. It would be incorrect, however, to characterize the scroll simply as agreeing with 𝔐. Skehan's early (1965) judgment that it is "quite near to the received text, with only slight concessions to the tendency towards expanded readings for the sake of clarity and smoothness" (p. 99) now needs to be refined on the basis of his own, Sanderson's, and my research.

Gen-Exod[l] belongs to the general textual tradition of the book of Exodus which I term "edition I" (because we have no earlier editions extant) and which is represented also by both 𝔐 and the text-base from which 4QpaleoExod[m] and 𝔴 developed. The "revised edition" (or "edition II") of Exodus, witnessed by 4QpaleoExod[m] and the text which the Samaritans accepted for their Scriptures, was produced by the addition of 16 major expansions and a different order of text in two places.[12]

While the reconstruction of this scroll strongly suggests that it did not contain any of the major expansions, the remains are too fragmentary to demonstrate that conclusively. But it is a conservative and careful text which, though probably agreeing with 𝔐𝔊

---

12   4QpaleoExod[m] agrees with 𝔴 in 13 extant typological readings and in 5 reconstructed typological readings. For a detailed discussion of both similarities and differences between 4QpaleoExod[m] and 𝔴, see Sanderson, *An Exodus Scroll*, 196-220.

in its textual *edition*, agrees in *individual* variants sometimes with
𝕸, sometimes with 𝔀, sometimes with Exod^m, and sometimes
preserves a unique reading. It exhibits a slight tendency to expand
by one word or element of a word (approximately 8 times beyond 𝕸),
as do most texts, including 𝕸 (approximately 4 times beyond Gen-
Exod^l) and 𝔀 (approximately 9 times beyond Gen-Exod^l).

In the edition, those readings are catalogued among the
"variants" which are extant on the leather and for which any one
of the four Hebrew witnesses (Gen-Exod^l, Exod^m, 𝕸, or 𝔀) show
disagreement beyond pure orthography. Gen-Exod^l preserves 50 such
variants. Only one of them involves a major feature of the Exod^m𝔀
tradition: after Exod 26:35 the scroll agrees with 𝕸 against Exod^m
and 𝔀 in lacking the passage containing the instructions for the
incense altar. 𝕸 places that passage at Exod 30:1-10, but Gen-Exod^l
is not extant at that point, and though it is possible, one cannot be
certain whether the scroll originally had it at that point. Only 6 of
the 50 variants involve a phrase (e.g., אל אחיו אׄי[שׁ with 𝕸 rather
than א[חד אל אחד with Exod^m𝔀, 25:20). The remaining 43 variants
involve only a single word (e.g., the tetragrammaton with 𝕸
rather than אלהים with 𝔀, 3:4; נח[שׁת with 𝔀, which is lacking in 𝕸,
27:12). Thus Gen-Exod^l does not offer much of significance with
regard to textual content.

In 26 variants Gen-Exod^l agrees with 𝕸 against 𝔀, in 9 it agrees
with 𝔀 against 𝕸, in 14 it disagrees with both, and in 1 it agrees
with both against Exod^m. But it is interesting to push a bit further
and note that in 11 of those 23 disagreements with 𝕸, the scroll
agrees with either 𝕸^q or 𝕸^mss, and in three agreements with 𝕸 it
disagrees with either 𝕸^q or 𝕸^mss.

There are very few passages where both Gen-Exod^l and Exod^m
are preserved, only 9 variants of the total of 50: in 2 Gen-Exod^l
agrees with Exod^m𝕸; in 1 with 𝕸𝔀; in 1 with Exod^m𝔀; in 3 with 𝕸
alone; in 1 with 𝔀 alone; and in 1 Gen-Exod^l preserves a unique
reading.

Thus, it is plain that the most that can be said here is that there
are an early and a revised edition of the book of Exodus, that 𝕸𝕲
and probably 4QpaleoGen-Exod^l are witnesses to the early edition,
and that 4QpaleoExod^m and 𝔀 are witnesses to the revised,
expanded edition, but that each of the texts shows some development beyond the main lines of its textual parentage.

4QpaleoGen[m]

Features of the Manuscript

Of 4QpaleoGen[m] only a single small fragment, containing ten (or nine) complete words and eight (or nine) parts of words from Gen 26:21-28, survives. The fragment is only 4.5 cm high and 2.9 cm wide. Horizontal ruling with dry lines is visible and perhaps also vertical ruling; the distance between lines is 0.6 cm. As was customary in scrolls inscribed with the Palaeo-Hebrew script, the scribe used a dot to divide between words and probably divided words between lines. There are ca. 73 letters per line (but see below concerning lines 4 and 5).

Palaeography and Date

The manuscript displays a regular, practiced palaeo-Hebrew hand. McLean offers a palaeographic chart and a description of the script. He considers this manuscript one of the three earliest biblical manuscripts in the palaeo-Hebrew script, together with 4QpaleoDeut[s] and 4QpaleoJob[c], although he thinks that 4Qpaleo-Gen[m] has developed beyond the other two. His suggested date is "in the middle of the second century" BCE.[13]

Orthography

The orthography of 4QpaleoGen[m] differs from that of 𝔐 𝔊 in three of its 18 words:

26:22   אֹחֲרִית 𝔊 ed. Ken, mss (cf. also 26:21)] אחרת
𝔐 𝔊 ed. vGall, mss (var. or orth.?)

26:22   ולא] ולוא 𝔐 𝔊

26:25   ויט] ויטʾן 𝔐 𝔊

The phonological orthography seen in ויטʾן is paralleled, for example, in:[14]

---

13   McLean, "The Use and Development," plate 3, line 3, and pp. 57-60, esp. 60 [designated 4QpaleoGen].

14   See A. Sperber, *A Historical Grammar of Biblical Hebrew* (Leiden: Brill, 1966) 486 (§65); and R. Macuch, *Grammatik des samaritanischen Hebräisch* (Berlin: Walter de Gruyter, 1969) 36 (§14d). I am grateful to Esti Eshel for searching out these parallels.

Num 24:4	יחזי $ɯ^{mss}$] יחזה $\mathfrak{M}ɯ$
Gen 6:14	עשׂי $ɯ^{ms}$] עשׂה $\mathfrak{M}ɯ$
Gen 29:35	אודי $ɯ^{mss}$] אודה $\mathfrak{M}ɯ$

Textual Character and Affiliation

The small amount of text preserved is frustrating. For one word in Gen 26:21, the manuscript has ו[יֿחפר] and then breaks off at the left edge of the fragment, still within the *res̲h̲*; thus it cannot be determined whether the word here was plural with $\mathfrak{M}ɯ\mathfrak{C}\mathfrak{S}\mathfrak{V}$ or singular with $\mathfrak{G}$; note that in the next verse $\mathfrak{M}$ has ויחפר and $ɯ$ has ויחפרו. Though we cannot determine some details such as that, for some other questions speculation becomes a bit more possible. The ends of seven lines from the left side of a column do allow an attempt at least at quantitative reconstruction of the text that had been present. For most lines, the corresponding text in $\mathfrak{M}ɯ$ has ca. 73 letter spaces per line (counting both letters and the spaces between words). But for line 4 the number of letters in 4QpaleoGen^m is 10 less than that in the corresponding text in $\mathfrak{M}ɯ$, whereas for the next line the count is ca. 14 letters longer in 4QpaleoGen^m than in $\mathfrak{M}ɯ$. It is probably safer to conclude that in line 4 the manuscript possibly had an interval, because, although $\mathfrak{M}$ has no interval, $ɯ$ does have קצה. For line 5, however, one is forced to conclude that the manuscript simply had a shorter reading than $\mathfrak{M}ɯ$, omitting a phrase (perhaps such as והרביתי את זרעך) entirely or possibly inserting an omitted phrase supralinearly.

With so little text preserved, it is nearly impossible to determine or describe the textual character in any meaningful way. Some might say that it is "like $\mathfrak{M}$ with a few minor exceptions." A less misleading description, however, using more accurate terminology, would be to say, first, that though there is too little text to support major conclusions, 4QpaleoGen^m appears to be in general a witness to the same general text tradition to which $\mathfrak{M}$ in Genesis is also a later witness. But it is important to note that in the small amount of text preserved it disagrees orthographically with $\mathfrak{M}$ rather frequently (in three out of eighteen words) and is thus comparatively more divergent from $\mathfrak{M}$ than $ɯ$ is from $\mathfrak{M}$.

4QpaleoExod^m

Features of the Manuscript

4QpaleoExod^m has justifiably received a good deal of advance announcement concerning its great significance.[15] It was originally designated 4QEx$^\alpha$, Greek superscripts having been provisionally chosen to denote scrolls in the palaeo-Hebrew script. It is one of the most extensively preserved of the biblical scrolls from cave 4. Fragments from 43 out of 45 consecutive columns are preserved, spanning from Exod 6:25 to Exod 37:16.[16]

The introduction to the edition of this scroll extends to about 17 pages. Here we can note only a few items of interest. 4QpaleoExod^m was originally a beautiful scroll of fine, thin, creamy tan leather. Reconstruction of the layout of the full scroll suggests that seven columns would have preceded the first of the 45 columns partly preserved, and that five columns would have followed, thus totalling 57 columns for the complete book. The height of the scroll is estimated at 35 cm or slightly more, the inscribed portion measuring ca. 25–27.5 cm, with a top margin of at least 3.3 cm and a bottom margin of at least 4.5 cm. The number of lines per column was 32, or in some columns 33. The distance between ruled lines for script fluctuates from 0.7–1.0 cm, averaging 0.85 cm. The width of the columns varies within an estimated range of 12.2–14.7 cm. Note that the height of this scroll is about the same as that of 4QpaleoGen-Exod^l (36–38 cm), but that the latter has almost double the number of lines per column (55-60).

Preliminary study of the patterns of physical deterioration of the scroll suggests that the conclusion of Exodus was at the center of the scroll as it lay rolled in the cave. This would preclude the possibility that the text of Leviticus followed but would leave open

---

15   See the bibliography in the edition, especially: P.W. Skehan, "Exodus in the Samaritan Recension"; "Qumran and the Present State"; "The Biblical Scrolls from Qumran and the Text of the Old Testament," *BA* 28 (1965) 87-100, esp. fig. 14 on p. 98 [= cols. I-II, Exod 6:25–7:19] [repr.: *Qumran and the History of the Biblical Text* (ed. F.M. Cross and S. Talmon; Cambridge, MA: Harvard University Press, 1975) 264-77]; "Fragments of Another Exodus Scroll," *Scrolls from the Wilderness of the Dead Sea* (A Guide to the Exhibition, *The Dead Sea Scrolls of Jordan*, Arranged by the Smithsonian Institution in Cooperation with the Government of the Hashemite Kingdom of Jordan and the Palestine Archaeological Museum; London: Trustees of the British Museum, 1965) 16, 26 [= cols. I-II, Exod 6:25–7:19]; J.E. Sanderson, *An Exodus Scroll*; E. Tov, "Proto-Samaritan Texts and the Samaritan Pentateuch," *The Samaritans* (ed. A.D. Crown; Tübingen: J.C.B. Mohr, 1989) 397-407.

16   For the full list of contents of the manuscript see Sanderson, *An Exodus Scroll*, 321-23.

the possibility that the text of Genesis preceded (cf. 4QGen-Exod[a] and 4QpaleoGen-Exod[l]), though there is no evidence or any particular reason to think that the scroll contained Genesis.

There was a patch stitched on the bottom of column VIII to repair it during the Qumran period. It is grayish tan (whereas the leather used for the original scroll was creamy tan), roughly circular, ca. 6.5 cm in diameter, and was sewn behind the original leather. Both the script and the orthography on the patch differ from those of the main scribe.

The scribe used dots for word division, and occasionally split words at the end of a line.

There were several methods of signalling paragraph divisions. The largest divisions were signaled by a threefold pattern: (1) leaving the remainder of the line at the end of a section blank, (2) with an enlarged palaeo-Hebrew *waw*, the initial letter of the new section, usually placed at the approximate center of that interval, and (3) the rest of the first word following at the right margin of the next line.[17] Again, it is probably legitimate to consider this an equivalent of the "open" section (פ) in 𝔐. But of the approximately 23 times that this pattern occurs in 4QpaleoExod[m], only 17 times does it correspond to an "open" section in 𝔐, whereas twice it occurs where 𝔐 has only the *ʾatnaḥ*. Twice 𝔐 has no interval, once it lacks the entire passage (a major expansion), and once it has a "closed" section (ס). All 23 times 𝔐 agrees with 𝔐 and thus also disagrees with 4QpaleoExod[m] 6 times. There are three places where divisions in 4QpaleoExod[m] overlap with those in 4QpaleoGen-Exod[l], and all four Hebrew texts agree in marking a large division at all three points.

Lesser divisions were signaled by a short interval with the first word of the new section on the same line. Of the 19 occurrences of this type of division in the scroll, only twice does 𝔐 have a "closed" section (ס), and only once does 𝔐 have קצה. 𝔐 again lacks one of the passages. In the remaining 16 occurrences 𝔐 has: an unmarked interval once (after 6:27), merely verse division 12 times, only the *ʾatnaḥ* twice, and a larger "open" section (פ) once.

There are several other patterns for larger divisions which occur less frequently, but the general conclusions drawn concerning 4QpaleoGen-Exod[l] continue to apply to 4QpaleoExod[m], as indeed they apply to most of the biblical scrolls in general.

---

17   See column I line 6 for a clear example: in P.W. Skehan, "The Biblical Scrolls from Qumran," fig. 14 on p. 98.

Palaeography and Date

McLean suggests a date in "the first half or first three-quarters of the first century BCE" for 4QpaleoExod[m] as well as for Gen-Exod[l] and a third unidentified manuscript (4Q124). But of these three he considers Exod[m] to "display the latest features and the greatest number of novel features which will see subsequent development."[18]

Orthography

The orthography of 4QpaleoExod[m], like that of 𝔐 and 𝔐, is at the same time mixed yet prone toward characteristic features. It tends toward a more full orthography, but remains in the moderate range. E.g., the words אלהים, כל, and לא are consistently spelled without *waw*, whereas אהרון, אותך, and לאמור are consistently spelled with *waw* (𝔐 and 𝔐 both normally have אלהים, אהרן, כל, and לא).

On the other hand it is apparent, just as it is in 𝔐, that the scribe is not attempting to put into practice a grammatically systematic orthography. He wrote ויאמר, without *mater lectionis*, five times on the extant fragments where the lack of *waw* is clear, once where the *waw* is probably lacking, and once in the plural, ויאמרו, where the long *o* is no longer accented. In contrast, he also wrote ויאומר, with *mater lectionis*, five times where the *waw* is extant and clear, and once where it is probable.[19]

In the few places where 4QpaleoGen-Exod[l] and 4QpaleoExod[m] overlap, 4QpaleoExod[m] always displays the fuller reading:

Exodus	Gen-Exod[l]	Exod[m]	𝔐	𝔐
16:33	אתו	אותו	אתו	אתו
18:21	שנאי	ש[ו]נאי	שנאי	שנאי
19:24	ואה[ר]ן	ואהרון	ואהרן	ואהרן

Another interesting feature which at first appears to be an orthographic matter turns out to be illuminating. As in 𝔐 and 𝔐, so in this manuscript the expected form מצרים often occurs (6:26, 27[bis], 28, 29; 7:4[bis]; etc.) meaning "[the land of] Egypt" (occasionally preceded by ארץ or מלך). In contrast to 𝔐 and 𝔐, in this manuscript another form מצריים also occurs five times where the double *yod* is

---

18   McLean, "The Use and Development," plate 3, line 12, and pp. 73-78, esp. 78 [designated 4QpaleoExod[m]].

19   The subsequent scribe of the patch wrote יאמר in its sole occurrence there (VIII 28).

sufficiently clear (7:18ᵇ; 9:5ᵇ, 6; 12:35, 36), 𝔐𝔖 invariably reading
מצרים (always vocalized in 𝔐 מִצְרַיִם, or pausally מִצְרָיִם). This is not
simply a pair of orthographic alternatives, but two morphological-
ly distinct forms. In all the latter five instances, "the Egyptians"
(the people, as opposed to the land) is either the clear meaning or a
reasonable interpretation, and in all five 𝔊 and 𝔖 have the plural
Αἰγύπτιοι and ܡܨܪ̈ܝܐ, as opposed to Αἴγυπτος and ܡܨܪܝܢ (7:18ᵇ and
9:5ᵇ are major expansions in 4QpaleoExodᵐ and 𝔐, thus not in 𝔊𝔖,
but 𝔊𝔖 have the plural in the source texts, 7:18 and 9:4, for those
expansions). In further confirmation 𝔗 has מצראי at 7:18, 9:4, and 9:6.

Textual Character and Affiliation

4QpaleoExodᵐ is the only scroll found at Qumran that combines all
three of these distinctive characteristics: palaeo-Hebrew script,
relatively fuller orthography, and text in the proto-Samaritan
tradition. It is a carefully copied scroll with only four scribal errors
in the portions of the 43 columns that have been preserved, as well
as five other unique cases of shorter text that may either reflect
parablepsis or retain the preferable, unexpanded text.

The text of Exodᵐ belongs to the text-type or tradition which
previously was known to us only in its later representative, the
Samaritan Exodus. The scroll shares all major, typological features
with 𝔐 with the single exception of the new tenth commandment
regarding the altar on Mount Gerizim inserted in the Samaritan
Exodus 20 from Deuteronomy 11 and 27. Thus, the expanded textual
tradition now known to us as the Samaritan Pentateuch, rather
than being a creation *de novo* of the community that worshiped at
Gerizim, is instead a somewhat later representative of a tradition
that was already known elsewhere in Palestine and that was used
in other communities without special allegiance to Gerizim. The
presence of 4QpaleoExodᵐ in cave 4 at Qumran is evidence that a
somewhat earlier representative of the same expanded textual
tradition was presumably accepted and used by at least some in the
Qumran community. The Gerizim expansion, proper to Samaritan
theology, was made only in the Samaritan community, and that
was the only major expansion which it made in Exodus.

To determine the detailed relationship between 4QpaleoExodᵐ
and 𝔐 and their contrast with 𝔐, it is necessary to look at the
pattern of both agreements and disagreements, in secondary,
preferable, and synonymous variants, among all four witnesses,
Exodᵐ, 𝔐, 𝔐, and 𝔊. To describe all this adequately requires great

length and nuance, and fortunately Sanderson has already published such a description.[20]

4QpaleoDeut[r]

Features of the Manuscript

4QpaleoDeut[r] has 44 extant fragments with identifiable text from chapters 7, 10–15, 19, 22–23, 28, and 31–34, and other fragments possibly from chapters 1, 17, 21, 29, and 30.

4QpaleoDeut[r] in most ways is similar to the other scrolls. There are ca. 32 lines per column, and the distance between lines of script is fairly uniform, at 0.8–0.9 cm. Its height is thus approximately 27.2 cm for the inscribed portion, plus ca. 3 cm for the top and the bottom margins, totalling ca. 33 cm. The width of the columns is difficult to assess, but where the evidence is clearest, the estimate is 10.2 cm. Deuteronomy 32 was apparently written stichometrically, with two hemistichs to the line.

The scribe occasionally split words at the ends of lines. Unlike the scribe of 4QpaleoDeut[s], who observed the left marginal ruling so scrupulously that he divided individual words, leaving a single letter at the end or beginning of a line, this scribe followed the custom of other scribes and left at least two letters together, at least in the three instances which have been preserved.

However, this manuscript also has a number of unusual characteristics: its scribe did not use dots for word division as all the other scribes writing palaeo-Hebrew did, but separated words only by leaving a space of ca. 0.2 cm; its surface appears to crumble in a manner not common at Qumran; and one of its fragments has a right-angled cut that appears possibly to be deliberate (otherwise, it is an amazingly coincidental geometric happenstance!). With respect to the lack of dots for word division, one should bear in mind that some inscriptions in the Phoenician script also did not use word dividers.

The paragraph divisions of this scroll are difficult to assess because of its fragmentary nature. Only one type is extant, a short interval within a line. Of the 5 such occurrences, 𝕸 has a "closed" section all 5 times and 𝔴 has קצה twice. One larger interval, of about a half line prior to chapter 34, is mostly reconstructed, but there 𝕸 also has a "closed" section, while 𝔴 has קצה. On the other hand, there is 1 place where 𝕸 has an "open" section not shared by

---

20   For a full analysis of the textual character and textual affiliation of this scroll, see Sanderson, *An Exodus Scroll*.

Deut^r, and 2 places where 𝔐 has a "closed" section not shared by Deut^r.

Palaeography and Date

The palaeo-Hebrew script is written in a small, firm, and practiced hand, employing fairly thick, even strokes. For some reason McLean does not seem to have known or studied this manuscript. It is, however, closely akin to the hand of 4QpaleoExod^m, but the hand of 4QpaleoDeut^r is slightly more compact and rounded than that of 4QpaleoExod^m. The features of the script indicate a date roughly contemporary with 4QpaleoExod^m, thus approximately in the first half or first three-quarters of the first century BCE.

Orthography

The orthography of 4QpaleoDeut^r is similar to that of 4Qpaleo-Gen-Exod^l, that is, a moderate balance between conservative and full in its use of *matres lectionis*, and not fully consistent. The forms אלהיך, כל, and לא are consistently spelled so (but הלוא is spelled with *waw*, as expected in 32:6, as it is in 𝔐 there), and the divergent forms found in the manuscript are such as one customarily encounters at other places in 𝔐𝔰. Often the forms in this manuscript are longer than those of 𝔐, but sometimes they are shorter (note בצים [22:6] and וחפרת (vid) [23:14]). This manuscript tends to use *waw* noticeably more frequently than either 𝔐 or 𝔰 (though often 𝔰^{mss} attest the same fuller form) to mark long *o*, especially in the fem. pl. and the *Qal* ptc., and infrequently to mark long or short *u*. But again, the orthographic practice is not systematic, since, e.g., unaccented long *o* sometimes is, and sometimes is not, represented by *waw*. The manuscript also uses *yod* somewhat more than 𝔐 (but again note בצים) or 𝔰, especially for the *Hif^cil*. Though either 𝔐 or 𝔰 occasionally has a *mater lectionis* when this manuscript does not, there seems to be no instance in which both 𝔐 and 𝔰 have one when 4QpaleoDeut^r does not.

Textual Character and Affiliation

4QpaleoDeut^r appears to have agreed with 𝔐𝔊 in lacking the typological features of the Samaritan Deuteronomy. In minor variants the manuscript most often presents a unique reading, less often agrees with 𝔰, and least often agrees with 𝔐.

Though the scroll has not been preserved in any of the passages where 𝔰 has a typologically significant reading, there are two fragments which at least allow reconstruction of such a variant and which suggest that the manuscript did not belong to the 𝔰 tradition. The reconstruction at Deut 11:30 suggests that מול שכם as in ᵚᵘ was probably lacking; and that at Deut 12:5 suggests that this manuscript read יב[חר with 𝕸 rather than בח[ר with ᵚᵘ (and therefore, presumably, at the other 20 similar passages in Deuteronomy).

There are 23 variants preserved in this scroll. Though 22 involve only one word or part of a word, one variant involves an entire verse. Deut[r] uniquely lacks 28:19. This could be seen as an omission because it occurs in a series of curses introduced by ארור. But since it is the last of the series and its content quite jejune, it is also possible that Deut[r] is original and the curse of v 19 merely a generic addition. Of the 23 variants, in 3 minor variants Deut[r] agrees with 𝕸 against ᵚᵘ. In 8 minor variants Deut[r] agrees with ᵚᵘ against 𝕸. In 10 variants Deut[r] disagrees with both 𝕸 and ᵚᵘ (in the one significant absence of verse 28:19 plus 9 minor variants). In the final 2 variants Deut[r] disagrees with 𝕸 and ᵚᵘ, which also disagree with each other.

Thus reconstruction suggests that Deut[r] agreed with 𝕸𝕲 against ᵚᵘ in lacking both the "sectarian" features and one moderate expansion of the latter tradition. But in minor variants the scroll agrees with ᵚᵘ against 𝕸 8 times, agrees with 𝕸 against ᵚᵘ only 3 times, and most often (12 times) presents a unique reading.

Out of the 44 identified fragments of this manuscript there is very little overlap with the cave 4 scrolls of Deuteronomy in the Jewish script edited by Sidnie White and Julie Duncan. In those few places a preliminary reading sees the texts as almost identical, except for some minor orthographical differences. Two textual variants tentatively emerged: in one manuscript there is one metathesis of two letters in a word where this commonly happens, and in another there is the substitution of one common preposition for another synonymous one.

4QpaleoDeut[s]

Features of the Manuscript

Of 4QpaleoDeut[s] only a single small fragment survives, measuring only 4.2 by 4.4 cm and containing only six complete and five partly preserved words from Deut 26:14-15. Word dividers are used regularly, and the left marginal ruling is so strictly followed that the word at the end of each of the three extant lines is divided. There is one interval of approximately a half line following Deut 26:15, which would normally be considered an "open" section but at this point 𝕸 has a "closed" section (ס); ᵚᵘ has קצה.

Palaeography and Date

This manuscript is inscribed in a slender, practiced bookhand, written higher along the ruling than normal. To McLean 4QpaleoDeut[s] appears to be the earliest of the biblical scrolls in the palaeo-Hebrew script. According to his typological schema it is "roughly contemporary with or slightly older than" 4QpaleoJob[c].[21] Though seven letters are not available for comparison because it is so small, he notes the relationship with the *yhd* coins, especially for *dalet* and *yod*, and judges that "Overall, the available forms seem earlier than" those of 4QpaleoJob[c], thus indicating a date "in the second half of the third century BCE."[22] This would mean, of course, that the manuscript was copied elsewhere and brought about a century later to Qumran.

Orthography and Textual Character

Again, there are only six complete and five partial words extant. Both the orthography and the text are very ordinary and straight-forward, and both agree with the orthography and text of both 𝔐 and 𝔰𝔰 for those few words.

4QpaleoJob[c]

Features of the Manuscript

Of 4QpaleoJob[c] only three small fragments survive, containing Job 13:18-20, 23-27; 14:13-18. The three fragments seem to have been from well-prepared leather and retain their flexibility, ruling, and clarity of script. The distance between lines of script was 0.8–0.9 cm, and one can estimate approximately 25 lines per column. The text was written stichometrically, with each stich beginning a new line, and the dots customary for word division in palaeo-Hebrew manuscripts were used. No instances are preserved where a word is split between lines, but that observation is meaningless, since the fragments are from a poetic passage written stichometrically, and the scribe may well have split words in the narrative sections.

Palaeography and Date

McLean considers this manuscript one of the two earliest biblical scrolls in the palaeo-Hebrew script, roughly contemporary with, but with a few tendencies slightly later than, 4QpaleoDeut[s]. He

---

21 McLean, "The Use and Development," plate 3, line 2, and pp. 53-7, esp. 53 [designated 4QpaleoDeut[β]].
22 Ibid., 57.

detects "little development in either form or stance... from the sixth century BCE formal scripts," though he pinpoints five characteristics which "indicate a passage of time." He suggests an "approximate date between 225 and 150 BCE with an emphasis on the earlier end of the scale."[23]

Orthography

4QpaleoJob^c displays a very conservative orthography, using no internal *matres lectionis* except possibly in יְמ[וֹת (14:14, which may reflect the radical), and in יְדִיךְ (14:15, which may reflect the historical spelling of the diphthong, *yadayk*). In contrast, for the few words preserved, 𝔐 has *waw* 6 times to indicate long *o* or long *u*:

13:24	ל[איב [לאויב 𝔐	
13:26	עונת [עונות 𝔐	
13:26	נערי [נעורי 𝔐	
13:27	ארחותי [ארחתי 𝔐	
14:16	תספור [תספר] 𝔐	
14:17	בצרור [ב]צרר 𝔐	

Textual Character and Affiliation

There is only one variant of one letter preserved, in 14:14. Its reading is clearly different from 𝔐, but it involves a single letter at the edge of the fragment, and the determination and significance of the disagreement involved is admittedly speculative. One cannot base any detailed arguments on this variant.

II. THE MANUSCRIPTS COMPARED

Features of the Manuscripts

Most or all of the features observed on these manuscripts fit into the patterns already familiar from the broader spectrum of manuscripts found at Qumran.

   The leather prepared and used for the palaeo-Hebrew manuscripts, except possibly for 4QpaleoDeut^r, appears to be similar to that used for the biblical manuscripts inscribed in the Jewish (square) script, and no differences are apparent between those

---

23   Ibid., plate 3, line 1, and pp. 47-52, esp. 52 [designated 4QpaleoJob^x].

manuscripts predating the Qumran settlement and those possibly copied at Qumran. For example, the ink used for 4QpaleoGen-Exod[l] had acid in it, just as the ink for some other manuscripts did, such as 4QLev[d] and 4QDan[d].

4QpaleoDeut[r] has a number of unusual characteristics: its scribe did not use dots for word division as did all the other scribes writing palaeo-Hebrew; its surface appears to crumble in a manner not common at Qumran; and one of its fragments has a right-angled cut with straight edges along the top and left sides which seems too geometrically regular to be unintentional. Nonetheless, its size, format, and text can be considered normal for a Qumran manuscript. Moreover, ancient inscriptions in the Phoenician script sometimes did not use dots for word division, and the surface crumbling of 4QpaleoDeut[r] could be due to unrelated factors such as type of damage or deterioration.

Concerning paragraph divisions, all the manuscripts except the tiny 4QpaleoGen[m] and 4QpaleoJob[c] are at variance with both 𝔐 and 𝔰𝔰 in their distribution. The conclusion that emerges from comparison of the extant divisions with the divisions preserved in 𝔐 and 𝔰𝔰 is that there was a common practice in the late Second Temple period of separating sections by longer and shorter divisions, but that the placement of these divisions was made more on a free and logical basis than according to a traditional schema that was standardized and widely accepted.

The palaeo-Hebrew *waw* used systematically by 4QpaleoExod[m] for division of some larger sections is used in 1QS at the top right of column V, apparently to mark the new section (though the square script *waw* is "repeated" in the initial word). A similar palaeo-Hebrew *waw* is found in 1QIsa[a], though both its placement and its function are unclear. It appears at line 22 between columns V and VI, and though it has been interpreted as marking column V,[24] it is possible that its placement may rather indicate (as in 1QS) reference to column VI at its left. Its function is not clear, but possibly it marks either the new section at 6:1 (if for column V) or the new oracle at Isa 7:7 (if for column VI).

Palaeography and Date

The palaeography of the six palaeo-Hebrew biblical manuscripts reveals six different hands, all well practiced. They display a familiarity with the script and an ability to write with "grace and

24   See E. Tov, "Hebrew Biblical Manuscripts from the Judaean Desert: Their Contribution to Textual Criticism," *JJS* 39 (1988) 5-37, esp. 26.

speed,"[25] which mark it as a reasonably common practice, not an unusual exercise. Though the palaeo-Hebrew script was probably a minority script, the minimalist view concerning its use needs to be revised, as McLean has noted, since all the main groups (except eventually the Pharisees) seem to have used it: the so-called "normative community" under the Sadduccees[26] and Hasmonaeans, the Qumran community, the Samaritans, and those of the First and Second Revolts.[27] Naveh makes the point, even if perhaps too strongly, that there was "a strong bond between a language and its script."[28] In the Persian period, Jews used both languages and both scripts—presumably the palaeo-Hebrew script for biblical texts and the Aramaic script for administration and trade. According to Naveh, the old script was in use well into the Hellenistic era.[29] On the other hand, insofar as McLean is also correct, there is scarcely a gap that separates the common use of that script in the early Hellenistic era from manuscripts such as 4QpaleoDeut^s, copied in the palaeo-Hebrew script ca. 250-200 BCE.

The dating of the manuscripts by McLean was done according to a typological schema, anchored at both ends by inscriptional evidence. Typological dating is open to some degree of questioning, but it must be remembered that with undated manuscripts there are only two avenues of estimating the date, namely, palaeography and archaeology. Archaeology can provide a *terminus ante quem*, the reliability of which depends upon the reliability of the methods, and luck, of the archaeological dating. The results of McLean's typological analysis of the scrolls fit with the archaeological dates. The dates assigned to some of the manuscripts predate the Qumran settlement (ca. 150 BCE), but so do some of those in the Jewish script, e.g., 4QExod^f, 4QSam^b, 4QJer^a, 4QXII^a and 4QQoh^a. This is not problematic, since most agree that some of the scrolls, especially biblical scrolls, were copied elsewhere, in Jerusalem or broader Palestine, and imported into Qumran as people came to join

---

25   Cross, "The Development of the Jewish Scripts," 189, n. 4.
26   D. Diringer, "Early Hebrew Script versus Square Hebrew Script," *Essays and Studies Presented to S. A. Cook* (London: Taylor's Foreign Press, 1950) 46-49.
27   McLean, "The Use and Development," 20.
28   Naveh, *Early History of the Alphabet*, 114.
29   "The various national versions of the Aramaic script began to appear only about a century after the fall of the Persian empire.... The Aramaic script was at that time so deeply implanted that the various nations continued to use it.... Different nations began to develop their own versions.... It seems likely that the Jews began to write Hebrew texts in the Aramaic script only when they felt that their form of the Aramaic script was distinctively Jewish" (ibid., 122).

the community.[30] The fact that there are no clear distinguishing features between the general Palestinian Jewish scrolls and the particularly Qumran scrolls suggests that scrolls were produced at Qumran according to conventions similar to those common in Jerusalem and Palestine in general.

The chronological order of the manuscripts in McLean's (and Cross's) view is 4QpaleoDeut[s], 4QpaleoJob[c], 4QpaleoGen[m] (all three predating the Qumran settlement), 4QpaleoGen-Exod[l], 4QpaleoExod[m]. McLean did not analyze 4QpaleoDeut[r], but in my view it should be dated to roughly the same time as 4QpaleoExod[m]. Thus, the simple conclusion would be that the first three were presumably copied somewhere in Palestine outside Qumran and that the latter three could have been copied either at Qumran or elsewhere in Palestine. Since there were a number of other palaeo-Hebrew manuscripts in four other caves at Qumran, and since no physical features distinguish these manuscripts from the other manuscripts in Jewish script (a number of which must have been copied at Qumran), there is no evidence to rule out a conclusion that some of the palaeo-Hebrew manuscripts were also copied at Qumran. If this is true, the further conclusion is also logical, that there appear to be no characteristic differences between those palaeo-Hebrew manuscripts copied at Qumran and those imported into Qumran. I must reiterate that we do not have strong evidence to support this as a firm conclusion, but the conclusion is logical and plausible.

Most or all of the palaeographic features observed on these manuscripts also fit into the patterns that indicate no observable differences between manuscripts copied outside Qumran (i.e., those assigned dates prior to the settlement at Qumran) and manuscripts presumed to have been copied at Qumran. But it is necessary to consider this conclusion from the perspective of orthography as well.

Orthography

Study of the orthography of each of the three larger palaeo-Hebrew manuscripts tells us something also about 𝕸. The orthographic practice at work in the Qumran manuscripts, just as in 𝕸, shows somewhat distinctive tendencies but also a degree of inconsistency in each manuscript and in the various books in 𝕸.

---

30   The last clause clearly distances my view from that proposed by N. Golb, "Khirbet Qumran and the Manuscripts of the Judaean Wilderness: Observations on the Logic of Their Investigation," *JNES* 49 (1990) 103-14.

The orthography of the six palaeo-Hebrew manuscripts can be charted on a spectrum arranged this time, not primarily by chronology, but by fullness in use of internal *matres lectionis*. The most conservative use of internal *matres lectionis* is in 4QpaleoJob^c, which arguably has none. Perhaps 4QpaleoDeut^s may be ranked next, insofar as it has no spellings fuller than 𝔐 or 𝔴, but this is uncertain and almost meaningless. 4QpaleoGen-Exod^l and 4QpaleoDeut^r display a slightly fuller use, and 4QpaleoExod^m a yet fuller use, though still within a fairly moderate range. Perhaps 4QpaleoGen^m should be placed with or slightly beyond 4QpaleoExod^m on this spectrum, but we have too little evidence for a firm decision. 4QpaleoGen^m alone among these manuscripts does write לוא with *waw*, whereas 4QpaleoExod^m writes לא without *waw*; but 4QpaleoExod^m sometimes, e.g., writes ויאומר with *waw*, while we do not know whether 4QpaleoGen^m may have written ויאמר without *waw*. At any rate, though there is a spectrum of orthographic practice in the Qumran manuscripts, virtually all forms are of a type routinely found in other known biblical manuscripts, including 𝔐, 𝔴, and other Qumran manuscripts in the Jewish script.

If we then compare the chronological spectrum charted by the palaeographically assigned dates with the spectrum drawn according to orthographical usage, we get—not a logically satisfying correlation that shows a regular chronological development of orthographic practice—but a picture that is actually more real and believable. In the short period with which we are concerned, a moderate range of orthographic practice seems to have been acceptable. 4QpaleoJob^c cooperates best by having a very conservative orthography that most would tend to date early, and by having one of the earliest palaeographical dates. Analogously, 4QpaleoExod^m has a more liberal orthographic profile together with a date near the later end of the spectrum. But 4QpaleoGen^m has what we often think of as a later orthographic style, while being dated palaeographically as early. We should recall, however, that the Nash Papyrus also writes the negative as לוא, and it is commonly dated to the second half of the second century,[31] roughly contemporary with the date suggested by McLean for 4QpaleoGen^m. The conclusion to be drawn here, just as for the scrolls in the Jewish script, is that though earlier manuscripts may tend to have more conservative spelling, that is only a rule of

---

31   See W.F. Albright, "A Biblical Fragment from the Maccabaean Age: The Nash Papyrus," *JBL* 56 (1937) 145-76; Naveh, *Early History of the Alphabet*, 162 and fig. 147.

thumb, a tendency. The common view—that Hebrew orthography was never rigidly standardized and that it reached its fullest style of spelling in the Hasmonaean era—is exactly what one observes in the palaeo-Hebrew manuscripts from cave 4.

Orthography at Qumran is probably not to be distinguished from general orthographic practice in contemporary Palestine (4Qpaleo-Gen^m) and even perhaps in Egypt (Nash Papyrus). Emanuel Tov speaks of Qumran orthography and amasses impressive data to offer us a more multi-dimensional perspective.[32] But he is careful to say that we do not have sufficient evidence to know whether "'Qumran' orthography was practiced widely in Palestine."[33] Though there is little evidence available, nonetheless there is some, and it is quite diverse. There are, e.g., fourth-century jar handles alternating between יהד and יהוד; the Nash Papyrus from Egypt uses לוא; and even the Massoretic texts of Chronicles and Samuel in their parallel passages display more and less *plene* styles, respectively, though a form of Samuel was used as a source by the Chronicler. In light of these diverse sources, I think it may be preferable to expand the nomenclature of orthographic categories from "Qumran" and "non-Qumran" orthography to terms that would cover the entire late Second Temple period, or Hasmonaean-Roman period, since it appears that the fuller orthography reached its characteristic features then. I would then characterize the different orthographic approaches in biblical manuscripts as "traditional" vs. "contemporary," or "conservative" vs. "modernizing"—depending upon whether the scribes continued to copy the Persian period texts in the old orthography or (like the scribes of 4QSam^c, 4QIsa^c, and 4QDan^b)[34] modernized them in accord with contemporary practices. In short, just as I detect no difference in physical features or palaeography of the palaeo-Hebrew biblical scrolls between those produced throughout Palestine and those produced at Qumran, neither do I see any characteristic difference between them in orthography, except insofar as scribes had to make a decision whether to modernize or not to modernize the orthography of their manuscripts as they made new copies.

---

32 E. Tov, "The Orthography and Language of the Hebrew Scrolls Found at Qumran and the Origin of These Scrolls," *Textus* 13 (1986) 31-57; and "Hebrew Biblical Manuscripts," esp. 23-25.

33 Tov, "Hebrew Biblical Manuscripts," 24.

34 See E. Ulrich, "4QSam^c: A Fragmentary Manuscript of 2 Samuel 14–15 from the Scribe of the *Serek Hay-yaḥad* (1QS)," *BASOR* 235 (1979) 1-25; and "Daniel Manuscripts from Qumran. Part 2: Preliminary Editions of 4QDan^b and 4QDan^c," *BASOR* 274 (1989) 3-27.

Textual Character and Affiliation

The Massoretic Text, when one is speaking in scholarly rather than religious terms, should more properly be termed the Massoretic collection of texts. It has now become common knowledge that the Septuagint differs from section to section and from book to book, and sometimes even within a given book. The case is the same with the assortment of texts gathered into the Massoretic collection. The textual profile of the individual books varies significantly, both with regard to the soundness of the text (i.e., sound texts such as Genesis and Exodus vs. problematic texts such as Samuel and Hosea) and with regard to the successive editions transmitted (i.e., early editions for the book of Exodus and for the Hannah narrative in Samuel, vs. revised editions for the David-Goliath narrative also in Samuel and for the book of Jeremiah).[35] Thus, one cannot simply compare texts from various books of the Bible to "the text" of 𝔐.

The palaeo-Hebrew manuscripts exhibit what one would expect: they are primarily in agreement with the editions we have known, with predictable types of minor expansions, transposition, errors, etc., that distinguish them in minor ways from the specific texts that happen to have been preserved. One could point out that only 4QpaleoExod[m] has a demonstrably proto-Samaritan text-type, whereas the remainder are close to 𝔐. But it must be remembered that this distinction is irrelevant for one of the six manuscripts (4QpaleoJob[c]), is unable to be determined for two others (4QpaleoGen[m] and 4QpaleoDeut[s]), and is reached primarily by reconstruction for the remaining two (4QpaleoGen-Exod[l] and 4QpaleoDeut[r], though one can rely on the conclusion about the latter two with reasonable confidence). Thus, we are left with the ratio of two texts in the same early edition as that in 𝔐 to one text in the revised edition as in 𝔰𝔪. A base that narrow cannot support very weighty conclusions. As is all too often the case, the fragmentary evidence is not extant where it is needed or sought. There is almost no overlap of the palaeo-Hebrew scrolls with each other or with other cave 4 scrolls, and when there is, there is very little of significance in the contrast.

---

35   See E. Ulrich, "Double Literary Editions of Biblical Narratives and Reflections on Determining the Form to Be Translated," *Perspectives on the Hebrew Bible: Essays in Honor of Walter J. Harrelson* (ed. James L. Crenshaw; Macon, GA: Mercer University Press, 1988) 101-16 [= *Perspectives in Religious Studies* 15/4 (Fall 1988) 101-16]; and "The Canonical Process, Textual Criticism, and Latter Stages in the Composition of the Bible," *Shaᶜarei Talmon: Studies in the Bible, Qumran, and the Ancient Near East Presented to Shemaryahu Talmon* (ed. M. Fishbane and E. Tov with W. W. Fields; Winona Lake, IN: Eisenbrauns, 1992) 267-91.

In sum, except for their script, the palaeo-Hebrew biblical manuscripts from Qumran cave 4 do not appear to form a group distinguishable from the other biblical scrolls in either physical features, date, orthography, or textual character. Moreover, though certainty is even more elusive for this contrast, there seems to be no great distinction in any of those four categories between manuscripts copied outside Qumran (or predating Qumran) and manuscripts copied at Qumran.

THE ANGELIC SONG OVER THE LUMINARIES IN THE QUMRAN TEXTS

Moshe Weinfeld

There are in the Qumran Psalms Scroll (11QPs[a]), in addition to the Psalms themselves, fragments of other hymns and prayers the nature and essential characteristics of which have so far not been investigated. In this study we shall analyze the so-called "Hymn to the Creator" (col. 26:9-15).[1]

The "Hymn to the Creator" appears in the scroll immediately after Ps. 150.[2] In this hymn we find in 26:12 the angels singing at the coming of dawn, with the appearance of the morning light. This is the very phenomenon upon which the *Yoṣer Qedushah* of the morning[3] is based and which, as we shall see, is further reflected in the books of Ben Sira and Jubilees.

---

1   J.A. Sanders, *The Psalms Scroll of Qumran Cave 11 (11QPs[a])*, Discoveries in the Judean Desert (=DJD) vol. 4 (Oxford: Clarendon Press, 1965); J.A. Sanders, *The Dead Sea Psalms Scroll* (Ithaca: Cornell University Press, 1967). See DJD 4.40, 47, 76-79, 89-91.

2   On the importance of this position see my article "Traces of Kedushat Yozer and Pesukey De-Zimra in the Qumran Literature and in Ben Sira" (Hebrew), *Tarbiz* 45 (1976) 23-26.

3   For the *Yoṣer Qedushah* cf. recently J. Heinemann in I. Elbogen, התפילה בישראל בהתפתחותה ההיסטורית (Tel Aviv: Dvir 1972), 52-53. The argument that the *Yoṣer Qedushah* does not appear in the Genizah documents is now refuted by the significant number of Genizah fragments which contain *Yoṣer Qedushah* liturgies (cf. e.g. the fragments listed by J. Heinemann, ibid., 53). Very instructive are the passages from the Genizah published by S. Schechter, *Gedenkbuch zur Erinnerung an D. Kaufmann* (Breslau: S. Schottlaender, 1900) 54 (Hebrew) and S. Asaf, מסדר התפילה בארץ ישראל, *Sefer Dinaburg* (Jerusalem Kiryat Sepher, 1949) 120 (Hebrew). The former reads: יוצר משרתים אשר משרתיו אלף עומדים לפניו: רבו רבי רבבות סובבים את כסאו. כלם אהובים... The latter reads אשר משרתיו אלף אלפי אלפים עומדים ברום עולם ומשמיעים... These passages, influenced by Dan. 7:10 and Ps. 68:18, are very close to the liturgical passage in the Epistle to the Corinthians of Clement of Rome 34:7: "Ten thousand times ten thousand were doing service to him crying out 'Holy, Holy, Holy, Lord Sabaoth, the whole creation is full of His Glory,'" and Apostolic Constitutions VIII xii 27: "Say together the thousand times ten thousand of angels, incessantly and with constant and loud voices, and let the people say it with them: 'Holy, Holy, Holy, Lord of Hosts, heaven and earth are full of His glory'" (*Didascalia et Constitutiones Apostolorum* [ed. F.X. Funk; Paderborn: F. Schoeningh, 1905], vol. I). On the reflection of the Jewish *Qedushah* liturgy in 1 Clem. and Ignatius to the Ephesians see D. Flusser, "Sanktus und Gloria," *Festschrift O. Michel* (Leiden/Köln: E.J. Brill, 1963), 132ff. For the Jewish *Qedushah* liturgy and especially the *Yoṣer Qedushah* embodied in the Apostolic Constitutions, Book VII, Chap. 35, see W. Bousset, "Eine jüdische Gebetssammlung im siebenten Buch der apostolischen Konstitutionen," *Nachrichten von der*

THE QUMRAN TEXT AND ITS PARALLELS IN COMMON JEWISH LITURGY

Not only do we find in the Qumran passage that God's establishing of the luminaries of heaven is associated with the song of the angels; the very language of the hymn attests to its affinity to the various forms of the *Qedushah*, mainly to the *Amidah Qedushah* and the *Yoṣer Qedushah*. Let us analyse the text:[4]

Great and holy is the Lord	גדול וקדוש ה'
the holiest of holy ones	קדוש קדושים לדור ודור
for every generation.	
Majesty precedes Him,	לפניו הדר ילך
and following Him is the	ואחריו המון מים רבים
rush of many waters.	
Grace and truth surround His presence;	חסד ואמת סביב פניו
truth and justice and righteousness	אמת ומשפט וצדק מכון כסאו
are the foundation of His throne	
He separates light from darkness,	מבדיל אור מאפלה
by the knowledge of His mind	שחר הכין בדעת לבו
He established the dawn.	

Gesellschaft der Wissenschaften zu Göttingen, Phil. Hist. Kl., 1915, 435ff. It should be admitted that the angelic praise is an independent unit interpolated into the *Yoṣer* Benediction. The formula המחדש בטובו בכל יום תמיד מעשה בראשית with which the benediction closes (S. Singer, *The Standard Prayer Book*, [New York: Bloch Publishing Company, 1943] =*SPB*) 46-47) is almost identical to the opening phrase ובטובו מחדש בכל יום תמיד מעשה בראשית (*SPB*, 45), creating a *Wiederaufnahme*, bringing us back to the original theme the continuity of which has been interrupted. (On this phenomenon in biblical literature see C. Kuhl, "Die 'Wiederaufnahme'—ein literarkritisches Prinzip?" *ZAW* 64 [1952] 1-11). However, even if it is an interpolation (see also Flusser, ibid., 140 n. 1), this has no bearing on the dating and liturgical use of the interpolation. It is quite possible that the phrase quoted was repeated because the angelic-song section, itself ancient, disrupted the continuity of the benediction, rendering it necessary to compose an ending similar to the beginning; see L. Ginzberg, פירושים וחידושים בירושלמי 4.156 (New York: JTS, 1941). The extensive material collected by A. Büchler, "La Kedoucha du Yocer chez les Gueonim," (*REJ* 53 (1907) 220-30) affirms that this liturgy itself was well known and accepted, but that some authorities held that it was not to be recited by the private worshipper, just as is the case with the *Amidah Qedushah* (Maimonides, *Hilkhot Tefillah* 7:17). This led to the *Qedushah* being entirely omitted from the benediction in the *Siddur R. Saadia Gaon* (ed. Mekiṣe Nirdamim, 13).

4   J.A. Sanders, DJD 4, 26: 9-12. The translation is from Sanders' 1967 edition.

Then all His angels had witnessed (it)   אז ראו כל מלאכיו ויראנו
they sang aloud, for He showed them   כי הראם את אשר לוא ידעו
what they had not known.

He clothes the mountains with produce   מעטר הרים תנובות
good food for every creature.   אוכל טוב לכול חי

A.

The opening line גדול וקדוש ה' קדוש קדושים לדור ודור is clearly
reflected in the various forms of the *Qedushah* and the Benediction
of *Qedushat Hashem*:

1) לדור ודור המליכו לאל כי מלך[5] וגדול וקדוש אתה recited daily,
according to the *Seder Rav Amran Gaon*;[6]

2) לדור ודור נגיד גדלך ולנצח נצחים קדושתך נקדיש (*SPB*, 55), designated for the Reader only in most rites;

3) אתה קדוש ושמך קדוש וקדושים בכל יום יהללוך סלה (*SPB*, 55) recited
by the individual worshipper; and, in two Genizah versions:

4) אתה קדוש ושמך קדוש ולך יאמרו קדושים קדוש[7]
לך יאמרו קדוש קדושים ברוך אתה ה' האל הקדוש[8]

In the morning *Amidah Qedushah* for the Sabbath and holi-
days, according to the Ashkenazic rite, the reading is תתגדל
ותתקדש... לדור ודור ולנצח נצחים (*SPB*, 199). At the conclusion of the
Qedushah of the *Musaf* service for the New Year and Day of
Atonement: כי מקדישיך כערכך (בקדשתך or קדשת, נאה לקדוש פאר
מקדושים.[9] Finally, in an ancient version found in the *Qedushah* songs
of the Hekhalot literature, יתקדש שמך קדושתך יתגדל בגדולה לנצח
עד סוף כל הדורות כי גבורתך לנצחי נצחים.[10]

---

5   For the place of enthronement (המלכה) in the *Qedushah*, cf. my forthcoming
     study on the biblical and ancient Near Eastern background of the *Qedushah*.
6   *Seder Rav Amram Gaon* (ed. D.E. Goldschmidt; Jerusalem: Mosad Harav Kook,
     1971) 24.
7   J. Mann, "Genizah Fragments of the Palestinian Order of Service," *HUCA* 2
     (1925) 296.
8   Ibid., 335 n. 134. The Qumran text shows that קדוש קדושים is an epithet related to
     God.
9   Appearing as early as the poems of Yannai, see *Piyyuṭei Yannai* (ed. M. Zulai;
     Berlin: Schocken, 1938) 2.336. For a discussion on this passage and those
     accompanying it, see E.D. Goldschmidt, מחזור לימים הנוראים, vol. I, *Rosh Hashanah*
     (Jerusalem: Koren, 1970) 43.
10   A. Altmann, שירי קדושה בספרות ההיכלות הקדומה, *Melilah* 2 (1946) 23 (58a, lines
     16ff.). The *Qedushah* occurs very often in *Hekhalot* literature, cf. P. Schäfer, ed.,
     Synopse zur Hekhalot-Literatur (Tübingen: J.C.B. Mohr, 1981); see recently M. Bar-
     Ilan, קווי יסוד להתהוותה של הקדושה וגיבושה, *Daat* 2 (1980) 10-14.

All the components of the Qumran version— גדול וקדוש, לדור ודור, קדוש קדושים[11]—are thus present in the various forms of the benediction of *Qedushat Hashem* and in the *Qedushah* itself.

That גדול וקדוש was considered an essential element of the *Qedushat Hashem* benediction may be learned from the version of the *Amidah* found in a Cambridge Genizah fragment published by E. Fleischer,[12] which reads: נקדש את שמך... ויאמר והיה ה' למלך... צהלי ורני יושבת ציון כי **גדול** בקרבך קדוש ישראל... ברוך אתה ה' האל **הקדוש**. Since the publication of this version, E.S. Rosenthal has shown[13] that the passage in y. Ber. 1:5, 3d (=Ta°an. 2:3, 65c): "As for those who say צהלי ורני etc. (Isa 12:6), this is not considered a 'verse-benediction,'" deals with the recitation of a verse of Scripture as part of the benediction of *Qedushat Hashem* like the custom reflected in the Genizah passage. We may conclude, therefore, that the formula גדול וקדוש, "Great and Holy," was an accepted portion of the benediction of *Qedushah* in the period of the Palestinian Talmud.

Recently, N. Wieder has pointed out[14] that the same verse, צהלי ורני... (Isa 12:6), appears in the description of the *Amidah* in a Genizah fragment from the Adler collection after לדור ודור. Wieder thus demonstrates a connection between the formula גדול וקדוש and לדור ודור, and the verse צהלי ורני which contains the words "Great and Holy." Now it becomes evident that גדול וקדוש was recited together with לדור ודור already in the Qumran liturgy.

Alongside גדול וקדוש in the *Qedushah* benediction we find also קדוש ונורא, "holy and awesome:" קדוש אתה ונורא שמך.[15] The triplet גדול, נורא, קדוש is attested, in fact, in the liturgy of the Bible itself. In the enthronement psalm (Psalm 99), in which a triple "*Qedushah*," in the form of three separate refrains echoes

11 קדוש קדושים is congruent in meaning and construction with אדיר אדירנו which is found in the *Musaf Qedushah* on the festivals and High Holy Days (see Elbogen, 66, 521). The pleonastic type of the construct state of two nouns of the same root encountered in קדוש קדושים and אדיר אדירנו is especially prevalent in later literature; cf. Y. Avishur, *The Construct State of Synonyms in Biblical Rhetoric* (Jerusalem: Kiryat Sefer, 1977) (Hebrew), 83, 175 (for קדוש קדושים see the reference there to פיוטי ינאי).

12 E. Fleischer, "לנוסחה הקדום של קדושת העמידה," *Sinai* 63 (1968) 240-41.

13 E.S. Rosenthal, "Two Comments," *Tarbiz* 41 (1972) 450 (Hebrew).

14 N. Wieder, "On an Obscure Passage in the Palestinian Talmud," *Tarbiz* 43 (1974) 46-52 (Hebrew). On צהלי ורני in the *Qedushah* of the Karaites, see Bar-Ilan (above, n. 10) 15-16.

15 *Sifre Deut.* 343 (ed. Finkelstein, 395), cf. *Pirqe de-Rabbi Eliezer* 31 and the Genizah versions: J. Mann, "Genizah Fragments of the Palestinian Order of Service;" *HUCA* 2 (1925) 269-338; S. Schechter, 'Genizah Speciments,' *JQR* 10 (1898) 656-59; Asaf, *Sefer Dinaburg*, 117.

throughout (vv. 3, 5, 9), we read: שמך גדול ונורא קדוש הוא 16יודו, "Let them praise Your name, Great and Awesome One! Holy is He!." The formula גדול וקדוש, then, existed alongside that of קדוש ונורא found in the Sifre,[17] and it was the former which became normative in the Qumran service and has remained so ever since.

The combination of גדול, קדוש and נורא appears again in the formal responsive prayer chanted prior to the reading of the Torah (*SPB*, 216). As part of this prayer it is customary to recite the *Shema* followed by the verses beginning רוממו ה' אלהינו from Psalm 99 (vv. 5, 9) just quoted. It thus appears that the refrains of this psalm, יודו שמך and the two רוממו verses, provide a basis for a liturgy, combining *Shema* with *Qedushah*.[18]

The verse with which the "Hymn to the Creator" opens thus constitutes a formula of the *Qedushah* type and shows that the *Qedushah* rite was already existent in the Second Temple period.[19]

B.

לפניו הדר ילך ואחריו המון מים רבים, "Majesty precedes Him and following Him is the rush of many waters." Such imagery is known to us from the various biblical descriptions of theophanies. "Glory and splendor" (הוד/הדר) precede God in Ps 96:6, while the sound of "many waters" accompanying His appearance is well known from the description of the heavenly chariot in Ezek 1:24 and especially 43:2. The latter verse describes the Glory (כבוד) of God coming from the East while its sound is like the sound of "many waters," and the earth shone with His glory: והנה כבוד אלהי ישראל בא מדרך הקדים וקולו כקול מים רבים והארץ האירה מכבדו. This is similar to what we find in the hymn discussed here. In this hymn as well the coming Glory (הדר)[20] is accompanied by the rush of "many waters"[21] and following its appearance comes the light (lines 11-12). Moreover, like the

---

16   Taking יודו as jussive, as vv. 5 and 9 are imperative.

17   For a combination of both formulae cf. המלך הגדול והגבור והנורא קדוש הוא in the *Yoṣer Qedushah* (SPB, 46).

18   On the combination of the *Shema* unit with the *Qedushah* see my forthcoming study on the ancient Near Eastern background of the *Qedushah*. (For the time being, cf. S.N. Kramer, M. Weinfeld, הספרות השומרית וספר תהילים-מבוא למחקר השואתי, *Beth Mikra* 57 [1974] 138-9).

19   Therefore, the origin of גדול וקדוש in 11QPs[a] is not to be sought in linguistic association with Pss. 149-150, as proposed by P.W. Skehan, "A Liturgical Complex in 11QPs[a]," *CBQ* 35 (1973) 203.

20   הדר is synonymous with כבוד and constitutes an identical concept; see my article כבוד in *ThWAT* (ed. H. Ringgren, G.S. Botterweck; Stuttgart: W. Kuhlhammer, 1982), vol. IV, cols. 25-27.

21   המון מים in Jer 10:13, 51:16 and מים רבים in Jer 51:13 are associated with rain and, therefore, are irrelevant for the context of vv. 2-3 of the hymn where theophany and God's throne occur (contra Sanders in his edition and Skehan, 204).

theophany of Ezekiel, which revolves around the throne and chariot (chapters 1, 10), so also here we find next to the "many waters," the throne (מכון כסאו) and its attributes (vv 3). The image of God's throne upon the waters[22] which occurs in Rev 4:6 and b. Ḥag. 12b-13a indeed belongs to the *Merkabah* tradition, incipient in the book of Ezekiel,[23] and may be traced back to more ancient times.[24] Moreover, the "many waters" in Ezekiel come to illustrate the rush and sound of angels' wings (1:24; 10:5), and it seems that in our hymn also the rush of the "many waters" in v 2 already anticipates the angels of v 5. According to the Targum of Ezek 43:2 "the sound of many waters" actually constitutes the angels' praise: "the voice of those blessing his name" (קל מברכי שמיה). This view is already found in 1:24 where כקול מים רבים is explained by the Targum as the sound of angels praising the Lord and קול המולה כקול מחנה is interpreted as the voice of the camp of heavenly angels (כקול משרית מלאכי מרומא). An identical explanation is given by the Targum for the קול רעש גדול in Ezek 3:12.[25] The same conception lies behind the LXX translation of Ezek 43:2. וקולו כקול מים רבים is rendered καὶ φωνὴ τῆς παρεμβολῆς, ὡς φωνὴ διπλασιαζόντων πολλῶν, "and the sound of *the camp* like the sound of many redoubling (their shouts)." The *camp* which is added here is based on Ezek 1:24 whereas the *redoubling* draws upon the tradition that the angels continually praise the Lord (cf. Rev 4:8).[26] The notion that the wings of the angels are, as it were, their instruments for singing is reflected in the "Angelic Liturgy" of Qumran: והמון רנה ברום

---

22 "The sound of many waters," שאון מים רבים in Isa 17:12-13 is paralleled there by the sound of the roaring seas, כהמות ימים, and according to the *Merkabah* traditions God's throne is upon the sea. Cf., e.g., the Moslem tradition of Ibn Ṣayyād taken from the *Merkabah* literature: "I see a throne upon the sea (var. upon the water) and around it *al-Ḥayyat*." For the latter see D. J. Halperin, "Ibn Ṣayyād Traditions and the Legend of al-Dajjal," *JAOS* 96 (1976) 217.

23 This view is correctly illustrated by D.J. Halperin, "The Exegetical Character of Ezek. X 9-17," *VT* 26 (1976) 129-41.

24 For the biblical roots of this idea, see my article "Divine Intervention in War in Ancient Israel and in the Ancient Near East," *History, Historiography and Interpretation,* (eds. H. Tadmor and M. Weinfeld; Jerusalem: Magnes Press, 1983) 121-47.

25 ...קל זיע סני דמשבחין ואמרין בריך יקרא..., "a great roaring sound of those who praise and say 'Blessed'...."

26 Cf. Apost. Constit. VIII xii 27: "ten thousand times ten thousand of angels *incessantly...* say: 'Holy, Holy, Holy'..." (see above, n. 3). For Rabbinic parallels and for an analysis of the LXX version of Ezek 43:2 see D.J. Halperin, "Merkabah Midrash in the Septuagint," *JBL* 101 (1982) 351-63. According to Halperin, this concept goes back to Ps 68:18 where שנאן is derived from שנה, "repeat." Ps 68:18 is incorporated in the *Qedushah* passage of Apost. Constit. VII xxxv 3 and in the Genizah (see n. 3).

כנפיהם, "and there is a roar of singing as they lift their wings."[27] The same conception prevails in the rabbinic sources (b. Ḥag. 13b; *Gen. Rab.* 65:21 [ed. Theodor-Albeck, 737-40] and parallels). It should be remembered that in Isa 6:4 we find that the doorposts shook from the sound of the praising angels: וינעו אמות הספים מקול הקורא. It is therefore not impossible that the above interpretation in Ezekiel reflects a kernel of authentic interpretation.

That the "sound of the many waters" has been associated with the *Yoṣer* liturgy may be learned from a Genizah fragment of the *Yoṣer* benediction. Here we read: בא מדרך הקדים וקולו כקול מים רבים והארץ האירה מכבודו, קומי אורי כי בא אורך וכבוד ה' עליך זרח בא"י יוצר המאורות, "He comes from the way of the East, and His sound is like the sound of many waters; the earth shines from His Glory. Arise, shine, for your light has come and the Glory of the Lord has shone upon you. Blessed are You... Creator of·the luminaries."[28] This passage is a combination of two verses, one taken from the theophany in Ezek 43:2 and the other taken from Isa 60:1. As has been argued by S. Lieberman (see below), the latter seems to correspond to the morning prayer of the Essenes as described by Josephus (War 2.128). As will be shown below, the Isaianic verse incorporated in the *Yoṣer* benediction reflects the eschatological concept implied in the praise of the renewal of the luminaries which is prevalent in the sectarian literature.

C.

חסד ואמת סביב פניו, אמת[29] ומשפט וצדק מכון כסאו, "Grace and truth surround His presence, truth and justice and righteousness are the foundation of His throne." As has been indicated, the throne of God is part of the theophany presented here, and the theme of the throne is indeed prominent in the various *Yoṣer* hymns. Thus we find in the famous *El Adon* hymn[30] (*SPB*, 187-8) a glorious description of the Lord's chariot,[31] and, as in the Qumran hymn, it is associated there with grace, justice and uprightness:

---

27   C. Newsom, *Songs of the Sabbath Sacrifice—A Critical Edition* (Atlanta, GA: Scholars Press, 1985) 315.
28   Cf. Mann, 292.
29   אמת in this hemistich seems to be redundant; cf. Skehan, 203 n. 26.
30   On the early date of this poem see E. Fleischer, "The Diffusion of the Qedushah of the Amida and the Yoṣer in the Palestinian Jewish Ritual," *Tarbiz* 38 (1969) 270 (Hebrew).
31   המתגאה על חיות הקדש ונהדר בכבוד על המרכבה, "Who rises high on the holy Chayoth, majestic in glory on the chariot." The throne occurs also in another *Yoṣer* hymn of the Sabbath liturgy, לאל אשר שבת, where we read: ביום השביעי נתעלה וישב על כסא כבודו, "on the seventh day He exalted himself and sat upon the throne of His glory" (*SPB*, 188).

El Adon

חסד ורחמים (מלא) כבודו

זכות32 ומישור לפני כסאו

Grace and compassion are
 before His Glory
Justice and uprightness (are)
 before His throne[33]

11QPs[a]

חסד ואמת סביב פניו

(אמת) ומשפט וצדק מכון כסאו

Grace and truth
 surround His presence
(Truth) and justice
 and righteousness (are)
 the base of His throne

This theme has its origin in Ps 89:15,[34] "Righteousness and justice are the base of Your throne, grace and truth stand before You," צדק ומשפט מכון כסאך חסד ואמת יקדמו פניך. The hymnic part of this psalm, which preserves an ancient angelic liturgy,[35] shows affinities to the *Yoṣer Qedushah* pattern in other respects as well. Thus we find there at the beginning a section (vv. 1-5) which revolves around the formula לדור ודור (vv. 1, 5), found in line 1 of the Qumran hymn and discussed above in connection with the benediction of *Qedushat Hashem*. Then comes the praise of the angels (vv. 6-9) followed by the creation theme (vv. 10-15) in which the throne associated with grace, truth and justice appears (vv. 15). The next verse speaks about the "light" of God's presence, אור פניך (vv. 16). Now the question is: what is the meaning of the grace in the cosmic angelic context found here?

COSMIC RENEWAL AS GRACE, TRUTH, RIGHTEOUSNESS AND COMPASSION

A characteristic feature of the hymns and prayers of the *Yoṣer* liturgy is the various expressions of benevolence, grace and truth which occur so often there:

---

32   צדק has been transformed into זכות as a result of the late Hebrew use of זכות. Cf., for example, Gen 15:6: ויחשבה לו צדקה, Targums: וחשבה לה לזכו (Onkelos and Pseudo-Jon.); 2 Sam 19:29: ומה יש לי עוד צדקה, Targum: ומה אית לי עוד זכו. The well-known Mishnah in Mak. 3:15 so interprets Isa 42:21: רבי חנניא בן עקשיא אומר רצה הקדוש ברוך הוא לזכות את ישראל לפיכך הרבה להם תורה ומצוות שנאמר ה' חפץ למען צדקו יגדיל תורה ויאדיר. צדקה in the quoted verse served as the basis for the idea of זכות. I owe this last observation to Dr. Baruch Schwartz.

33   Similar descriptions are found in the Hebrew book of Enoch, H. Odeberg, 3 *Enoch* (Cambridge: Cambridge University Press, 1928) ch. xxxi, 106 (Hebrew, 48), and in various midrashim; cf., for example, אותיות דרבי עקיבא in II [ed. A. Wertheimer, Jerusalem: Mosad HaRav Kook, 1952] 343.

34   The expression in 11QPs[a] "surrounding his presence," סביב פניו, recalls also Ps 89: 8, 9: סביבותיך, סביבו.

35   See my forthcoming study mentioned in n. 5.

1) המאיר לארץ ולדרים עליה **ברחמים**[36] **ובטובו** מחדש בכל יום (תמיד) מעשה בראשית, "He Who brings light to the earth and to them that dwell upon it with *compassion*, and in His *goodness* renews each day (always) the work of creation" (*SPB*, 45).

2) הכין ופעל זהרי חמה **טוב** יצר כבוד לשמו, "He has established and made the rays of the sun and thus has formed *goodness*, glory to His name" (*SPB*, ibid., the hymn of אל ברוך).

3) ומאיר לעולם כולו וליושביו שברא **במדת הרחמים**, "Who brings light to the whole universe and its inhabitants whom He has created with *the measure of compassion*" (*SPB*, 187, the poem הכל יודוך).

4) גדלו וטובו מלא עולם... **זכות ומישור** לפני כסאו **חסד ורחמים** לפני כבודו. **טובים** מאורות שברא אלהינו, "His greatness and *goodness* fill the universe.... *Justice and uprightness* are before His throne, *grace and compassion* are before His glory. *Good* are the luminaries which our God created..." (*El Adon* Hymn, *SPB*, 187-8).

5) דרש הכין והתקין חמתו... פועלי **צדקו** קרובי **רחמיו** שיר תשבחות שוררו למלכם, "He sought, established and made the radiance of His sun.... Those who perform His *righteousness*, those who are close to His *mercy*, sang a song of praise to their king" (אשר ברוב חכמה of the Genizah, see below).

6) אשר במאמרו ברא שחקים וברוח פיו כל צבאם, חוק וזמן נתן להם שלא ישנו את **תפקידם**... פועל **אמת** שפעלתו **אמת**, "Who created the heavens by His command and all their hosts by the breath of His mouth; He has given them fixed statute and season so that they should not alter their task..., the One who performs *truth*, Whose work is *true*" (benediction over the New Moon, *SPB*, 437).

In a Qumran passage to be cited below, in which God's knowledge (דעת) is associated with the luminaries, the divine attributes of justice, צדק, and mercy, רחמים, are also mentioned (1QS 10:11-12): "I shall call God 'my righteousness' (צדקי) and the Most High 'establisher of my goodness' (מכין טובי), 'fountain of knowledge'

---

36   Compare in the Eucharistic prayer of Addai and Mari: "Who created the world and its inhabitants in His lovingkindness." This prayer is considered "the most ancient Christian eucharistic composition to which we can have access today" (L. Bouyer, *Eucharist, Theology and Spirituality of the Eucharistic Prayer* [Notre Dame: University of Notre Dame Press, 1966] 147). According to G. Dix (*The Shape of the Liturgy* [London: 1945] 186) it is to be dated to later second or early third century. Cf. also J. Vellian, "The Anaphoral Structure of Addai and Mari compared to the Berakoth Preceding the Shema in the Synagogue Morning Service," *Le Museon* 85 (1972) 201-223. (This article refers constantly to the Second benediction before Shema as "ahuba," but it should be called "ahabah").

(מקור דעת)."[37] The *goodness* and *grace* of the Lord in all these passages may be explained in the following manner. The rising of the sun is due to the gracious force of the Creator: המחדש בטובו בכל יום מעשה בראשית (תמיד), "Who renews *through his goodness* the creation every day continually (*Yoṣer* liturgy, *SPB*, 45, 46; cf. b. Ḥag 12b). This notion is in fact expressed in the continuation of the Qumran hymn discussed here: "He clothes the mountains with produce, *good food for every living creature*," מעטר הרים תנובות אוכל טוב לכול חי (line 6). With the rise of the dawn everything is, as it were, newly created. Angels as well as men praise God for the renewal of creation and especially for the regeneration of the luminaries (cf. the benediction יוצר המאורות). חסד and אמת / אמונה in this context express the benevolent, constant creation of God as found in *Gen. Rab.* 78:1 (ed. Theodor-Albeck, 915): "It is written (Lam 3:23) 'They are new every morning, great is Your truth' (lit. 'steadfastness = אמונתך'),"[38] חדשים לבקרים רבה אמונתך. Because You renew us every morning, we know that great is Your truth to redeem us/ to revive our dead.[39] The juxtaposition of awakening in the morning with awakening in the afterlife is likewise expressed in the אלוהי נשמה prayer and in the hymns of the Qumran Hodayot.[40]

Regeneration of the lights in the morning, described as the "eternal grace" of the Lord, is found in the song about changing seasons in 1QS 10:1-4:

> When the luminaries shine forth from the holy height...when they are being renewed (בהתחדשם)... a sign... for eternal grace (חסדי עולם; lines 3-4).

---

37 For דעת and צדק associated with the heavenly bodies, cf. 1QM 17:8: ושמח צדק במרומים וכול בני אמתו יגילו בדעת עולמים, and see Y. Yadin, *The Scroll of the War of the Sons of Light against the Sons of Darkness* (Jerusalem: Mosad Bialik, 1955) (Hebrew) 259, n. 8.

38 The preceding verse speaks about God's uninterrupted grace and compassion: חסדי ה' כי לא תמנו כי לא כלו רחמיו, which is echoed in the *Modim* benediction of the *Shemoneh Esreh*, the main topic of which is thanks to God for His wondrous deeds every day. There we read: הטוב כי לא כלו רחמיך והמרחם כי לא תמו חסדיך, "You are the Benificent One for Your compassion has never ceased, You are the Compassionate One for Your grace/kindness has never ended" (*SPB*, 63).

39 Cf. the parallels in *Lam. Rab.* and *Midrash Tehillim* for which see Theodor-Albeck, *Gen. Rab.* 915-16. Compare also the prayer מודה אני recited upon waking from sleep: "I thank You... Who restored my soul within me mercifully, great is Your steadfastness." For the history of this prayer cf. A. Berliner, *Randbemerkungen zum täglichen Gebetbuch* (Berlin: M. Poppelauer, 1909) 31.

40 Cf. my article, "The Morning Prayer in Qumran and in the Conventional Jewish Liturgy," *RQ* 13 (*Memorial J. Carmignac;* 1988) 81-94.

Renewal of creation linked to the praise of the angels, as in the *Yoṣer* prayer, is actually found in the Hodayot Scroll (1QH 11:3-14):

> I thank you my God, that you have dealt wondrously with dust[41] to raise from the dust of the worms of the dead (להרים מעפר תולעת מתים) to the everlasting foundation (לסוד עולם)... to stand in Your presence together with the eternal hosts... to be renewed together with the whole creation (ולהתחדש עם כל נהיה)[42]

"Raising from the dust of the worms of the dead" in this context is to be associated with the idea of revival from death in the morning.[43] The "renewal" here is the renovation of creation every morning when men and angels unite together to praise the Lord, a union which has eschatological overtones, as indicated above.

The rebirth of the luminaries associated with the idea of "truth" and combined with eschatological revival is clearly expressed in a Jewish prayer to be said at the appearance of the new moon: [44]

> Blessed be You, O God... Who created the heavens... (and) all their host. He assigned to them order and season.... They are glad and rejoice to do the will of their Master (רצון קונם ששים ושמחים לעשות),[45] the Worker of truth Whose work is true (שפעולתו אמת פועל אמת);[46] He commanded the moon to renew itself (שתתחדש) as a crown of glory to those carried from the womb (לעמוסי בטן) who likewise are destined to renew themselves and to glorify their Creator.[47]

---

41   For this idea in the morning prayers of the cited Qumran sect as well as those of the conventional Jewish prayers, see my article in the Carmignac Memorial (above, n. 39).

42   For נהיה, cf. 1QS 3:15: כל הויה ונהיה which means "whatever exists," i.e. the whole universe. See J. Licht, מגילת הסרכים (Jerusalem: Mosad Bialik, 1965) 90 and the references there.

43   See my article (above n. 40).

44   Quoted in b. San. 42a and *Soferim* 19:10 (ed. M. Higger, *Massechet Sopherim* [New York: Deve Rabbanan, 1937] 337-8); cf. *SPB*, 437.

45   For such phrases in the *Qedushah* liturgy compare the *El Adon* hymn (*SPB*, 188): שמחים בצאתם ושבים בבואם באימה רצה קונם, "They (the luminaries) rejoice in their going forth and are glad in their returning, they perform with awe the will of their master." For the heavenly host performing the will of its master, cf. in the *Yoṣer* liturgy (*SPB*, 45): "and all of them in awe and fear do the will of their master," וכלם עשים באימה וביראה רצון קונם. Cf. Slavonic Enoch 6:4: "The heavenly host... stand before God and perform His will."

46   An alternative formula: פועלי אמת שפעולתם אמת, ascribes the work to the luminaries themselves. A variant in a Schechter manuscript reads: פעלו צדק ואמונה. See Higger, *Massechet Sopherim*, 338, n. 76.

47   In *Maḥzor Vitry* (ed. S. Hurvitz: Nürenberg, 1889, sec. ed. 1923) 183: להתחדש ולפאר יוצרם כמותם, "to renew themselves and to glorify their Creator *like them*" (i.e., like the luminaries).

The "work of truth" here has been rightly understood by Rashi on San. 42a: שאינם משנים את סדרם, "that they do not change their course." That concept is actually expressed in the prayer itself: שלא ישנו את תפקידם, "that they should not change their task," to which compare Ben Sira 39:31: בצותו אותם ישישו ובחקם לא ימרו פיו, "they are glad to (carry out) his order and they do not disobey the laws."[48]

The notion of eschatological renewal is here clearly expressed and it is quite possible that this idea, which was originally linked to the sun and associated with the *Yoṣer* liturgy, was shifted to the moon and the moon blessing because of opposition to Essene practice.[49] In fact, the original tradition in which an eschatological motif was appended to the morning liturgy may be discerned in the concluding section of the *Yoṣer* benediction. As indicated above, S. Lieberman[50] has observed that the Genizah fragment of the *Yoṣer* benediction which reads: קומי אורי כי בא אורך וכבוד ה' עליך זרח, בא"י יוצר המאורות, "Arise, shine, for your light has come and the glory of the Lord has shone upon you. Blessed are You, O Lord, Who created the luminaries,"[51] seems to reflect a liturgical custom similar to that of the Essenes.[52] We may add that in light of what has been said before about the eschatological aspect of the renewal of the luminaries in the Qumran writings, Lieberman's view gains strength, especially since the verse quoted in the Genizah fragment is taken from an explicitly eschatological chapter (Isa 60). This tradition has indeed penetrated the prevalent *Yoṣer* liturgy which contains at the end a clear eschatological address: אור חדש על ציון תאיר ונזכה כלנו במהרה לאורו, "Cause a new light to shine on Zion, so that we may all soon have a share in its light."[53] In spite of the

---

48 Cf. also 1 Enoch 2:1-3 and *Sifre* Deut. 306 (ed. Finkelstein, 332); see recently the discussion of M. Kister, "Metamorphoses of Aggadic Traditions" *Tarbiz* 60 (1991) 196-7 (Hebrew).

49 Josephus, War 2.128.

50 S. Lieberman, "Light on the Cave Scrolls from Rabbinic Sources," PAAJR 20 (1951) 398-9.

51 Mann, 292. This comes after the verse וקולו כקול מים רבים והארץ האירה מכבדו which is reflected in the Qumran hymn under study (see above). It is therefore not impossible that behind the Genizah fragment lies a liturgical tradition consisting of elements similar to those of the Qumran hymn.

52 According to Lieberman the קומי אורי..., said at dawn, could have been taken by Josephus as a real invocation of the sun, "as if entreating it to rise" (ὥσπερ ἱκετεύοντες ἀνατεῖλαι).

53 In some of the Genizah fragments the phrase נר משיחך תאיר לנו is appended to the אור חדש formula; cf. Elbogen, 15. For other forms of this formula see E. Fleischer, *The Yoṣer, Its Emergence and Development* (Jerusalem: Magnes Press 1984) 35-36 (Hebrew).

objections raised to the inclusion of this formula,[54] it could not be eliminated, apparently because of its strong roots.

In addition to this prayer for "new light" we find at the end of the *Yoṣer* benediction other formulae found in the Qumran liturgies associated with the luminaries. After המחדש בטובו בכל יום תמיד מעשה בראשית, and before the prayer אור חדש, we find the verse לעושה אורים גדולים כי לעולם חסדו (Ps 136:7). This verse actually stands behind the liturgical passage quoted above from the Manual of Discipline: בהתחדשם... גדול לקודש קודשים ואות למפתח חסדי עולם. The Qumran exegetes interpreted כי לעולם חסדו of Ps 136:7 in an eschatological sense, as did the composer of the *Yoṣer* liturgy who attached the אור חדש to the verse לעושה אורים גדולים כי לעולם חסדו.[55]

The notion of the creation of new luminaries in the eschaton was prevalent in the sectarian literature. Thus we read in the book of Jubilees that when God builds the new Temple in Zion,[56] *"all the luminaries will be renewed* for the salvation, peace and blessing of all the chosen of Israel" (1:29). Similarly, in 1 Enoch 91:16 we find that the heavens will change, a new firmament will appear, and *the host of the heavens will shine sevenfold.*

The renovation of the luminaries in the recreated world is attested also in rabbinic literature.[57] It occurs likewise in the blessing said at the appearance of the new moon quoted above. As in Jub. 1:29, where it says that the luminaries will be renewed for the salvation of the chosen of Israel, so we find here that the moon will be renewed as a crown of glory for those who have been carried from the womb (= the chosen ones): שתתחדש עטרת תפארת לעמוסי בטן (*SPB*, 437). By the same token the *perfect light* (אור תום) mentioned in 1QH 18:29 (cf. 4:6) alludes to the *light* reserved for the righteous and the chosen in the future life (1 Enoch 58) and to the light of the seven days (אור שבעת הימים) known from rabbinic literature.[58]

The joy (שמחה) and gladness (ששון) of the luminaries while fulfilling their function, found in the *El Adon* prayer (שמחים בצאתם ושישים בבואם) quoted above, as well as in the blessing said at the appearance of the new moon (ששים ושמחים לעשות רצון קונם), is also reflected in Qumran literature. In 1QM 17:8 we read that the archangel Michael will be sent to help the holy warriors with eternal light (באור עולמים) to illuminate *with joy* the house of Israel for peace and blessing to those of the divine lot (שלום וברכה לגורל

---

54   It was especially Saadiah Gaon who fought against the inclusion of the formula, see Elbogen, ibid., 15.
55   Cf. Elbogen, ibid.
56   Ibid., 15-16.
57   Cf. L. Ginzberg, *The Legends of the Jews* (Philadelphia: JPS, 1967) 1.23-24.
58   Ginzberg, ibid.

(אל),[59] and that צדק will rejoice in heaven (ושמח צדק במרומים), which undoubtedly refers to the luminary which represents justice (compare שמש צדקה in Mal 3:20).[60] Joy caused by the luminaries is clearly expressed in the phrase which concludes the *Yoṣer* liturgy (Sephardic version): והתקין מאורות משמח עולמו אשר ברא, "and He established luminaries to gladden the world that He created."[61]

D.

Creation of the luminaries through knowledge (דעת), followed by the song of the angels, is a characteristic feature of the *Yoṣer* liturgies:

11QPs^a	El Barukh (*SPB*, 45)

מבדיל אור מאפלה[62]

שחר הכין בדעת לבו

אז ראו כל מלאכיו וירננו

אל ברוך גדול דעה[63]

הכין ופעל זהרי חמה...

מאורות נתן סביבות עזו

פנות צבאיו קדושים...

מספרים כבוד אל וקדושתו

Separating light from darkness
by the knowledge of His mind
He established the dawn
When all *His angels* had
witnessed it, they *sang aloud*

Blessed God, great in *knowledge*
He established and made *the rays
of the sun*...
He set luminaries round His glory
The chiefs of His host, *the holy
ones*...
They *recount the Glory* of God
and His holiness

El Adon (*SPB*, 188)	Genizah[64]

טובים[65] מאורות...

אשר ברוב חכמה גדולה

---

59 Cf. Jub. 1:29 quoted above: "the luminaries will be renewed for salvation, peace and blessing for all the chosen of Israel."

60 For the identification of the light with צדק cf. 1 Enoch 58:4 concerning the righteous in the world to come: "they will look for light and will find justice."

61 Cf. Elbogen, 15.

62 This formula recalls אור עולם באוצר חיים אורות מאפל אמר ויהי which opens the *Yoṣer* benediction in today's rite on the high holy days only, but which, according to the Palestinian tradition, is to be recited daily; see Mann, 295.

63 The acrostic here matches that of the *El Adon*: ברוך ומברך=ברוך; אל אדון=אל; דעת ותבונה=דעה; גדלו וטובו=גדול. See Z. Jawitz, *Mekor Haberakhot* (=*Die Liturgie des Siddur und ihre Entwicklung* [Berlin: 1910] 53).

64 The acrostic for *ṭet* and *yod* matchs in *El Baruch*: טוב, יצר (*SPB*, 45)

65 Mann, 323; I. Levi, "Fragments de rituels de prières provenant de la guéniza du Caire," *REJ* 53 (1907) 241.

יצרם בדעת בבינה ובהשכל...
פאר וכבוד נותנים לשמו...
שבח נותנים לו כל צבא מרום...

דרש הכין והתקין זיו חמתו, פועלי צדקו
קרובי רחמיו שיר ותשבחות שוררו למלכם

Good are the luminaries...	the One Who with great wisdom
He has formed them with	has explored, *established* and
knowledge, understanding and	made the *radiance of His* sun,
insight...	those who perform His
they give glory and honor to	righteousness
His name...	*those close to His mercy sang*
all the hosts of heaven give	to their King songs and
Him praise...	praises

The idea of the creation of light and the luminaries through knowledge is frequently attested in the writings of Qumran,[66] especially those which speak explicitly of the changing of times and seasons. Thus in 1QH 12:4ff. we find the following section of a prayer on the changing of the seasons:

At the departure of the	למוצא לילה ומבוא יום
night and the coming of the	תמיד בכל מולדי עת
day, unceasingly, at the birth	יסודי קץ ותקופת צועדים
in time of all the established...	
through the course of the seasons	
in their order appointed by their signs,	בתכונם באותותם
for the whole of their rule...	לכל ממשלתם...
for the God of knowledge has established it.[67]	אל הדעות הכינה

In a prayer from the Manual of Discipline,[68] which represents a similar liturgical tradition,[69] we encounter, immediately after a list of the changes of time—day and night, seasons of the year, Sabbatical and Jubilee years—the words אזמרה בדעת, "I will sing of knowledge,"[70] followed later by references to the recitation of the

---

66   On the concept of דעת in the writings of the sect, see W.D. Davies, "Knowledge in the Dead Sea Scrolls and Matthew 11:25-30," *HTR* 46 (1953) 113-140;. J. Licht, מגילת ההודיות (Jerusalem: Mosad Bialik, 1957) 42-43; H.W. Kuhn, *Enderwartung und gegenwärtiges Heil* (Göttingen: Vandenhoeck & Ruprecht, 1966) 139ff.

67   For translation see S. Holm-Nielsen, *Hodayot, Psalms from Qumran* (Universitetsforlaget Aarhus, 1960) *ad loc.*

68   1QS 10:9-14.

69   See S. Talmon, "The 'Manual of Benedictions' of the Sect of the Judean Desert," *RQ* 2 (1960) 475ff; cf. Licht's discussion in his מגילת הסרכים, (Jerusalem: Mosad Bialik, 1965) 204-8.

70   אזמרה בדעת וכול נגינתי לכבוד אל (1:9). The subject here is *divine* knowledge; see Licht in his commentary, *ad loc.*

morning and evening prayers: עם מבוא יום ולילה אבואה בברית ועם מוצא
ערב ובקר אמר חקיו. בראשית משלח ידי ורגלי אברך שמו, בראשית צאת ובוא לשבת
ורקום, עם משכב יצועי ארננה לו, "With the coming of day and night I
shall enter God's covenant[71] and when evening and morning appear
I shall recite His laws.[72] When I begin to send forth my hands and
my feet I will bless His name; at the beginning of my going and
coming when I sit down or rise, when I lie down on my bed I will sing
unto him."[73] In another passage from the War Scroll (10:15-16) we
read: מועדי קודש ותקופות שנים וקצי עד... אלה ידענו מבינתכה, "holy
festivals, seasons of the years and endless epochs... *these we have
come to know from Your wisdom.*" This last phrase appears again in
1QH 1:21: אלה ידעתי מבינתכה. In the same hymn we find the words
(line 11): מאורות לרזיהם כוכבים לנתיבותם, "luminaries by their
mysteries, stars in their courses," and in the concluding passage
dealing with the establishment of seasons and epochs *through
God's knowledge* (lines 18-19): למספר דורות עולם ולכל שני נצח... ובחכמת
דעתכה הכינותה תעודתם. אלה ידעתי מבינתכה. "To numerous generations and
eternal years... by Your skillful knowledge You did establish their
function.... *These I have come to know from Your wisdom.*"

Since in the writings of the sect the struggle between good and
evil is compared to the war of light and darkness, it is no wonder
that the expression "God of knowledge," אל הדעות, appears in
connection with the separation of truth from falsehood: מאל הדעות
כל הויה ונהייה ולפני היותם הכין כול מחשבתם. וישם לו שתי רוחות... האמת והעול.
במעין אור תולדות האמת וממקור חושך תולדות העול,[74] "From the God of
knowledge exists all that is and will be; before they came into being
He established their entire design... And He Made for Himself two
spirits... truth and perverseness. From a spring of light come the
generations of truth, but from a fountain of darkness come the
generations of perverseness."

Especially telling is the fact that in most of these passages
which speak of the creation of the luminaries through knowledge,

---

71   In this context, entering into the covenant refers to reciting the daily *Shema*
      which is associated with the *Qedushah*. On the *Shema* and its connection with
      the covenant see my article, "Prayer and Liturgical Practice in the Qumran
      Sect," *The Dead Sea Scrolls, Forty Years of Research* (ed. D. Dimant and U.
      Rappaport; Jerusalem: Yad Ben Zvi and Magnes, Leiden: E.J. Brill, 1992) 242-43.
72   Cf. בשכבו ובקומנו נשיח בחוקיך in the Evening Prayer (*SPB*, 131): the reading is
      identical in the Genizah; see Mann, 307.
73   Cf. Talmon, "Manual of Benedictions," 475-500, on morning, afternoon, and
      evening prayers reflected in this passage and the parallel passage in the
      Hodayot scroll.
74   1QS 3:15-19.

the verb used is הכין,[75] "institute, establish." In 11QPs^a: שחר הכין בדעת לבו; Hodayot 13:10: כי אתה הכינותמה; the poem El Barukh: גדול דעה הכין; the Genizah Hymn: אשר ברוב חכמה הכין והתקין זיו חמתו. Significantly, the use of הכין in connection with the heavenly bodies appears in Ps 74:16: אתה הכינות מאור ושמש, though there is no mention of wisdom or knowledge.

The image of God as ordering seasons and separating light from darkness through wisdom and knowledge is in fact incorporated in the Evening Service in the המעריב ערבים *benediction*: בחכמה פותח שערים ובתבונה משנה עתים ומחליף את הזמנים... ומבדיל בין יום ובין לילה, "*In wisdom* He opens the gates and *in understanding changes* the seasons... and distinguishes between day and night" (*SPB*, 130). This distinction between light and darkness linked to knowledge finds its clearest expression in the liturgy in the prayers אתה חוננתנו למדע תורתך and ותודיענו recited at the close of the Sabbath, the former when a weekday follows (*SPB*, 140), the latter when a festival commences (*SPB* 328).[76] Both these prayers begin with the theme of דעת and proceed to enumerate the distinctions between holy and profane, light and darkness, Sabbath and weekday. The rabbis, at least as far as the first of the two is concerned, prescribed its recitation as part of the Benediction of Knowledge, אתה חונן... דעת (m. Ber. 5:2).[77]

The ability to discern and to make distinctions, which originates in the possession of knowledge,[78] refers not only to the distinction

---

75 Cf. the LXX's addition to Solomon's prayer (1 Kgs 8:12) [vs. 53 in LXX]: ἥλιον ἐγνώρισεν ἐν οὐρανῷ, "He acknowledged the sun in the heavens." Scholars tend to assume that the translator misread (בשמים) הבין for הכין. If this were so, this would be another case of the use of הכין in a cosmological context. But הכין is never translated by γνωρίζειν and there is thus no place for assuming the reading הבין in this verse. On the contrary, the association of דעת with the creation of the luminaries is likely to increase the possibility that the reading שמש הודיע is original.

76 Called by the rabbis: מרגניתא בבבל, "the jewel (=precious prayer) of Babylonia, b. Ber. 33b.

77 The expression חנן דעת appears in 1QH 14:25: ואני עבדך חנותני ברוח דעת, which follows upon פשע פשע (line 24). In the preceding passage (14:8-22) we find מתן בינה (line 8) followed by הגשה and קרבה (lines 13-14), all of which recall the benediction triplet of: דעת, תשובה (repentance) and סליחה forgiveness which open the petitionary part of the *Shemoneh Esreh*. On דעת, קרבה and תשובה as a basic pattern in the Qumran prayers, see my article, "The Prayers for Knowledge, Repentance and Forgiveness in the 'Eighteen Benedictions'—Qumran Parallels, Biblical Antecedents, and Basic Characteristics," *Tarbiz* 48 (1979) 186-200 (Hebrew).

78 Cf. the rabbis' incisive statement, אם אין דעה הבדלה מנין, "Without knowledge, whence distinction?" y. Ber. 5:2 9b. The association of הבדלה with דעה is evident also in the Damascus Covenant: ולהבדיל בין הטמא לטהור ולהודיע בין הקדש לחול (6:17-18; 12:19-20). The influence of Ezek 22:26 is apparent, which in turn draws upon Lev 10:10-11; however, in the latter source the verb ידע does not appear in the parallelism.

between light and darkness, holy and profane, but also to the distinction between Israel and the gentiles, the clean and the unclean.[79] Such ideas bring us again to the Dead Sea sect, for whom such distinctions between light and darkness symbolized the difference between truth and falsehood, righteousness and evil.[80]

The concept of "distinction" in both the cosmic and the religious spheres is well known from the other religions of the first century CE. We read, for example, in the oath of allegiance of a Mystery[81] (first and third century CE papyri) that the oath is to be sworn by "the god who has separated heaven from earth, darkness from light, day from night, rising from setting of the luminaries, death from life, black from white, dry from wet, hot from cold, bitter from sweet, and body from soul."[82]

The luminaries, and the changes of time associated with them, originate in the highest, peculiarly divine knowledge. Thus, the Qumran liturgy dealt with here closes by saying: כי הראם את אשר לא ידעו, "for He showed them what they did not know;" the angels acquire the revelation of secret things by their closeness to God. Indeed, the very same sentence is found in 1QH 13:1-2 in which we find the idea of revealing רזי פלאים, "wondrous mysteries" (cf. 1:21), and the host of God's spirits and the assembly of His holy ones, צבא רוחיך ועדת קדושיך. At the end of the hymn we find the proclamation: יספרו כבודך בכל ממשלתך כי הראיתם אשר לא [ידעו], "Let them recount Your glory throughout Your dominion, for You did show them that which no other [flesh] had seen before."[83] The

---

79 Cf. b. Pes. 104a, as well as in the Genizah (Mann, 323); N. Wieder, "The Old Palestinian Ritual—New Sources," *JJS* 4 (1953) 30-37.

80 דעת is essentially the power enabling man to distinguish between good and evil, to identify the seasons and time periods. It thus has both cosmic and moral associations. On the relation of the concept of דעת to the Greek (γνῶσις) in Hellenistic religions, see my article "Loyalty Oaths in the Ancient Near East" *UF* 8 (1976) 408 n. 262. On דעת in the apocalyptic-visionary sense, cf. I. Gruenwald, "Knowledge and Vision," *Israel Oriental Studies* 3 (1973) 63-107.

81 See M.P. Nilsson, *Geschichte der griechischen Religion* (2nd edition; Munich: C.H. Beck, 1974) 2.695-6 for additional references and the Greek text.

82 Compare the הבדלות in b. Pes. 104a: (1) קדש וחול (2) אור וחושך (3) ישראל ועמים (4), מים עליונים ותחתונים (7) ים וחרבה (6) טמא וטהור (5) יום השביעי וששת ימי המעשה. These appear in the old Palestinian *Havdalah* (Mann, 323; Wieder, 36). It is interesting that while the Greek document enumerates ten distinctions, the rabbis limited the הבדלות to seven, apparently due to a tendency to make use of a typological number. For the religious significance of הבדלה, cf. the Nabatean text: פילען פרש לילא מימכא מן די ינפק יתהם לעלם, "and let the one who separates day from night curse forever those who will remove them" (the bodies from the sepulchre). See J.C. Greenfield, "Studies in the Legal Terminology of the Nabatean Funerary Inscriptions," ספר זכרון לחנוך ילון (Jerusalem: Kiryat Sepher, 1974) 64-83.

83 In light of the parallel from the Psalms Scroll, it would appear that the hymn here speaks of angels, not members of the sect. It remains difficult to be certain,

entire thanksgiving hymn (13:1ff.), it should be noted, bears many similarities to the first hymn of the Hodayot quoted above in connection with luminaries, knowledge, and time changes.

ANGELS, LUMINARIES AND KNOWLEDGE

Angels as possessors of "knowledge" is a very common motif in Qumran literature and especially comes to the fore in the context of heavenly praise dealt with here. Thus, in Hodayot 3:22-23 the praising angels are called רוחות דעת, "spirits of knowledge," while in 11:14 and in fragment 10:6 they are called ידעים. Most important in this respect is text 4Q400 frag. 2 from cave 4.[84] There we read that God's glory is praised by אלי דעת,[85] "angels (lit. divine beings) of knowledge," "while standing in their abodes" (במעוני עומדם), and that they praise the Lord's glory together with men, according to their knowledge, אלוהים ואנשים יספרו הוד מלכותו כדעתם.[86] In a fragment from the Benediction of the Chief Priest (1QS^b 4:22-28)[87] we read that the chief priest is like the מלאך פנים, "angel of the presence,"[88] in the holy abode (במעון קודש) who serves in the "king's palace" (היכל המלך)[89] and that he shares his lot with the "angels of the presence," as a result of which he becomes "the great luminary of the world of knowledge" (למאור גדול לתבל בדעת). This text identifies, then, the chief priest with the "angel of the presence" (who has direct access to the Lord)[90] as well as with the great luminary (i.e. the sun) of knowledge.[91]

---

however, for the members of the sect see themselves as partners of the angels in God's revelation (see below).

84   Cf. Newsom, *Songs of the Sabbath Sacrifice*, 110.

85   Compare קרובי דעת in fragment 1 of the same text (line 7) and צבא דעת in 1QH 18:23.

86   The passage is fragmentary and runs as follows: להלל כבודה **באלי דעת** ותשבוחות מלכותה בקדושי ק[ד]שים... המה נכבדים בכול מחני אלוהים ונוראים למוסדי אנשים פ[לא... מאלוהים ואנשים יספרו הוד מלכותו ורוממו [...שמי מלכותו וכל מרומי רום תהלו פלא לפי כול [...כבוד מלך אלוהים יספרו במעוני עומדם... נרוממה **לאלהי דעת** [ק]ודש **ובינתו** ככול ידע...

87   For this passage and the identification of the blessed there with the chief priest, cf. Licht, מגילת הסרכים, 282-3.

88   Cf. the blessing to Levi in Jub. 31:14: "And may the Lord cause you and your descendants from among all flesh to approach him to serve in his sanctuary as the *angels of the presence and as the holy ones.*" מלאך פנים occurs in 1QH 6:13. For מלאך פנים in apocryphal literature, cf. Licht, *Hodayot*, 284 and Holm-Nielsen, *Hodayot*, 114 n. 110.

89   For this term denoting Temple, cf. Ben Sira 50:2, 8.

90   See 1QH 6:13 where the members of the sect are compared with the מלאכי פנים who do not need any mediator nor intercessor (מליץ בנים).

91   Cf. also Test. Levi 4:2-3 where it is said that Levi will serve before the Lord and will spread "the light of knowledge" upon Jacob, being like the sun for Israel. The comparison of the priests with the angels and luminaries seems to support the thesis first suggested by J. Maier, "Zum Begriff יחד in den Texten von

This latter identification of the chief priest with the great luminary should not surprise us. As has been indicated above, the angels are paralleled with the morning stars in Job 38:7, a view which is also reflected in Psalm 148 where (vv. 3) we find the sun, moon and the כוכבי אור (bright stars or morning stars)[92] together with the angels and the Lord's host (מלאכיו, צבאיו, vv. 2). The identification of the luminaries with the angels is most clearly expressed in the book of Job in the passages about the culpability of angels and men. In the verses in which men are compared to angels, by way of *a minori ad majus*, there is an interchange of מלאכים and קדושים (4:18, 15:15) with the moon and the stars (25:5):

Even His servants He distrusts
charges His angels with errors
how much more those who dwell in clay houses (4:18)

Even His angels he distrusts	Even the moon is not bright
the heavens are not pure in His sight	*nor the stars pure in His sight*
how much more a man...	how much more a man...
(15:15)	(25:5)

That the celestial bodies constitute God's host may be learned too from Isa 40:25-26 (cf. also 1 Enoch 18:13; 21:3), and the same view is found in the first hymn of the Hodayot:

> You have stretched out the heavens to Your Glory... (put) the strong winds according to their ordinances into angels of holiness before they were created, into eternal spirits over their dominions, bodies

---

Qumran," *ZAW* 72 (1960) 148-60 that the notion of the communion of the sect with angels is rooted in "Tempelsymbolik." Cf. also K.G. Kuhn, *RGG*, 3rd edition, V (1961), 748-50 and Kuhn, *Enderwartung*, 66-70. For a comparison of the priests with angels cf. y. Ber. 1:1, 2c: אמר רב הונא זה שרואה את הכהנים בבית הכנסת בברכה ראשונה צריך לומר ברכו ה' מלאכיו. The idea of the priests being like the luminaries because of their association with the shining Urim and Thumin occurs also in 4QpIsa[a] in the Pesher to Isa 54:12, "As to that which is said: 'And I will make as agate all your pinnacles (שמשתיך),' this refers to the twelve (priests) who give light by the judgment of the Urim and Thumim... which shine forth from them like the sun in all its radiance." See J. M. Baumgarten, "The Duodecimal Courts of Qumran, Revelation, and the Sanhedrin," *JBL* 95 (1976) 61-62. Cf. n. 10 there referring to Rashi regarding the association of שמשתיך with ישמשונה in אלף...ה in Dan 7:10.

92   אור may be rendered "morning," cf. Job 24:14; Neh. 8:3 and hence M. Dahood's proposal (*Psalms*, III, Anchor Bible, New York: Doubleday, 1970, 353) to consider כוכבי אור in Psalm 148 as synonymous with כוכבי בקר in Job 38:7.

of light according to their mysteries, stars according to their courses...[93]

Besides the equation of angels with luminaries we find here the angels equated with winds and spirits (cf. 13:8: צבא רוחיך), a phenomenon encountered also in Ps 104:2-3): "He makes the winds his messengers/angels" (עשה מלאכיו רוחות), and in the heavenly vision in 1 Kgs 22 where the רוח appears as one of the members of the divine council.

That the luminaries fulfill a role identical with that of the angels may be learned from the way the position of both in the heavenly abode is described in the Qumran writings. Thus, in 1QM 12:1-2 we read that the hosts of the angels are stationed in the "holy habitation," מזבול כבודכה/בזבול קודשכה/במעון קודשכה. The same is said about the luminaries: "In the morning they shine forth from the holy habitation (מזבול קודש) and in the evening they enter into the glorious abode (למעון כבוד)" (1QS 10:2-3; cf. 1QH 12:5-7).

The overlapping function of the luminaries with that of the angels is clearly attested in 1 Enoch 41:7 and in the *El Adon* hymn. In both sources the luminaries, like the angels, praise the Lord and extoll him. In 1 Enoch: "They (sun and moon) praise and extoll and do not cease."

In the *El Adon* hymn:

נאה זיום בכל העולם	מלאים זיו ומפיקים נגה
עושים באימה רצון קונם	שמחים בצאתם וששים בבואם
צהלה ורנה לזכר מלכותו	פאר וכבוד נותנים לשמו

Full of spendor and emanating radiance, their splendor shines over the whole world. Joyous at their rising and glad at their setting, they perform with fear the will of their Master. They give honor and glory to His name, jubilation and exultation at the mention of His kingdom.

And in the poem לאל אשר שבת:

[94]מאורות אשר יצרת (עשית) יפארוך

Lights You have created will praise You.

The connection between angels and knowledge is to be traced back to the literature of the First Temple period. Thus we read in 2 Sam

---

93   For translation and comments see Holm-Nielsen, *Hodayot*, 17, 21.
94   See *Seder Rav Amram Gaon* (ed. Goldschmidt), 71; cf. A. Rofé, *Israelite Belief in Angels* (Diss. Hebrew Univ., 1969) 53ff. (Hebrew).

14:17 that the king is like a *divine angel to discern between good and evil* or that he has wisdom *like the divine angel to know everything on the earth* (ibid., vv. 20). Similarly, we read in Prov 9:10 and 30:3 about דעת קדושים, "knowledge of the angels" (cf. LXX), a "knowledge" reflected in Job 15:8 where reference is made to the myth about man's stealing wisdom from the divine council.[95] A similar background lies behind Gen 3:5, "You will be like divine beings who know good and evil,"[96] והייתם כאלהים ידעי טוב ורע, and Gen 3:22, "Now that the man has become like one of us, knowing good and evil,"[97] a tradition which may be linked to the story of Ezekiel 28 about an angel or cherub "full of wisdom" (מלא חכמה) in charge of the garden of God (vv. 12).

Finally, we should refer to Mal 2:7. Here, as in 1QS[b] 4:22-23 quoted above, the priest is compared to the angel of the Lord of Hosts who imparts knowledge and Torah: "For the lips of a priest guard knowledge and men seek instruction from his mouth, for he is a מלאך of the Lord of Hosts," כי שפתי כהן ישמרו דעת ותורה יבקשו מפיהו כי מלאך ה' צבאות הוא. Here we find the priest, the angel and knowledge combined as in Qumran with the only exception being that no luminary is mentioned.

In the Qumran writings, as well as in other Jewish contemporaneous circles, there existed, then, a correlation between angels, knowledge and luminaries. It seems that the idea of celestial bodies endowed with mind and knowledge found in the Pseudepigrapha,[98] Philo,[99] and various midrashic legends,[100] was already prevalent in Jewish circles of pre-Christian times. Maimonides follows the same line when stating:

> All the stars and planets are endowed with soul, wisdom and insight, and they live and exist and recognize the One Who spoke and the world came into being. All of them, everyone according to

---

95   See the commentary of N.H. Tur-Sinai (Torczyner), *The Book of Job, A New Commentary* (Hebrew; Tel Aviv: Yavnet, 1957).

96   Cf. Targum Pseudo-Jonathan: ותהוון כמלאכין רברבין דחכמין למנדע בין טב לביש, "And you will be like the great angels that know to distinguish between good and evil" and cf. Neofiti Targum.

97   Cf. *Gen. Rab.* 21, 5 (ed. Theodor-Albeck, 200): "Rabbi Pappias expounded 'the man has become like one of us,' as one of the serving angels."

98   See Pss. Sol. 18:10-12 (considered as a separate psalm); compare the blessing for the new moon (b. San. 42a) and Syriac Apocalypse of Baruch 48:9.

99   Plant. 3.12; Opif. 24.73; Somn. 1.135. It should be noted, however, that by expressing this opinion he might refer to the prevalent view and is not necessarily speaking in his own name; cf. H.A. Wolfson, *Philo* I (Cambridge: Harvard, 1947) 363-85.

100 Cf. Ginzberg, *Legends of the Jews*, 1.100, 112.

its eminence and rank, praise and extol their Creator like the angels.[101]

The last sentence about the rank and hierarchy in the divine choir accords with the above mentioned statements from Qumran about the rank and order of the angels in praise (cf. 1QH 3:20-23; 11:13; 4Q 405 20 II-21-22, line 14).[102]

THE ANGELS' PRAISE IN BEN SIRA

The angelic song, associated with the appearance of the luminaries and the changes of time, appears in Ben Sira also, here again connected with divine knowledge. A song of praise of God and His creations reads there as follows (42:16-20):

The brilliant sun shines forth upon everything,	שמש זהרת[103] על כל נגלתה
And God's Glory fills His creations.	וכבוד אדני מלא מעשיו
God's Holy ones were unable to completely recount His wonders,	לא השפיקו קדשי האל לספר כל נפלאותיו
The Lord has strengthened His hosts To stand firm before His glory...	אמץ אדני צבאיו להתחזק לפני כבודו...
For the Most High knows everything and observes the eternal signs,	כי ידע [ע]ליון כל [דעת] ומביט אותיות עולם
Discloses past and future, and reveals secret things,	מחוה חליפות נהיה ומגלה חקר נסתרות

---

101   הלכות יסודי התורה, 3:9. cf. *Guide for the Perplexed* II, 5. Maimonides is here influenced by Neoplatonic thought, especially by Plotinus; see A.L. Ivri "Neoplatonic Currents in Maimonides' Thought," *Perspectives on Maimonides, Philosophical and Historical Studies* (ed. J. L. Kraemer; Oxford: 1991), 115-40.

102   Cf. Newsom, *Songs of the Sabbath Sacrifice*, 303.

103   Cf. זהרי חמה in the prayer אל ברוך גדול דעה and זיו חמה in the Genizah passage אשר ברוב חכמה quoted above.

Knowledge does not escape Him...[104]   ...לא נעדר מפניו שכל

Here we see both stylistic and thematic similarity to the Qumran passages we have quoted,[105] from which we may conclude that the prayers we are dealing with are indeed all quite early and do reflect ancient versions of a sort of *Yoṣer* prayer.

The idea expressed in the Ben Sira passage, that the angels are unable to sufficiently recount God's wonders, appears as well in 1QH 12:29-30: וגבו[רי פל]א המה לא [יוכלו] לספר כל כבודכה, "and the wondrous mighty ones, they cannot recount Your full glory," and in frag. 1:1-4: מלאכי קודש אשר בשמים... והם לא יוכלו... ולא יעצורו לדעת בכל,[106] "[the holy] angels in heaven... they cannot... they are not able to know all...."

The passage from Ben Sira above also helps to determine the sense of a passage from Qumran cave 6[107] which reads: ... [מל]אכי צדק [לעו]למים לא יכלו..., "the righteous angels that strength- en themselves with the spirit of knowledge forever cannot" Just as in Ben Sira 42:16-20, we have here the strength of the angels, and at the same time their inability to praise God fully. What is true in heaven is all the more obvious of man, as we see in the apocryphal Psalm 151 from the Qumran Psalms Scroll: את מעשי (אדון הכל) כי מי יגיד ומי ידבר ומי יספר, "For who can proclaim, who can tell, who can recount the Lord's works?"[108] as well as in Ben Sira 18:4-5, "For who

---

104   According to the version found at Masada 5:3-9 = 42:16-20; see Y. Yadin, "The Ben Sira Scroll from Masada," *EI* 8 (Sukenik Memorial Volume; 1968) 27-28 and J. Strugnell, "Notes and Queries on 'The Ben Sira Scroll from Masada,'" *EI* 9 (Albright Volume; 1969) 116 (English section).
105   Yadin, ibid., 27.
106   Restoration according to Licht, מגילת ההודיות, 219.
107   6Q 18, Fragment 5, DJD III, 134.
108   Cf. Sanders, *The Psalms Scroll of Qumran Cave 11*, 28:6-7. According to the verse division of A. Hurwitz, "Adon Hakkol," *Tarbiz* 34 (1965) 224, we should read: ומי יספר את מעשי אדון הכול. F.M. Cross, "David, Orpheus, and Psalm 151:3-4," (*BASOR* 231 (Oct. 1978) 69ff., who reads in lines 5-6 *lu* instead of *lo*, understands מי here in parallel with *lu* as "would that someone (tell)," arguing that a different rendering, viz., the mountains cannot tell, would be "nonsense in a biblical or early Jewish context" (70 n. 6). However, the problem is one of exhausting the praise and not the mere telling of it: although the mountains etc. praise God (cf. Ps 148:9-10, rightly adduced by Cross), they are not able to recount all His praises; cf. Ps 106:1-2: "Praise the Lord... who can tell the mighty acts of the Lord, proclaim *all* His praises," and cf. also Ps 40:6: "You, O Lord... have done many things... I would rehearse the tale of them but they are more than can be told." The passage from Psalm 151 of 11QPs[a] should then be thus translated: "The mountains do not witness to Him, nor do the hills. The leaves of the trees do not recount my words, nor does the flock my deeds. For who can tell..." For the reading "leaves of the trees," cf. Skehan, *CBQ* 25 (1963) 407-8. This reading may be supported by a liturgical fragment from the Genizah: "Your praise supercedes in number the dust of the earth... more than every plant, every leaf and seed..." (TS NS 198, 20).

can fully[109] recount His works, and who can trace His great deeds? No one can measure His majestic power and who can tell in full all His mercies?"

The same theme recurs in the so-called Benediction of the Song (ברכת השיר), the *Nishmat* prayer (*SPB*, 182-183; see b. Pes. 118a), which according to Genizah versions, was recited daily:[110] אילו פינו מלא שירה כים ולשוננו רינה כהמון גליו ושפתותנו שבח כמרחבי רקיע... אין אנו מספיקים להודות לך... ולברך את שמך על אחת מאלף אלפי אלפים ורבו רבבות פעמים הטובות שעשית..., "Though our mouths were full of song as the sea, and our tongues of exaltation as the multitude of its waves, and our lips of praise as the widely extended firmament..., we should still be unable to thank You and bless Your name for one thousandth of thousand thousands... of the bounties which You have bestowed....[111]

An identical *topos* is found in the Hekhalot literature in connection with the praise of the angels:[112] כי מי יכול להגיד אחת מאלף אלפי אלפים ורבי רבבות גבורתיך מלך מלכי המלכים... שהחיות נצבות לפניך... מלך גדול וקדוש אתה שיכול לדעת את מעשיך ולחקור את גבורתיך, "Who is able to recount one thousandth of thousand thousands... of the marvelous deeds of the King of Kings... when the angels stand before You... because You are a King great and Holy that one may know Your deeds and explore Your mighty acts...."

This *topos* is already attested in the Homeric liteature. Thus, we read there in connection with naming the ships and the troops that participated in the war at Troy,

> Tell me now, you Muses... for you are godesses and... know all things..., who were the captains of the Danaans..., but the common folk I could not tell, nor name, not *though ten tongues were mine and ten mouths and a voice unwearing...*
>
> Homer, The Iliad II 485-494

---

109   ἐξεποίησεν has to be translated as הספיק as may be learned from 42:17 where the Hebrew has השפיק and LXX ἐξεποίησεν.

110   Cf. Mann, 279, 325.

111   For a parallel in Mandaic liturgy, cf. J.C. Greenfield, "A Mandaic 'Targum' of Psalm 114," *Studies in Aggadah, Targum and Jewish Liturgy in Memory of Joseph Heinemann* (Jerusalem: Magnes Press, 1981) 29: "If our mouths would be like the sea, and our lips like the waves, and our tongues like steep mountains."

112   Cf. *Pirke Hekhalot Rabbati, Bate Midrashot* I (ed. A.J. Wertheimer; Jerusalem: Ktav Wasepher, 1950) 111. Cf. P. Schäfer, *Synopse zur Hekhalot Literatur* (Tübingen: J.C.B. Mohr, 1988) 276.

Here the muses (=the angels)[113] who know everything can recount the story but not men. Similarly, we find in Virgil's Aeneid (vi 625-627):

> Nay, had I a hundred tongues, a hundred mouths and a voice of iron
> I could not sum up all the forms of crime.

This topic is also found in the hymn of Lucius to Isis:

> My voice has no power to utter that which I think of your majesty.
> No, not if I had a thousand mouths and many tongues and were able
> to continue forever... (Apuleius, *Metamorphoses*, XI, 25).

Most recently a Greek inscription was discovered in Ḥammat Gader that has on it a poem by the Empress Eudocia (fifth century CE). Here we read:

> In my life many and infinite wonders have I seen. But who, however
> many his mouths, could proclaim... your strength.[114]

THE PRAISE OF THE ANGELS IN THE BOOK OF JUBILEES

P.W. Skehan[115] has shown that Jub. 2:2-3 parallels 11QPs^a 26:4-5. Furthermore, the verbal congruency between the passages led him to the conclusion that the Qumran hymn influenced the book of Jubilees:

Jubilees	11QPs^a
He created... day and dawn[116] which He established in the *knowledge of His heart.* Thereupon we *saw His work and praised Him...*	He established the dawn by the *knowledge of His heart.* Then *all His angels saw and were jubilant.*

Although both sources speak about creating *dawn* and not the luminaries, as in the liturgies quoted before, this should not be viewed as a different tradition since the light created on the first

---

113   For the muses functioning as angels see my article, "The Heavenly Praise in Unison," *Meqor Hajjim, Festschrift für Georg Molin zum 75. Geburtstag* (Graz: Akademische Druck und Verlagsanstalt, 1983) 427-33.

114   J. Green and Y. Tsafrir, "A Poem of the Empress Eudocia," *IEJ* 32 (1982) 79-80. Cf. the parallel to this *topos* adduced by A. Scheiber, "Parallels to a Topos in Eudocia's Poem," *IEJ* 34 (1984) 180-1.

115   P.W. Skehan, "Jubilees and the Qumran Psalter," *CBQ* 37 (1975) 343-7.

116   Following the Greek version of Epiphanius (Skehan, 345).

day was considered identical with that of the heavenly bodies (cf. b. Ḥag. 12a).

The Hymn to the Creator in 11QPs^a 26:9-15 contains the basic elements of the *Qedushah* liturgy in the conventional Jewish morning prayer (*Yoṣer* liturgy) as well as in the book of Jubilees and in Ben Sira. The opening sentence of the Hymn to the Creator: גדול וקרוש ה׳ קרוש קדושים לדור ודור, "Great and holy is YHWH the holiest of holy ones for every generation," overlaps the conventional and the Genizah formulae of the Benediction of the *Qedushah*.

Furthermore, the basic formula of the Qumranic hymn: שחר הכין בדעת לבו, "He established the dawn (=the light) by the knowledge of his mind," occurs in the book of Jubilees 2:2-3, in Ben Sira 42:16-20, and in the *Yoṣer* liturgy; cf. especially גדול דעה הכין ופעל זהרי חמה, "(the God) great in knowledge formed and established the rays of the sun."

The cosmic renewal of the luminaries accompanied by grace, truth, and justice is found both in the Qumran literature and in the *Yoṣer* liturgy.

STUDIES ON THE TEXTS
OF THE DESERT OF JUDAH

DATE DUE

			Printed in USA